TRAVELS IN ARABIA
TRAVELS IN OMAN

OMAN IN HISTORY

JAMES RAYMOND WELLSTED

INTRODUCTION & EDITOR
TONY WALSH

CONTENTS

Introduction This Edition — v
Introduction Original Edition — xxiii

1. Arrival in Muscat — 1
2. Muscat's Population and Trade — 7
3. Journey from and Return to Muscat — 13
4. Travel from Muscat to Bani bu Ali — 20
5. Bani bu Ali's History and Environs — 28
6. Culture of Jaalan — 34
7. Travel through Bidiyyah — 42
8. Meeting Lieutenant Whitelock in Samad Al Shan — 51
9. Ascent from Nizwa to Jabal Akhdar — 61
10. Descent from Mountains to Nizwa — 71
11. Violent Fever grips the Party — 81
12. Moving from Burka to Suwayq — 88
13. From the Coast to the Mountains — 96
14. Barriers to Farther Travel — 102
15. Description of Northern Oman — 109
16. Seaborne Conflict — 116
17. Culture of Persian Gulf — 123
18. Agriculture of Batinah Coast — 128
19. Agriculture and Livestock — 134
20. Commercial Aspects of Oman — 145
21. Festivals and Ornaments of Women — 154
22. Arab Culture and Governance — 161
23. The Imam of Oman — 168
24. Political Relations of the Imam — 174
25. Arrival in Balhaf Yemen — 181
26. Ruins of Nakab Al Hajar Fortress — 189

Appendix - Letters from Said bin Khalfan — 197
Appendix - notations — 201
Photographs & Images — 207
INDEX — 209

INTRODUCTION THIS EDITION

As well as the few original illustrations from the book and its superb map by John Arrowsmith, supporting period and modern images have been included.

This edition has been retyped; fortunately, despite the book being 200 years old, the nationally accepted spellings & grammar for British English had coalesced into a form comparable to the style used in the 21st century. Even in its original form the book reads clearly. However, Wellsted's spellings of the same place-names and terms vary within the book - a familiar by-product of transliterating Arabic into English, even now. Examples include the words *felegi / feletch / falodge / falj* for the Omani structure *falaj* (the man made water channel).

To ease clarity, modern spellings of peoples names, places and other nouns are used - with his original spelling bracketed in the first instance. I have used the current preferred spelling of Makkah within Saudi Arabia, for Mecca. This use of modern names means not only is there consistency - but modern mapping can also be referred to. Wellsted used the word *kamaline* (the Anglo rendering of *kambali* - Indian woven cloaks or blankets) to mean a *bisht* (cloak) and also a rug - in the text the correct meaning has been used.

Equally Wellsted also wrote names whose modern version is not clear - for example he mentions "the Towaylee, from the Zanzibar coast who are known by having their teeth filed" - it is likely that he means the "Makonde" but certainty is not possible, so the Towaylee name is not altered.

Errors creep into many books, Wellsted's is no different. Wellsted appears to have conflated the names of Oman's rulers. Without certainty who was meant, no change has been made in these instances. Wellsted's book also notes "Acting Commander J. B. Aines, in charge of the Hon. Company's brig *Palinurus* " refused to offer Wellsted "every possible assistance". At the time it was actually Commander S. B. Haines who was in command of the *Palinurus*. The hand compositor or copyholder may have misread Wellsted's normally clear handwriting. The refusal to offer assistant is an indication of the long term antipathy between the two men. A sign of the stress Wellsted must have been under while writing is that he included 30th February in his dating, though in March was correct in his day and dates.

Both the Maria Theresa Thaler and the Spanish/Mexican dollar circulated in Oman in the 1830s; usage varied between the coast which used Spanish dollars and interior which used Maria Theresa Thalers; however Wellsted only mentioned dollars - and came from Muscat therefore he may not have been using any Maria Theresa Thalers and in all cases his mention of dollar must mean the Spanish dollar.

The book by Wellsted is initially written as a dated diary of a journey whose destination was intended to be Diriyah, in central Arabia. Wellsted's insights into the people he met on his journey, together with their culture, are key elements of the narration. The later chapters offer a wider perspective of the culture, agriculture and politics of Oman and southeast Arabia. Finally, a visit to an archaeological site in southern Yemen is included.

He covers Oman's Ibadhi Islam, as he understood it - using a more general term for the sect that modern Omanis do not accept, Khuwarijites (Kharijites). This sect developed in the late 7th century AD - and spread through Omani inhabitants in Iraq, to Oman, North Africa, Yemen and later into Zanzibar.

~

James Raymond Wellsted

James Raymond Wellsted was born in 1805. His father, also named James Wellsted, worked as an upholsterer. James Wellsted senior may have been among the first tenants of Molyneux Street, Marylebone - part of the Portman Estate of north-central London, developed for the Portman family, descendants of Sir William Portman, a Tudor magnate and royal servant.

Little is known of our James Wellsted's early life. His sister, Sophia Matilda Wellsted - later the wife of solicitor J. D. Marsden - was the mother of Kate Marsden, the explorer and Christian missionary. Kate somehow secured a personal audience in 1890 with Queen Victoria and, later that same year, with Princess Alexandra, the future Queen - and, even more improbably, with the Empress of Russia, who thirteen years earlier had honoured her for humanitarian work with wounded soldiers in Bulgaria. James Wellsted had an earlier close encounter with Queen Victoria; the family possessed either remarkable chutzpah or an extraordinary "six degrees of separation."

James Raymond Wellsted entered the East India Company's (EIC) naval service, the Bombay Marine, in 1823 as a Volunteer; the cadet grade from which officers advanced. The term dated from the eighteenth century and denoted young men offering service without a formal commission: "volunteers" not in the modern sense of unpaid helpers, but in contrast to those "press-ganged" into service. His first ship was HCS Ternate, a 237-ton, 18-gun brig launched in 1801. Though used as a survey vessel, the Ternate had taken part in the British attack on Ras Al Khaimah in 1819.

British Troops attacking Ras Al Khaimah 1809 J. Thirtle

Wellsted's next few years were spent in the Persian Gulf, on what was a multi-purpose assignment. The Bombay Marine brig/sloop Ternate was primarily a survey vessel, though it was also used for armed attacks and for diplomatic dispatches. With perhaps 150 men and no more than 20 officers, it wasn't a large ship. From 1827, Wellsted gives a snapshot of its work - and of himself.

"While cruising on this coast in 1827, I was proceeding with dispatches to the Sheikh of Sharjah, Sultan bin Saqr, when a strong breeze unexpectedly set in...our boat...was capsized... After landing, the gale increased, and for three days we could not attempt to put off to the vessel (the Ternate)... Sultan was unremitting in his attention to me... On one occasion he invited me to dine... a small room... a rude table, two or three chairs, given him by the commanders of our vessels... [and] coffee, which the Sheikh himself made and handed round. A storyteller was then called in... but I was then too ignorant of the language to understand it."

This small episode reveals the traits that made Wellsted a perceptive traveller: calm in a capsize, curious in a majlis, and courteous enough to take the carpet over the gifted chairs. Wellsted understood his environment and was eager to fit in.

Wellsted was one of a compact cohort of contemporaries - junior officers who would criss-cross the Indian Ocean and the Persian Gulf. Henry Lynch, joined the Ternate on the same day as Wellsted; Henry Ormsby, joined 7 June 1823 and served in the 387-ton Elphinstone; and Edward Wyburd, who became 2nd Lieutenant in the 420-ton Amherst on 9 July 1825. These men were part of what was a surprisingly small number of officers in the Bombay Marine (Indian Navy). In 1830 there were probably fewer than 160, all European, from the Superintendent (Sir Charles Malcolm) down to the Midshipmen. Indian sailors crewed the ships. The total crew number on the 18 ships of the Bombay Marine was between 2,100 & 2,700.

In City of the Caliphs, Wellsted reflected on his contemporaries restless range: 'It is a singular fact that so small a service as the Indian Navy should, in one and the same year, have seven midshipmen, four of whom have traversed more of the East than probably the same number of individuals alive; Ormsby, Lynch, W[yburd], and, may I add, the editor of these volumes.' Their choice of the EIC's service (the Bombay Marine until 1830, when it was retitled the Indian Navy) was likely helped by the Royal Navy's post-Napoleonic contraction: many British naval ships were laid up, and opportunities afloat narrowed.

Sir Henry Creswicke Rawlinson, writing in 1873, placed Lynch 'of the school of Ormsby, Wellsted, and Wyburd'-an accurate and daring observer, and, he thought, the most gifted of the group as a scholar and linguist.

The East India Company's strategic outlook had shifted after the Napoleonic Wars. The 1799 defeat of Tipu Sultan, whose father had seized the throne of Mysore, removed a principal adversary within India; Napoleon's failure in Egypt and the French evacuation in 1801 blunted the immediate French threat to India. Although Napoleon later sent Jean-Baptiste de Cavaignac to Muscat in 1803 to try and gain wide-scale support, he returned empty-handed. After Waterloo, British command of the sea from London to Bombay was unchallenged, and within India the EIC held sway. Yet in Travels in Arabia Wellsted warned that the French spectre had given way to anxiety over Russia's southward reach: he wrote 'The Russian frontier now extends to within 120 miles of the sources of the Euphrates... the passage of an army along its banks to the shores of the Persian Gulf might be accomplished without any considerable difficulty.' From Bombay's vantage point, the Great Game was beginning.

Steam-power changed the tempo at sea. After early coastal experiments, and with deep-sea passages proven from the 1810s onward, Bombay's Government grew keen to employ steam for its own long-distance routes. The arrival from London, in 1825, of the auxiliary paddle steamer Enterprise, into Calcutta, showed what might now be possible between London and Bombay via the Cape, though it turned out that the Red Sea would become critical.

The Malcolms - Sir John Malcolm, appointed Governor of Bombay on 1 November 1827, and his brother Captain Sir Charles Malcolm, brought in as Superintendent of the Marine-pressed for 'full steam ahead' in policy and propulsion. Charles Malcolm, a 45-year-old Royal Navy officer, seasoned in the Indian Ocean, the West Indies, South America, and the Atlantic, reached Bombay on 1 June 1828 and took up his post on Wednesday, 4 June. The young Wellsted served as his secretary.

Steam power to serve India had powerful champions with the Malcolm brothers and their brother Sir Pulteney Malcolm, naval Commander-in-Chief in the Mediterranean. The 411-ton paddle-steamer HCS Hugh Lindsay was launched at Bombay on 14 October 1829 in the Malcolms' presence (and, one suspects, that of the Superintendent's secretary).

In 1829 the survey sloop HCS Thetis escorted a single collier up the Red Sea, depositing hard Welsh "steam coal" that burned hot, with low ash and little smoke, at Aden, Jeddah, Quseir and Suez; the collier was wrecked on the return-an object-lesson in why Moresby's charts, completed soon after, were not a luxury but a necessity. The coal was to allow the Hugh Lindsay to make its maiden voyage from Bombay.

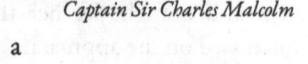

Captain Sir Charles Malcolm

From Bombay, Hugh Lindsay made its proving voyage in March 1830 to Suez. With almost all spare space in the ship given over to coal, her twin 80-horsepower engines burned roughly seventeen tons a day. The round voyage-Bombay-Suez-Bombay-took forty-one days door-to-door. Underway, she averaged about six knots (11 km/h); the coaling halts pulled the overall average down. Modern expedition-type small cruise ships run at around 15 knots, so Hugh Lindsay was no speedster. Even so, the verdict was clear to the Malcolms - and soon the EIC: steam was the future. Hugh Lindsay made regular mail runs up the Red Sea, for onward delivery to London and eventually worked in the Persian Gulf and Shatt Al Arab.

When Hugh Lindsay later cruised in the Persian Gulf, she drew both amazement and dismay. In waters long ruled by monsoon and shamal winds - where the wind direction can come from one direction for months, steam power promised year-round navigation to any point of the compass. However, the ship was only half the story: steam demanded coal depots and soundings - bunkering stations and hydrographic surveys - the essential foundations of naval supremacy.

In 1830, aged twenty-five, Wellsted was sent to chart the Arabian coasts aboard HCS (Honourable Company's Ship) *Palinurus* - aptly named for Aeneas's helmsman - as the classical Erythraean Sea was mapped so that modern steam could run through ancient waters.

From 1830 the EIC split the work between two small brigs: HCS Palinurus (8 guns; 192 tons bm "builder's measurement") under Captain Robert Moresby for the northern Red Sea, and HCS Benares (14 guns; 230 tons bm) under Captain Thomas Elwon for the southern half.

James Raymond Wellsted joined Palinurus as second lieutenant in October 1830. On that service he noted the brig carried seventy men; twenty-five Europeans and forty-five lascar ratings - a distribution shaped by survey work with multiple cutters, shore parties, instrument-keepers, and draughtsmen.

A survey lieutenant's core duties were to fix latitude and longitude by observation (with chronometers rated to Greenwich), run systematic lines of soundings from the cutters or more often by negotiating with local boat owners, lead shore parties to establish points and sketch coastal profiles, and compile boat-sheets and fair copies. Wellsted also compiled details of the supplies available at ports, From these, Captain Moresby, with Lieut. T. G. Carless, produced the detailed sea charts, that were refined in Bombay and usually sent to John Walker's office in London to be engraved as the finished Red Sea series. Wellsted's logs also fed the Sailing Directions for the Red Sea (issued with Horsburgh's India Directory, 5th ed., 1841), forming the new hydrography into practical routing.

Palinurus was a compact vessel - roughly the size of the 180-ton Mayflower. Her size and draught let her thread among coral reefs and sand bars, hazards that increased on the approaches to major ports such as Jeddah. As was usual in the early 19th century, copper sheathing would give protection against marine wood-borers, but minimal protection against grounding on coral reefs that were so common in the Red Sea.

Beyond the charts, Wellsted produced sailing directions, coastal views, and narratives that circulated within the Bombay Marine. Two centuries on, his descriptions of inland journeys still matter for understanding the EIC's forward planning, most notably his weeks on Socotra, then under active consideration for one or more coaling stations between Bombay and Suez. The portrait that emerges is of a confident - at times overconfident - but non-judgmental observer of the places he passed through.

Wellsted was explicit about the practical aim of the Red Sea work: "To ascertain how far its passage could be made available for steamers was one of the principal objects to which our attention was directed during the late survey of the Red Sea." He also wrote with a frank Anglo-centric confidence: "Egypt, the high-way between Europe and India, must, sooner or later, be ours. How gladly its present wretched inhabitants would hail the change, let those answer who have visited it, instead of drawing their ideas of the government of its enlightened ruler from reports current in Europe."

Like many nineteenth-century travelogues, his narrative of these surveys jump-cuts - sometimes zigzagging like a dhow beating into a headwind-so the sequence and even the spellings shift on the page. Thus Cosseir appears as Kosa'ir on the next page (I used Quseir as the most usual today); Terhan becomes Tiran. The Palinurus first sailed down the Arabian coast (modern Saudi Arabia) from Ras Muhammad at the Sinai tip, then went across to the Tiran narrows and south to Al Muwaylih with its fort. The fort, built around AD 1560, dates from soon after the Ottoman's control of the Hijaz. It was one of a string of forts built not only to control the region but also to provide support to Hajj pilgrims. The Hajj pilgrims travelled in vast caravans from Egypt and Syria that followed the coastline, while those from India and beyond would use one of the ports serving Madinah and Makkah.

On land, Muhammad Ali Pasha held Egypt to an extent from 1805, but indisputably from his massacre of the Mamluks in the Cairo Citadel in 1811; the Hijaz was an historical possession of whoever ruled Egypt. However, after the naval battle at Navarino (20 October 1827) and the Egyptian and Ottoman defeat, Britain enjoyed de facto maritime supremacy in the Red Sea as well as the Mediterranean. The increasing use of steam-power needing physical coaling stations and the imminent charts would only increase that domination.

The Palinurus coasted south to Jeddah, in effect parallel to the Egyptian Ḥajj road; Wellsted put arriving sea-borne pilgrims from Egypt at around 20,000, and India had 2,000 arriving annually. Jeddah intrigued Wellsted for its people and its markets - "goods and food" in profusion - but his understandable focus was the dynamics and interplay of Muhammad Alī's officers, the Sherifs of Makkah and the recent exclusion of the Ottomans.

In 1832, the Palinurus shifted north to survey the Sinai, where Wellsted made excursions in biblically resonant terrain, where he wrote about Moses & Elim in the belief that southern Sinai was a location for both. With Lieutenant Thomas G. Carless (the draughtsman), he also travelled overland between Quseir and Luxor in Egypt.

Quseir - Luxor - Cairo - Alexandria offered one conceivable overland/river bridge between London and Bombay, but the Suez-Cairo-Alexandria route won out. The Red Sea survey work by Palinurus was completed between 1830 and 1833. The resulting charts-compiled by Moresby and Carless and published by John Walker-appeared in 1836.

Lieutenant Wellsted's next assignment was under Captain Stafford B. Haines, still in Palinurus. In October 1833, they set off for a survey of southern and eastern Arabia, starting from Ras Madrakah (then styled by British chart-makers as Cape Isoletta) in Eastern Oman. Moving south to Qishn in Mahra in Yemen, Haines sought a formal agreement from the Mahra tribe's Sultan Umar bin Tawari to survey Socotra, which the Mahra tribe ruled. From 9 January to 14 March 1834 the ship's boats traced the island's coasts; ashore, Wellsted, who was then Assistant-Surveyor, and Midshipman Charles Cruttenden crossed the interior.

Wellsted's Memoir on the Island of Socotra covers 10 January-7 March 1834. His party comprised Hamid who was the guide (though dismissed mid-journey for obstructiveness), Sulayman who ultimately proved to be the most useful guide, a Nubian boy named Sunday, an Indian cook, and two enslaved men from the island for general duties. Their start coincided with Ramadan 1249 AH (11 Jan-9/10 Feb 1834), which inevitably complicated how the journey was managed. Transport was by camel (*Camelus dromedarius*). Luggage was lashed high, and somehow "beds" were balanced onto the top of that luggage. Wellsted quips that it resulted in him perched fourteen feet above the ground; he must have swayed dramatically with the stride of the animal. At Hadibu (then Tamarida - the name is linked to tamar, the Arabic for the date palm *Phoenix dactylifera*), a local sheikh objected to the party's wanderings and Cruttenden stayed with him as a good-conduct hostage during the midpoint of the circuit. Even with the almost inevitable hindrances, the exploration achieved its essential aims.

The surveys triggered the Government of India to attempt to purchase Socotra as a coaling-station and authorised an offer-up to 10,000 Maria Theresa thalers (the regional trade coin originally from Austria) - but the Sultan refused outright. Nonetheless, a small mixed detachment (European and Indian) under Captain R. A. Bayly had already been sent and landed at Hadibu in late 1834. Disease soon ravaged their camp; contemporary accounts remarked that scarcely a sound man remained to dig his comrade's grave. The detachment was shifted up into the hills, then withdrawn in stages between April and November 1835. British interest in Socotra as a coal depot faded, and with Aden taken in 1839, Socotra regained its former obscurity, making Wellsted's account even more valuable.

Wellsted spent the rest of 1834 & much of 1835 surveying the southern coasts of Arabia between Ras Madrakah and Aden. Once again Crittenden joined Wellsted on a several-day journey of exploration into a valley 370km northeast of Aden. This turned out to have been a near disaster. "It was not indeed until afterwards that we ascertained the extreme risk we had encountered on this journey; for the Diyabi Bedouins, finding we had passed through their territory, lay in wait for us, under the impression we should return by the same route. But the ship fortunately took up a second station, about twenty miles to the westward of the former one, and on receiving intelligence of that, we returned by another and more direct road to her."

By mid-1835 Wellsted had left the Palinurus on the Aden-Mokha sector and returned to Bombay. There, he must have used his earlier service as Sir Charles Malcolm's secretary (1828-29), as he secured Bombay Government permission for an inland exploration of Oman - that he also hoped would enable him to visit the capital of what is now termed the Second Saudi State in Riyadh (he referred to it as their previous capital Diriyah).

Wellsted wrote, "After obtaining the necessary permission, I embarked at Bombay on board a small schooner (the Cysene) for Muscat, at which port, after a pleasant passage, we arrived on the 21st of November. I found Sayyid Said, the Imam of Muscat or sovereign of Oman, ready, with his characteristic liberality, in every way to forward my views. Letters were prepared under his own direction to the chiefs of the different districts through which I had to pass, and on November 25th I quitted that port to proceed to Sur."

Travelling, supported by a small party through Oman, often into areas known to be hostile to any traveller, Wellsted displayed an almost naive trust, which enabled him to undertake his journeys. This trust was his characteristic outlook, but it was tempered with some preparedness. In Yemen he 'knew that the natives of this district were considered especially hostile to those of a different creed; and that they had some years ago cut off the whole of a boat's crew of the only vessel that had previously touched on their coast, by seducing them with promises from the beach, I could not, therefore, but accuse myself of rashness, in thus venturing with no better pledge for our safety than their promised fidelity'. Though while in Socotra, he noted when an Arab 'suggested, indeed, that any individual, seated, as he was, near me, could seize me by the wrist or throat, so as to render me powerless, while his companions might plunder the baggage; but a sight of the pistols, which I always wore concealed at my girdle, convinced him that I was anything but defenceless against open attacks.'

Irrespective of the location, the inhabitants of most towns and villages he visited in Oman were reluctant to support the onward travel of Wellsted. This was either from their stated belief that the journey itself was dangerous or to show hospitality and keep him with them - in traditional Omani society, 3 days was considered appropriate stay. Nonetheless, Wellsted usually overcame their arguments and continued with his travels.

Arriving in Bani bu Ali, Oman, the location of two intense battles between the eponymous Arab tribe and British forces 15 years earlier, he received 'a reception so truly warm and hospitable not a little surprised me. Before us lay the ruins of the fort we had dismantled, my tent was pitched on the very spot where we had nearly annihilated their tribe, reducing them from being the most powerful in Oman to their present petty state. All, however, in the confidence I had shown in thus throwing myself amidst them, was forgotten.' Wellsted's confidence and presumably manner almost acted as a guarantor of his safety. He travelled alone, for several days, escorted by a party of Janaba Bedouin. They reached deep into the sand desert, enabling him to gain remarkable insight into their character and culture.

Wellsted was remarkably stoic; in Yemen, his guides abandoned him in a remote area. 'Unexpectedly, however, we fell in with an old woman, who, as soon as she was informed of our situation, without the slightest hesitation promised to conduct us to her house. We gladly followed her, but having wandered far from the path, we did not arrive there until midnight. We found our guides comfortably seated within a house, smoking their pipes and drinking coffee. Though excessively provoked, I was aware that remonstrance would be useless; and concealing my chagrin, I proceeded to secure a lodging for the night.'

He was a most observant and insightful traveller, remarking in Oman that

'Although the Grand Sheikhs of the principal tribes have in some cases the power of life and death, and also that of declaring war and peace, yet their authority in every instance is considerably abridged by the aged and other influential men of the tribe. In civil and criminal affairs they act rather as arbiters than as judges, and cases of importance are sometimes debated by the whole tribe'. This was the case in Oman until at least the mid-20th century, and in some instances of matters of social importance to a tribe, up-to the current day.

Wellsted's courtesy, good manners and confidence in those he met were ideally suited to the society he met. 'After their evening prayers, the young Sheikh, accompanied by about forty men, came to the tent, and expressed his intention of remaining with me as a guard during the night. To ask the whole party in was impossible, and to invite a few only would have displeased others, so I took my carpet outside amidst them.'

Unlike Wilfred Thesiger who in the mid-20th century travelled far more extensively in Arabia, but perhaps deliberately avoided the company or mention of women, Wellsted mixed easily with females. In Oman, 'The women were seated on an old carpet near a good fire, and I was invited to place myself between them. They were unveiled and entered freely into conversation with me. After answering a hundred questions connected with the English and their country, coffee, and then milk, were introduced.'

Wellsted frequently expressed considerable admiration of the women he met, perhaps no more so than in Suwaiq recounting when the Sheikh's wife, a sister of Oman's ruler Sayyid Said, 'heard the intelligence [of a planned attack by her brother Sayyid Said on the town during her husband's captivity, who was held by Sayyid Said in Muscat as hostage], she sent messengers to collect the various Bedouin tribes who were in the interest of her husband, and made other preparations to march in person against the dominions of the Imam; but before any succours could arrive, the latter had despatched a force to Suwaiq, in order to take possession of the fort, with an assurance, that unless it was given up, the Sheikh should be put to death. "Go back" said this spirited female, when the message was delivered to her; "Go back to those who sent you, and tell them that I will defend the fort to the utmost of my power; and if they choose to cut him to pieces before me, they will find it make no alteration in my resolution." She accordingly defended it with so much bravery and skill, that the Imam's force, after losing several men and wasting considerable time, were compelled to raise the siege and proceed to Muscat.'

Wellsted's attitude was not always one of admiration of all he met; 'It will apply as a general re-mark, that the Sheikhs of the towns in Oman are very personable men, with a dignified deportment and pleasing manners; but this was a sneaking, greasy-looking animal, who had more the appearance of a butcher than a Sheikh.'

Remarkably open to other cultures, Wellsted also accepted that individuals were not representative of a general population. In Yemen he explained; 'Our guides, as usual, having gone to seek shelter from the heat of the sun, had left us to make our breakfast on dates and water, in any sheltered spot we could find. The sun was nearly vertical, and the walls of the houses afforded us no protection. Seeing this, several of the inhabitants came forward, and offered with much kindness to take us to their dwellings. We gladly consented and followed one of them. Coffee was immediately served; and it was with some difficulty, after a promise to return if possible in the evening, that we prevented our host from ordering a meal to be immediately cooked for us. This circumstance, combined with several others which occurred on our return, convinced me, if we had been provided with a better escort, that after passing the territory of the Diyabis, we should have experienced neither incivility nor unkindness from the people'.

Wellsted had the account of the Socotra read to the Royal Geographical Society in London in 1835 and published his Red Sea/Southern Arabia travels in 1838 as Volume 2 of 'Travels in Arabia'. This is an amalgam of several visits to the Red Sea region over six years. The narrative includes Pharaonic history, Biblical history, and recent events, all wrapped in descriptions of the areas in which Wellsted travelled. He notes details constantly; 'Locusts are sold in the markets of Yanbu, and also at Jeddah. The Mukin or Red species, being the fattest, is preserved, and, when fried and sprinkled with salt, they are considered wholesome and nutritious food' - this practice has continued down to modern times. Continual references are made as to the relations of tribes with the Ottoman Turks and Egypt's Mohammed Ali, who were, at least nominally, the region's rulers.

Wellsted's publication of 'Travels in Arabia' cemented his reputation as an author. Published in 1838, it was dedicated in December 1837, with her permission, to the new Queen, Victoria, quite an audience for the former naval 'volunteer'.

The press highly commended the publication. After expressing its 'high admiration of the diligence and talent shown by Lieutenant Wellsted, ' one paper says, 'the Memoir does credit both to the author himself and to the Service to which he belongs'.

Wellsted however did not have good health on his journeys. In 1834, while travelling through Socotra, Wellsted and his party became ill with 'fever', possibly malaria. Again, while in Oman in the winter 1835/6, Wellsted, along with all his party, collapsed with 'fever', whose symptoms do suggest malignant (*falciparum*) malaria - requiring lengthy recuperation.

During the year following Wellsted's first exploration to Oman he continued working on the Palinurus. Once again the ship was surveying the coasts of southern Oman and Yemen, though given his published papers he must also have been writing on board. While surveying the Hallaniyat Islands, off the coast of Dhofar, the Palinurus rescued the crew of the whaling ship Reliance, which was hunting for whales, most likley Sperm Whales for their blubber. The Hallaniyat Islands seemed to be a magnet for ships destined to be wrecked, the most famous is probably the Portuguese vessel Esmerelda which sank in a storm in 1503.

Visiting Oman again in April 1837, he was again in an acute stage of 'fever'. A Victorian commentator wrote that; 'In a fit of delirium he discharged both barrels of his gun into his mouth, but the balls, passing upwards, only inflicted two ghastly wounds in the upper jaw.' He was transported from Oman aboard the Hugh Lindsay (that amazing steamship) to Bombay and thence returned to Europe on leave, reluctantly leaving his Arab horse behind.

Wellsted was a sought-after expert about the region, giving evidence to the House of Commons in 1837 about the Red Sea steamship route. He was retired from the Indian Navy on 9 May 1838 and, according to commentators, dragged on a few years in shattered health and with impaired mental powers, recuperating in France. Though despite that mention of Wellsted's health, he wrote extensively and fluently.

During this period he wrote 'Travels to the City of Caliphs', which was published in 1840. This book was compiled from Henry Ormsby's accounts to Wellsted of Ormsby's travels between 1826 and 1830 and a previous manuscript written by Ormsby. Wellsted, in effect, was acting as a mouthpiece for Ormsby. After his adventures, Ormsby re-entered the navy, he was, after all, one of those four acclaimed young men, so was a welcome returnee. Ormsby was rapidly rising up the ranks, even serving in the China war of 1840-1842 and must have been too busy to complete his memoir.

Wellsted, writing in the preface of 'Travels to the City of Caliphs' 'This work owes its origin to the following circumstance. Lieut. (Henry) Ormsby, of the Indian Navy, the hero of the first part of the work, voluntarily quitted that service at the early age of nineteen and devoted himself for three years to traversing various portions of the East. The buoyancy of spirit with which every hardship encountered by my friend was surmounted; his courage, and zealous perseverance, where others, amidst pestilence and famine, would have shrunk back, and the facility with which he filled up the variety of characters it was necessary he should assume, are perhaps unequalled even amidst the performances of the host of celebrated travellers to whom it has been the pride of Great Britain to have given birth. If the several incidents therefore are not portrayed with sufficient strength, the fault lies with the author and not the adventurer'.

Wellsted was considerate of others, even during his first fever in Oman. Then, while he was recovering in Seeb, he paid for the sea transport from Muscat to Seeb and subsequent care costs for a Frenchman who was ill in Muscat.

On 25 October 1842, Wellsted died at 13 Molyneux Street, aged 37. His will named his father, James Wellsted, as the only beneficiary - of £100, a modest sum in those days.

Wellsted's reputation was maligned in subsequent memoirs and marginalia. Captain Haines wrote in the Transactions of the Bombay Geographical Society, published 1852-53, 'the late Lieutenant Wellsted, of the Indian Navy, appears to have caused an erroneous account' [of Wellsted's role in Socotra]. Haines describes the context 'I decided, therefore, that, while I conducted the trigonometrical survey of the island, my assistant [he meant Wellsted] should travel leisurely through the interior; and, to assist him, I ordered Mr. Midshipman (now Lieutenant) Cruttenden, who understood the Arab language and character well, to accompany him. Having executed the commands of Government within the time specified, I forwarded a fair copy of my survey, with my own observations on its anchorages, and those of my officers during the cruise, consisting of papers from my assistant, Lieutenant Wellsted, the late Dr. Hulton, and Messrs. Cruttenden and Smith. It will therefore be evident that Lieutenant Wellsted was only a subordinate officer, acting under obedience to my orders.' To emphasise Haines feelings, Wellsted was not included in any thanks within Haines own papers, while all other senior personnel were listed. However - as a counterbalance - in his thanks within his Travels in Arabia neither did Wellsted include Haines, the pair did not gel.

Before Wellsted's publications, Haines had entrusted him with the leadership of Socotra's land survey and initial negotiations, presumably in Arabic, with Sultan Omar ibn Tawari. Wellsted appears, in fact, to have deferred to Haines in any decisions he made, even though Haines was absent. Indeed, Wellsted writes explicitly, 'My instructions directed me'. The glowing reception of Wellsted's publications might have been the cause of Haines's published irritation of 1844.

OMAN DURING WELLSTED'S TIME

The northern area of the modern Sultanate of Oman, in Arabia's south-east, has an ancient history. Its coasts traded with Mesopotamian and Indus Valley civilisations over 4,000 years ago. At various periods, the seaboard fell under dynasties from Persia, notably the Achaemenid Empire. After the arrival of Arab tribes some 2,000 years ago, the interior was dominated by those tribes rather than by foreign powers. Following the rise of Islam in the 7th century AD, a distinct religious tradition and local political dynasties developed along the northern mountain chain (often called "the interior") around Nizwa and Rustaq. These helped to set northern Oman apart from much of the rest of the Arabian Peninsula. Portugal's occupation of coastal towns from AD 1507 simply reinforced the long-standing separation of coast and interior.

With the rise of the Al Busaid (Al Said) dynasty from AD 1744, Oman remained a distinct polity, but the gap between coast and interior began slowly to narrow. Muscat emerged as the capital in the 1790s, its harbour becoming a shorthand for the state as a whole.

By the early 19th century, Oman was in a state of flux. In Muscat, Sayyid Said bin Sultan Al Said (variously described by contemporaries as Sultan, Sooltan, or Imam) had ruled this loosely held-together state since 1807. He depended on the support of Omani tribes for any serious military action. The rulers of the First

Saudi State (the Emirate of Diriyah) exploited this lack of central land power to raid, and at times occupy, large areas of what is now northern Oman. Wellsted refers repeatedly to these incursions. Mutlaq bin Mohammed Al Mutairi, the father of Saad bin Mutlaq who features frequently in Wellsted's writing, led raids into much of the territory, including Muscat itself, in these first decades of the 19th century under the ruler the Amir Saud bin Abdulaziz Al Saud. His successor as Amir, Abdullah bin Saud Al Saud, was less successful. His reign and his influence on Oman ended when Egyptian forces captured him at Diriyah and sent him to Constantinople for execution in 1819.

For Sayyid Said this was only a short-lived respite. In the east of the country he retained power, helped by British support through the East India Company, which assisted him in curbing the growing power of the Al Hamouda sheikhs in Bani Bu Ali. North-west of Muscat, the coastal town of Suwaiq and its environs, together with the historically important town of Nizwa and nearby settlements, were ruled almost independently by Sayyid Hilal bin Mohammed Al Said, a cousin of Sayyid Said, though twelve years his junior.

Sayyid Said bin Sultan

In the port of Sohar, Wellsted wrote of Ahmed bin Aisan—actually Sayyid Hamud bin Azzan Al Said, a second cousin of Sayyid Said—who ruled from the town's large fort. His authority extended over a wedge of territory inland towards, and including, the important town of Rustaq, some 130kms to the south-east. Sayyid Hamud's grandfather had created Sohar as an effectively independent territory from 1783. Oman's coastal-based rulers understood that amicable relations with Britain could help secure their own positions.

Britain, acting through the East India Company, had already demonstrated its strength along this coast. It attacked Ras Al Khaimah in 1809, Shinas in 1810 (with Omani support), and Ras al-Khaimah again in 1819. These expeditions underlined Britain's naval and marine power. The inland battle of Bani Bu Ali in 1820 was disastrous for Britain and its Omani allies, but a subsequent British victory there in 1821 showed that, when required, Britain could project force away from the shore. Over the space of some twenty years, Britain had become an important player over large areas of Arabia.

The Second Saudi State, the Emirate of Najd established in 1824 under Turki bin Abdullah Al Saud, continued to send forces into Oman and established a power centre at Buraymi. The "Wahhabi" forces of Turki's son and successor, Amir Faisal bin Turki bin Abdullah Al Saud, raided with near impunity into coastal Oman and much of the hinterland from their desert oasis base at Al Buraymi. That oasis lay about 920 kilometres from Riyadh (which Wellsted still calls "Diriyah", the name of the previous Saudi capital, now within modern Riyadh), only about 100 kilometres from Sohar on the Sea of Oman, and roughly 300 kilometres from Muscat.

This Wahhabi threat was only checked, under Ottoman instruction, in December 1838, when Egyptian forces under Khurshid Pasha captured Emir Faisal in Riyadh and sent him to Cairo. Though less extensive than the earlier Saudi occupation, this was the period in which James Wellsted travelled in northern Oman, repeatedly encountering the effects of these raids.

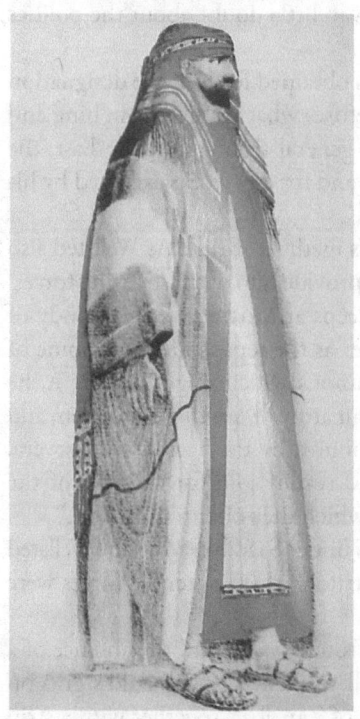

Abdullah bin Saud Al Saud - portrait in Constantinople

Despite his weakness on land, Sayyid Said commanded an impressive naval fleet. In the 1830s his European-style armed ships ranged from the *Liverpool*, a 74-gun ship later presented to King William IV of Britain (a prestige gesture - the nineteenth-century equivalent of a big-ticket "political donation"), through seven ships carrying 22 guns or more, down to a small six-gun vessel: in total, some fifteen warships and around sixty Arab-style gunboats. These ships used Muscat, Bombay, and Zanzibar as their principal home ports, though the *Henningshaw*, a 36-gun ship, was stationed at Calcutta. This navy enabled him to protect his merchant marine and the vessels of his subjects. More importantly, it allowed him to dominate Zanzibar and much of the East African coast.

In the first half of the 19th century this fleet enabled Sayyid Said to deal with Britain on terms no other regional ruler could claim, and his careful maintenance of good relations with visitors such as Wellsted helped to secure his position as an ally. In exchange (and perhaps to reduce the obligations that came with it) for the *Liverpool*, Britain presented the *Prince Regent*, a three-masted sailing royal yacht. The gift was commemorated on a Flight, Barr & Barr Worcester dinner plate made as part of a full service for Said bin Sultan; it depicts the yacht's arrival at Muscat, an elegant contemporary witness to the relationship.

Wellsted travelled as a British official and dressed accordingly, as he notes in his description of meeting Lieutenant Whitelock at Samad al-Shan: "He [Whitelock] has assumed the native dress, but I still retain that of England." Whitelock was probably directed to Samad al-Shan, as Wellsted himself had been, in a letter he received at Sur from Said bin Sultan. Supported by such introductory letters, Wellsted received a generally friendly welcome in most of the places he visited.

All the rivals of Sayyid Said at least wanted to be independent of Muscat. This was put plainly to Wellsted when he met women from a sheikh's family in Bani Bu Ali, who "expressed themselves highly delighted that an Englishman had, at last, come among them, but spoke of Sayyid Said with contempt, and did not conceal their desire to throw off their present very slight connexion with him." Though he admired Sayyid Said, and Wellsted was himself a recipient of Sayyid Said's generosity and clearly admired him: Wellsted was in little doubt about the politics of Oman.

"Speaking of Sayyid Said, whose liberality has obtained for him the designation of the second Omar, they observe that he never refuses what is asked from him; and that for the customary offering to a superior so general throughout the East, the Imam usually returns its value one hundred fold; and for any works executed by his order, he pays a higher rate than other individuals."

This generosity was a key part of Sayyid Said's method of rule. As Wellsted also wrote, he relied on the tribes and their sheikhs to provide him with a fighting force:

"The only permanent force that the Imam keeps at Muscat is a small body of four hundred men, accoutred in the same manner as the sepoys of India. Some of these are also his domestic slaves; but upon occasions which might require it, he could from Southern Oman collect in three days an army of ten thousand men, and afterwards increase the number to thrice the amount, by the accession of several Bedouin Sheikhs and their followers, who would readily join for the sake of the share in the plunder, and the occasional presents which they obtain from him."

Given the constant raiding by Wahhabi forces under Saad bin Mutlaq (Wellsted wrote Sayyid ibn Mutlak) throughout Omani territory, these potential forces were never used to decisive effect.

Internal family conflict, repeated incursions from Riyadh, and the absence of a disciplined land army under his direct control all weakened Sayyid Said's grip on Oman. At the same time, the Oman-ruled island of Zanzibar, together with a strip of the East African coast from Kilwa north to Mogadishu, offered him a more attractive economic and political base. He was constructing an Arabian Sea trading empire - a thalassocracy - and by the 1830s his capital had relocated from Muscat to Zanzibar.

Though highly profitable for Sayyid Said, Zanzibar further loosened his hold on Oman. As Wellsted observed:

"Yet, with all his able qualities, the Imam's government has on more than one occasion been placed in the greatest jeopardy. Ever restless, and incessantly on the lookout for some pretext to sanction their giving vent to a natural love of strife, his relations have usually taken advantage of his absence to Zanzibar to carry their views into effect."

It was into this Oman – looking out over the sea, fragmented on land, and pivoting between Muscat and Zanzibar with Riyadh trying to gain power - that James Wellsted travelled through and later wrote about.

∼

WELLSTED IN OMAN

After Wellsted's arrival in Muscat on 21 November 1835, he travelled southeast by sea, to the port of Sur. Though a small town, Sur regularly traded with East African ports as far south as Mozambique and Indian subcontinent ports through to modern Sri-Lanka. His intention was to travel from Sur towards the northwest, on the western side of the Al Hajar Mountains, to Al Buraymi, and then via Al Ahsa, near Bahrain, to the capital of the Al Saud ruler . Wellsted called the capital Diriyah; however, this had already been destroyed by Ottoman/Egyptian forces, and a new town, Riyadh, had superseded it.

Wellsted's initial route from Sur followed that of two British military expeditions in the early 1820s from Sur to Bani bu Ali, both had engaged in battles with the Bani bu Ali tribe. Remarkably, Wellsted was not attacked, but he was treated as an honoured guest and shown around the region. From Bani bu Ali he continued northwest, between the desert sand-dunes and the Al Hajar Mountains, visiting oasis settlements along the way. In one he met unexpectedly with Lieut. F. Whitelock, and the pair of British officers continued together to the important settlement of Nizwa. At Nizwa he spent some time, and then ascended the 2,000-meter Jabal Al Akhdar Mountains to its most important settlement, Sayq.

It was in Nizwa, after his descent from Jabal Akhdar, that the first of a series of misfortunes struck Wellsted and his party. The entire group was struck with what must have been malaria, and after several days recovering, they travelled east to the coast for what was intended to be a healthier location at Seeb, to the west of Muscat. A recovery was soon made, and they journeyed up the coast to the port town of Suwayq, from where they would take a route through the mountains to Ibri. Wellsted was aware that forces of the Emir Faisal bin Turki Al Saud, the ruler of Diriyah, under Saad bin Mutlaq were raiding in many areas of northern Oman. However, it was folly for Wellsted to assume that a letter from Oman's ruler, Sayyid Said bin Sultan Al Said, to Saad bin Mutlaq, would enable him to travel safely to Diriyah. At the time, Sayyid Said bin Sultan Al Said was paying a tribute (zakat) of 5,000 Maria Theresa Thalers a year to Emir Faisal bin Turki Al Saud (who ruled Riyadh intermittently between 1834 and 1865).

On reaching Ibri, the sheikh of the town made it clear that Wellsted should leave immediately as the town had 2,000 Wahhabi men, troops of the Al Saud, in effective occupation. Wellsted learnt that the Wahhabis, led by Saad bin Mutlaq, had also been raiding through areas of Oman that Wellsted had travelled through, to the south of Ibri. Wellsted took the only route available to him, a return east to the coast, which marked the end of his attempt to reach Diriyah.

'Travels in Oman' is not only a remarkable tale of discovery, but an insight into the foundation of modern Oman. It also gives an understanding of the type of men who, like Wellsted, built up Britain's influence in the region as individuals rather than simply part of an invading force.

**THANK YOU 🙏 for buying
"Travels in Arabia"
I do hope you find it informative.**

INTRODUCTION
ORIGINAL EDITION

With the exception of that portion relating to the peninsula of Sinai, the following volumes contain the Author's researches in parts of Arabia hitherto imperfectly or wholly unknown to Europeans. They may, therefore, derive a value from these considerations to which it is very certain they would otherwise have no claim.

In the personal narrative, he has endeavoured to convey to the reader the impressions produced on his mind at the moment of each particular occurrence. As to the rest, it was compiled from copious notes collected at various intervals, Many of the facts herein stated have never previously been made known to an European public, and it is on this ground of novelty alone that the Author diffidently hopes his researches may prove interesting to the philosopher and the naturalist, as well as those more immediately engaged in geographical pursuits.

The vindication of Bruce's reputation, being founded on self-evident facts, can scarcely be impugned. Such readers, however, as feel interested in the question, - and in this number the Author flatters himself the great majority are included, - will be gratified to know that one - by no means the least virulent of his detractors- did an act of tardy justice to the reputation he once actively laboured to destroy [1].

It remains but to acknowledge the assistance derived from others towards the completion of this work. The Author's thanks are especially due to John Arrowsmith, Esq.; to whose knowledge, skill, and industry, so many travellers have already recorded their deep obligations, for constructing and engraving the maps with which it is illustrated; to the Rev. J. Reynolds, Secretary to the Oriental Committee, for the translation of a valuable manuscript relative to the religion of Oman; to Lieut. H. A. Ormsby, I.N., whose intimate acquaintance with Bedouin habits and customs have aided him considerably in his account of that interesting people; to Captain R. Moresby, the author of the admirable Charts of the Red Sea and Coast of Arabia, which have excited the admiration of many learned societies in Europe; and to his esteemed and respected friend Admiral Sir Charles Malcolm, to whose personal regard, as well as to his enthusiastic zeal for the extension of geographical science, the Author was indebted for facilities which mainly contributed to the satisfactory issue of his long and arduous undertaking.

In the map of Oman, the routes of Lieut. Whitelock is added to his own; he accompanied the Author over the greater part of the province: and, after he left, succeeded in passing from Shinas (*Wellsted wrote Schinas*) to Sharjah (*Sharja*). For the drawing of the Bisharyan Camel (*of southeast Egypt*), which embellishes this volume, the author is indebted to J. Bonomi, Esq., who was kind enough to allow it to be taken from a model in his possession.

For the more complete illustration of the text, he has availed himself of several notes by the Rev. G. C. Renouard, which were attached to papers inserted in the Journal of the Royal Geographical Society. The mode of spelling Arabic proper names, adopted throughout, is also that advocated by the same gentleman [2] who has reduced Oriental orthography to a fixed standard, as far as those papers are concerned. Each letter has invariably its corresponding equivalent. The consonants are sounded as in English; the vowels as in Italian; the accents mark long vowels, and an apostrophe ['] the letter 'ain. *Gh* and *hh* are strong gutturals; the former often resembling the Northumbrian r, the latter the Welsh and Gaelic *ch*. *A, e, i, o*, are to be respectively pronounced as in far, there, ravine, and cold; *u* as in rude, or *oo* in fool; *ei* as *ey* in they; *ou* as *ow* in fowl; *ai* as *i* in thin; *ch* as in child.

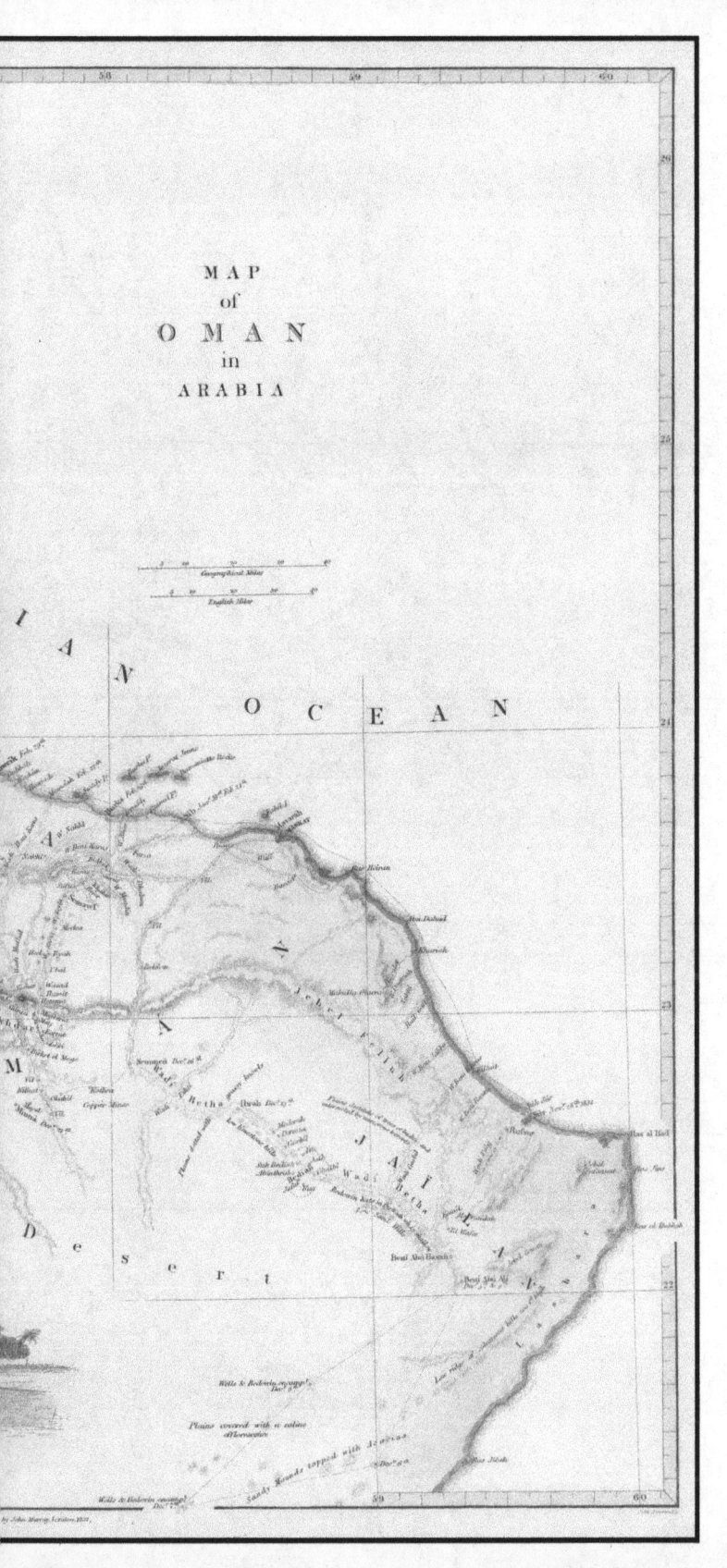

CHAPTER I
ARRIVAL IN MUSCAT

A spect of Arabia - its unexplored Districts - The Author's preparations for his Journey - Arrives at Muscat (Maskat) - Interview with the Imam - His presents - Personal appearance and generosity of character - Muscat; its ancient name and commercial importance - Position-Fortifications, Houses, &c.

Arabia has been aptly compared to a coat of frieze bordered with gold, since the only cultivated or fertile spots are found on its confines, the intermediate space being filled with arid and sandy wastes.

Nearly the whole of its Syrian or northern frontier has been examined. [Johann Ludwig] Burckhardt describes, from personal observation, the immediate vicinity of Makkah (*Mecca*) and Madinah (*Medina*) in the Hijaz; and [Carsten] Niebuhr, in the same manner, a small portion of Yemen; but the extensive provinces of Hadramaut and Oman, together with the western side bordering on the Persian Gulf, were still wholly unexplored.

During my employment for some years past on the survey of the southern and western coasts of Arabia, my attention was constantly directed towards attaining a knowledge of the provinces contiguous to them; but no opportunity for penetrating the country, which presented a fair chance of success, occurred within this period, until the commencement of the year 1835, when the restless and grasping disposition of Mohammed Ali induced him to despatch a force from Egypt, in order to take possession of the Coffee country. My proposal of accompanying his army to this point, and from thence to endeavour to reach Hadramaut, was immediately acceded to by the Indian government; but, before their sanction could be conveyed to me, intelligence arrived of the Mohammed Ali

Pasha (*Pacha's*) force having been led into a defile in the Asir (*Assair*) country, and there defeated with great slaughter; a miserable remnant alone reaching the seashore.

Foiled, therefore, in this quarter, on my return to Bombay I turned my attention towards Oman, which possesses claims not inferior in interest to the other provinces, but deterred, in all probability, by the known insalubrity of its climate, and the supposed hostile character of its inhabitants, no European traveller has hitherto penetrated it, and its people, with their country, remained wholly unknown to us. In the prosecution of this project, I was induced to hope that the political relations between its liberal and enlightened ruler and our own government were of such a nature as to leave little doubt but that he would afford every facility in his power to the object of the mission. After obtaining the necessary permission for this purpose, I passed a few days in procuring the requisite letters [3] and presents, and on November 9th, 1835, embarked on board a small schooner (the *Cyrene*), for Muscat [4], at which port, after a pleasant passage, we arrived on the 21st of the same month.

Shortly after our little bark had anchored within the cove, I went on shore and waited on the Imam; but finding that he had a full divan, I took the liberty of requesting a private audience on the morrow, which was immediately granted.

Muscat Harbour - 19th century

ARRIVAL IN MUSCAT

November 22nd. I found no one with his Highness (Sayyid Said) this morning but his son, and after delivering my presents, a few words sufficed to explain the objects of my proposed journey. Prepared as I was by my previous knowledge of Sayyid Said's characteristic liberality to meet with no unfavourable exception to these, I was surprised out of all former conception by the eagerness he displayed to further my views. 'it is occasions like these," he said, " which afford me real pleasure, since they enable me, by meeting the wishes of your government, to evince the strength of my attachment to them;" and he added, in a tone the sincerity of which there was no mistaking, "these are not words of the tongue, but of the heart." After a conversation of some length, in which I received every aid from his perfect knowledge of the country, it was arranged that as there was but one road to the southward, which I felt no desire to repass, that I should proceed first to Sur, land there, and go on to Bani bu Ali (*Beni-Abu-Ali*), thence cross in a line nearly parallel with the sea-shore, to the Jabal Akhdar, or Green Mountains, which are described as elevated, populous, and fruitful; and after investigating them, finish the remaining portion of Oman; and from thence, if the road should continue open, proceed to Diriyah (*Der'ayyah*) [5], the Wahhabi capital. Some other minor subjects were then discussed and arranged, and I took my leave, highly gratified with the prospect of success before me.

November 23rd. From his Highness this morning I received a fine Nejd horse for my journey, a brace of greyhounds, and a gold-mounted sword, together with an intimation, that so long as I remained in Oman, the best the country afforded should be mine; that all expenses of camels, guides, &c., would be defrayed by him, and that letters were prepared, under his own direction, to the chiefs of the different districts through which I had to pass, requiring them to receive me with all possible attention. Placing on one side every consideration which might have actuated this prince in furthering what he supposed the views of my government to serve me, there was, on this occasion, in the style and mode in which he exhibited it, a spirit in full accordance with the truly noble character which he bears.

Sayyid Said is fifty-two years of age and has reigned twenty-seven years. He possesses a tall and commanding figure; a mild, yet striking countenance; and an address and manner courtly, affable, and dignified. In his personal habits, the Imam has preserved the simplicity of his Bedouin (*Bedowin*) origin; he is frugal almost to abstemiousness; he never wears jewels; his dress, excepting in the fineness of the materials, is not superior to that of the principal inhabitants; and he is attended, on all occasions, without pomp or ostentation. It is noticed by the Arabs, as an instance of the warmth of his affections, that he daily visits his mother, who is still alive, and pays, in all matters, implicit obedience to her wishes. In his intercourse with Europeans, he has ever displayed the warmest attention and kindness; probably, if any native prince can with truth be called a friend to the English, it is the Imam of Muscat; and even on our side, the political connexion with him appears to have in it more sincerity than is generally supposed to exist.

The government of this prince is principally marked by the absence of all oppressive imposts, all arbitrary punishments, by his affording marked attention to the merchants of any nation who come to reside at Muscat, and by the general toleration which is extended to all persuasions: while, on the other hand, his probity, the impartiality and leniency of his punishments, together with the strict regard he pays to the general welfare of his subjects, have rendered him as much respected and admired by the town Arabs, as his liberality and personal courage have endeared him to the Bedouins. These splendid qualities have obtained for him throughout the East the designation of the Second Omar.

Sayyid Said is the son of Sultan (*Sooltan*), the third son of Ahmed Ibn Said, who, in A.D. 1730, rescued his country from the Persian yoke. Although the individuals in this line are not of the Yarubi (*Yaharabi*) [6] Al Azd (*el Azad*) tribe, by whom the sovereignty of Oman was held for about two hundred and fifty years, and to whom, in the person of Saaf, Ahmed Ibn Said, of the Yarubi Al Azd, succeeded, yet the two dynasties are collaterally descended from the same common ancestor, Azd, which is also the general appellation of the tribe in which both branches are included. The present sovereign of Oman, however, is not styled Imam by the Arabs. In order to attain this title, it is necessary, at the period of his election, that he should possess sufficient theological attainments to preach before the assembled chiefs, by whom he is chosen, and their followers; and also that he should not embark onboard ships. The latter, as in the case of Saaf, who took possession of the ports on the African coast and their dependencies, is, after installation, overlooked; but the former they consider so indispensably binding that Sayyid Said, who either does not possess the necessary attainments, or fancies so, has dispensed with the ceremony altogether, and, in consequence, receives from his subjects the title of Sayyid, or prince, only.

Reserving for a future section the details connected with the government, which apply generally to the greater portion of the towns in Oman, I shall first give an account of Muscat, and then proceed at once to the narrative of my travels. Various notices of this town may be found in the pages of Niebuhr, Hamilton, and others, but they mostly refer to a remote period, and are now, from the great change which its condition and commerce have experienced under its present ruler, scarcely applicable to it. I shall, therefore, give the result of my own observation and inquiries at some length.

It would appear that the ancient geographers [7] were acquainted at an early period with the position of Muscat [8]. It was probably Mokha (*Moscha*), a port of the Hadramaut, mentioned by Ptolemy: noticed also in the Periplus of the Erythraean Sea, as the grand emporium of the trade between India, Persia, and Arabia. But, notwithstanding this testimony, Muscat does not appear to have been a place of very considerable commercial importance until the Portuguese took possession of the town in 1508, and converted it into an intermediate port, where their ships might obtain supplies and refreshments in the passage between their Indian settlements and that on the Island of Hormuz (*Ormuz*) in the Persian Gulf.

With this view they fortified it with considerable labour and expense. When the latter city, on the 26th April, 1622, was taken possession of by the Persians, under the Emperor Shah Abbas, a great number of its wealthiest inhabitants sought shelter in Muscat; but, in 1658, the Arabs, having retaken the city from the Portuguese, put all the garrison to the sword, and the only vestiges of their settlement now remaining are the forts and two churches, one of which has fallen to ruins, and the other is converted into a palace for the Imam. From this period, until Sayyid Said obtained the government, the reigning princes only visited Muscat occasionally, and Rustaq (*Rostak*) was considered the capital of Oman.

The town of Muscat is situated at the extremity of a small cove in the gorges of an extensive pass, which widens from this point as it advances into the interior. On either side, the cove hills, to the height of from three to five hundred feet, rise almost perpendicularly from the sea, and appear lined with forts, which, considering they belong to the vicinity of an Arab town, are in a tolerable state of repair. The largest, and most commanding, are erected, on either side,-at the inner extremity of the cove; and within that on the western side state prisoners are confined. Two half-moon batteries also command the entrance: the guns appear well mounted, and the guard at all seasons on the alert. The distance across, from fort to fort, is only half a mile, so that an open attack in the day-time would be very difficult if these were well served.

To persons arriving from seaward, Muscat with its fort and contiguous hills, have an extraordinary and romantic appearance. Not a tree, shrub, or other traces of vegetation is visible, and the whitened surface of the houses, and turreted forts in the vicinity, contrast in a singular manner with the burnt and cindery aspect of the darkened masses of rock around. Similar in its aspect to most eastern cities when viewed from a distance, we first discern the level roofs of the dwellings, the domes of the mosques, their lofty minarets, and other prominent features, and the view retain these attractive features until we land when the illusion quickly disappears. Narrow crowded streets and filthy bazaars, nearly blocked up by porters bearing burthens of dates, grain, &c., wretched huts intermingled with low and paltry houses, the owners of which, seated on a small projecting part before their door, are merely sheltered from the heat of the sun by tattered canvas awnings; and other dwellings more than half fallen to decay, but which yet continue tenanted, meet the eye in every direction. There are, nevertheless, within the town several substantial, handsome houses; the palace of the Imam, and those belonging to the old princess, his mother, the governors, and several others, being of the latter description. The form of these edifices differs considerably from what is usually seen in the towns of Yemen and the Hijaz, and partakes more of the Persian style of architecture.

Muscat is built on a slope, rising with a gradual ascent from the sea, where the water nearly washes the bases of the houses. This side has no defence, but the others are protected by a wall fourteen feet high, with a dry ditch. The entrance is by two gates, which they close every night at sunset.

CHAPTER 2
MUSCAT'S POPULATION AND TRADE

A*bundance of Provisions - Natives - Balouchis - Persians - Manufactory of Arms - Intermarriages - Insalubrity of Muscat - Banians - Oriental Bankrupts - Banian Cows - Jews - Population - Customs - Exports and Imports - Pilgrims - Coffee trade - Dates - Distillation of Arak (Arrack).*

Notwithstanding its unpromising appearance, there are few parts where supplies may be obtained in greater profusion, or of better quality. Beef, mutton, poultry, fruit throughout the year, fish, &c., are all good in their several kinds. Muscat is supplied with water by means of a deep well, contiguous to which there is a fort, where a guard in time of war is constantly stationed, in order to prevent others from cutting off the supply. A newly constructed aqueduct conveys the water to the town. It is hard and of an indifferent quality. The cove abounds with fish.

The greater portion of the inhabitants of Muscat are of a mixed-race, the descendants of Arabs, Persians, Indians, Syrians, by the way of Baghdad and Basra (*Basarah*), Kurds, Afghans, Balouchis (*Beluches*), &c., who, attracted by the mildness of the government, have settled here, either for the purposes of commerce or to avoid the despotism of the surrounding governments.

This we discover has been the case from a very early period; two centuries before the birth of Mohammed, a powerful tribe, then residing on the shores of the Persian Gulf, sought refuge here against the oppression of the Persians, and, as late as 1828, a party of Jews, unable any longer to endure the exactions and tyranny of Dawud Pasha (*Daud Pacha*), were received by the Imam with much kindness.

Few Afghans make Muscat their permanent residence, those seen in the town being mostly pilgrims to or from Makkah. Hence they seldom enter into many commercial speculations and are further remarkable for keeping aloof from the other classes. The Balouchis, on the contrary, mix with all, and though a thrifty race, are in general very poor. A considerable number of the Imam's household troops are recruited from this class; others hire themselves as porters, an occupation for which their athletic forms well befit them, while some few engage as mariners on board *baghlas* (*bagalas*) [9] or ships, where they are much esteemed for their cheerfulness and activity. In consequence of the difference in their faith, the Oman Arabs and Persians seldom intermarry, but with the Balouchis the Arabs are less fastidious, since they not unfrequently obtain Arab wives, and reside here permanently, which they also frequently do, in the event of any of their slaves becoming mothers. It is only very recently that the former treachery of the Persians has been overlooked by the Arabs. During Imam Saaf's reign, a garrison of the latter were admitted into the town; but taking advantage of that prince's habitual vice of drunkenness, they on one occasion seized upon the forts, deposed him, and usurped the government. After they in their turn were dispossessed, they were not allowed in any considerable number to reside within the town; but since the marriage of the Imam with the Princess of Shiraz, that order, with several other restrictions, has been rescinded. Indeed, an offence committed by a Persian, whether it be of a civil or criminal nature, is permitted to go before their own *qadi* (*kadi*), and, according to his report, they are punished or acquitted. The Persians at Muscat are mostly merchants, who deal in India piece-goods, coffee, hookahs or *qalyans*, and rose-water. Others, from Bandar Abbas (*Bunder Abbas*), Lar, and Minab (*Menon*), manufacture swords and matchlocks, for which there is a great demand in the interior.

From their mixed descent, and also from the custom of intermarrying with their Zanzibar and Abyssinian slaves, the complexion of this portion of the inhabitants varies very considerably, but the higher orders, who have preserved untainted the purity of their Arabian descent, retain, in a remarkable degree, the peculiar characteristics of their race. In their persons they are mostly spare, and their skins are of a light, healthy brown colour, They rarely suffer from fevers, although the climate of Muscat is, in this respect especially, fatal to strangers, no European having been able to live there hitherto, and many fatal cases occur in such of our ships as are compelled to remain but for a few days. The lower classes are stout, with remarkably muscular limbs, and some of them afford the most perfect models of strength and symmetry. So little variation is to be found in the habits, disposition, and moral character of the Arabs who occupy the maritime towns, that I have preferred treating of them generally in a separate section. It remains to notice two other classes of foreigners in Muscat.

There are more Banians [*a 19th-century British term for Indian merchant, often Gujarati*] here than in any other city of Arabia. At the period of my visit it was calculated that they amounted to one thousand five hundred, and, under the mild administration of Sayyid Said, they were supposed to be rapidly increasing. They possess a small temple, are permitted to keep and protect a certain number of cows, to burn the dead, and to follow, in all other respects, the uninterrupted enjoyment of their respective religious tenets, without any of that arbitrary distinction of dress which they are compelled to adopt in the cities of Yemen. Here they appear to possess all the privileges of Muslim (*Mussulman*) subjects, with one single exception. The relation of a Banian slain by a Muslim can be compelled to accept a compensation for blood, while with the Arab it is a matter of choice.

They mostly embark at Porbandar (*Porebunder*) from the northwest provinces of India, and, in the prosecution of their commercial avocations, frequently remain for a period of fifteen or twenty years. They never bring their women with them, and, though it is well known that they occasionally intrigue with Arab females, there are few exceptions to their remaining unmarried for the whole of this period. It is, however, a singular fact in connexion with the history of this class, that, when occasional, though rare instances occur of their falling away from their own faith, and adopting that of the Muslims, the latter do not appear to pride themselves on their proselytes. A practice they have of proclaiming themselves bankrupt is a subject of considerable diversion to the Arabs. An individual thus situated seats himself in the open day in his shop with a candle burning before him. Those of his own class to whom he is indebted no sooner perceive this, than they come in and revile him in no measured terms, and sometimes even beat him. But, after this ebullition, he is not molested until he has again commenced business, and is in a fair way to retrieve himself when they again commence their importunities so that his failure in no wise releases him from his former obligations.

Accompanied by an Arab merchant and some Bedouins, I once went to look at the cows belonging to this sect. There were about two hundred in a large space, enclosed by a wall. The animals were well-fed, sleek, and mischievous. Myself and the merchant, being unarmed, were permitted to enter, but this was denied to the Bedouins, because they wore their *jambiyas*, and it was thought would not fail to use them in case the animals became at all mischievous. My companions immediately perched themselves, with several others who had collected, on the wall, and seemed to derive excessive amusement from observing the form of adoration which the Banians were paying to their cattle. When the animals fall sick, the Banian pays them the utmost attention, and, should they exhibit no symptoms of recovery, they are, as in the towns on many other parts of the coast, sent off to India. The habits of this class are, however, too well known to need any further mention here.

In Muscat the Banians constitute a body of the principal merchants, who almost exclusively monopolise the pearl trade from the Persian Gulf, amounting, it is calculated, to fifteen *lacks* [*lacs* - one *lack* = 100,000] of [Spanish] dollars annually. They enter as largely into the supply of grain from India and have also most extensive dealings in Indian cloths and piece-goods.

There are a few Jews in Muscat, who mostly arrived there in 1828, being driven from Baghdad, as we have before stated, by the cruelties and extortions of the Pasha Dawud. Nearly the whole of this race were compelled to fly. Some took refuge in Persia, while others, in their passage towards India, remained here. The same toleration exercised towards all other persuasions is extended to the Bani Israel, no badge or mark, as in Egypt or Syria, being insisted on: they are not, as in the town of Yemen, compelled to occupy a distant and separate part of the town, nor is the observance, so strictly adhered to in Persia, of compelling them to pass to the left of Muslims when meeting in the streets, here insisted on. Their avocations in Muscat are various, many being employed in the fabrication of silver ornaments, others in shroffing money, and some few retail intoxicating liquors.

Banian Hindus in 19thc James Forbes

I should fix the population of Muscat and Mutrah (*Matarah*) at sixty thousand souls.

This town is entitled to a high rank among Oriental cities, not only as the emporium of a very considerable trade between Arabia, India, and Persia but also, in reference to its extensive imports, of some note as the seaport of Oman.

The customs, fixed at five per cent. on all imported goods, are farmed at Muscat for one hundred and five thousand, and at Mutrah for sixty thousand Dollars, which give, collectively, an annual importation of three million three hundred thousand Dollars, or about nine hundred thousand pounds sterling. No duties of any kind are levied on exports. Although this does not sound very imposing when contrasted with the ports of India or Europe, it is very considerable for Arabia, the imports being chiefly cloth and corn; and, indeed, the amount exceeds that of any other town in the country, Jeddah (*Jiddah*) excepted.

The principal articles which are brought to, and afterwards exported from Muscat, and on which no duty is levied, are coffee and pearls. In the conveyance of the former eight or ten large, and double that number of smaller vessels, trade between Yemen and Muscat: they make but one voyage during the year. Some of these vessels are of two hundred and fifty tons, and upwards.

Freighted with dates, Persian tobacco, carpets, and generally filled with Persian pilgrims, they proceed along the Arabian Coast, and up the Red Sea, to Jeddah, where they land their pilgrims; and such of the crew who are desirous of doing so, proceed with them to the Hajj (Hadj) at Makkah. There they probably remain one or two months, according as the period may serve for the return of the pilgrims; but, after leaving that port, they make the best of their way to either Mokha or Hudaydah (*Hedeidha*), when they exchange the bullion received as passage money from the pilgrims for coffee, and manage to quit the Red Sea at the beginning or middle of the month of May, so as to avoid the first burst of the south-west monsoon. The coffee brought hither is then disposed of, and that which is not required for the consumption of the people in the town, or for sale to the Bedouins of the neighbouring provinces is shipped off in smaller boats to Bahrain, Basra, and the southern parts of the Persian Gulf. Formerly the trade to Basra was very extensive, Syria being almost exclusively supplied through this channel, but the importation of West Indian coffee into the Levant has now almost exclusively supplanted that from Mokha.

At Muscat the coffee trade is in the hands of the Banians, and is said to be very lucrative. The pearl fisheries in the Persian Gulf are estimated at forty *lack*s annually, and nearly two-thirds of that produce are brought hither in small boats, and from thence conveyed to Bombay in ships or *baghlas*. They mostly arrive sealed at Muscat, and very few are disposed of there. In Bombay the Parsis (*Parsees*) are the principal purchasers, and a great many are sent by them to China.

Baghla Muscat Harbour

Muscat yields but few exports and no duty is now levied on them. The principal are dates, taken to India, where large quantities are required to make the government Arak or are sold at the different ports on the southern coast of Arabia;

runas (*ruinos - Rubia tinctorum*), or red dye, much valued in India; sharks' fins, shipped off to China, where they are used for making soup, and a variety of other purposes; and salt fish, much esteemed by the lower classes of natives in India. The returns for these articles are made principally in bullion and coffee. A number of mules from Persia, and asses from the Island of Bahrain, are annually sent to Mauritius (*the Isle of France*).

CHAPTER 3
JOURNEY FROM AND RETURN TO MUSCAT

Excursion to the Hot Springs of Imam Ali - Cove of Muscat - Heat - Glassy surface of the Sea - The Laughing Gull - Visit on board a Bagala - Singular appearance of her Crew - Songs - Music - Dancing - Remarkable Echo - Scenery - Mutrah - Population - Arab Women - Bedouins - A Village - Watch Dogs - Caravanserai - Description of the Springs - Irrigation - Height of the Thermometer - Fine Climate - Return to Muscat.

November 23rd. Having obtained from his Highness this morning an officer to accompany me, I set out on a visit to the hot springs of *Imam Ali,* which are situated on the sea-shore, about seven hours to the westward of the town. Although the cool season was so far advanced, the day proved excessively sultry, and when we pushed off in our boat for Mutrah, notwithstanding a fresh breeze was prevailing outside, yet within the cove it was a perfect calm, and the heat thrown off from the sides of the mountains, along the base of which we were gliding, felt almost overpowering. At this time the sea presented a surface so smooth and glassy, that it reflected the dark hills, the whitened forts, the houses, and the shipping, with as much distinctness as from a mirror; and it required the slight motion communicated to their shadows by the long, undulating swell, which rolled slowly and lazily into the cove, to enable the beholder to determine the pictured objects from those which were real. Under the fierce glare of the noontide heat, the town, with its usually busy inhabitants, was silent, and at rest. Occasionally a long, slight canoe might be perceived, dotting the surface, as it rose on the summit of one of the rolling waves, with a single fisherman, seated near its stern pursuing his solitary occupation, while, hovering around him, and stooping occasionally to share in his "scaly spoil," the laughing sea-gull utters that wild, shrill, and piercing cry, distinguishable even at a distance, and which has given rise to its appropriate, but singular appellation.

On sweeping round an angle of the rock, we perceived a large *bagala* lying becalmed, and I will here introduce the scene which presented itself when I stepped on board, under an impression I should receive some letters. Let the reader picture to himself a huge misshapen vessel, of at least four hundred tons, with a long projecting prow, and an elevated and elaborately carved and ornamented stern, having but a single mast and single sail, the latter spread on a yard one hundred and fifty feet in length, and containing more canvass than the courses of the largest first-rates in his Majesty's navy. The decks appear crowded with beings of every hue, and from every clime. The Persian, distinguished by his flowing and richly-coloured dress; the Arab, with his coarse cloak of broad alternate stripes; the Balouchi, with his long hair and white garments; and the Armenian, who affects a costume bearing some resemblance to the unsightly garb of the Franks, are mixed up with and jostled by African negroes, who have but a piece of tattered cloth thrown around their waist. The latter compose the greater part of the crew, which may amount in number to one hundred and fifty men.

For their encouragement and recreation, whenever work is going on, about ten of their number are selected to sing to the remainder. A boy, with a sharp tenor voice, usually leads the concert, and to him his comrades reply in a deep, bass cadence, accompanying their voices with several rude instruments of music, and joining in a wild and picturesque sort of dance. These instruments are rude; one resembles the tom-tom of India (*Hindustan*); another, still more simple, the tambourine of Europe; but, when unprovided with these, I have observed them beating time upon one of their copper cooking dishes. To the European, scarcely any combination of sounds can appear farther removed from music, or, indeed, more thoroughly discordant, yet on these Africans, their effects appear indescribably exciting. The expression of the face, the contortions of the limbs and body, the yells with which their dancing gestures are accompanied, and the length of time they will continue the exercise, in fact until they sink down in a state of exhaustion, denote an intense sympathy with sounds to which we are equally strangers.

A light breeze sprang up, and, as they passed the forts on either side the entrance, two guns were fired, and the effects, contrasted with the former silence, were extremely magnificent. The reverberations, confined at first to the inner or nearer circle of hills, exceeded, rather than fell short of, the loudness of the original discharge; and might, as they broke in quick succession on the ear, be compared to the simultaneous and rapid firing of several heavy batteries of artillery. Nor was this diminished when they mingled with the secondary echoes, returned from more distant mountains, until, at length, the sounds became gradually more faint, and terminated in the former absolute silence. The rising breeze had wafted the smoke above the hills, and a strong beam of light was thrown on the shipping in the harbour, so that their masts, rigging, and even the lazy pendant, became, as it were, pencilled out upon the dark hills which formed the cove; but, owing to the peculiar nature of the scenery, the insignificance of works of art contrasted with those of nature, never appeared to me so striking as at this spot. The huge hulk of a seventy-four, and several scarcely less heavy frigates, with their spreading yards and lofty spars, are perfectly lost beneath the first range of what would otherwise appear low and insignificant hillocks.

After rounding the cape which forms the north-western extremity of the cove, we enter the neighbouring bay of Mutrah and pass a pretty town, situated on one of those low nooks which form a distinguishing feature in the scenery of this part of the world. Between the houses and the margin of the sea, so as to form a neat-looking promenade and landing-place, there is a broad belt of light coloured sand, which extends to the bold, gloomy cliffs overhanging either extremity of the town. The cove faces the prevailing breezes, and, in consequence of its exposed situation, is, at present, rarely frequented by vessels of any description; not a fishing-boat, nor even a canoe, was visible, and their absence added to the solitary, yet not unpleasing effect of the whole.

Nearly in a direction with Mutrah, a rugged islet rose before us. Its sides were splintered and shattered into curiously-shaped peaks, and on the very summit of these, where to the eye it appears difficult to conceive that the foot of man could have found a resting place, watchtowers have been erected. From one of the most elevated, a picturesque group of Arab soldiery, whose matchlocks and long lances glittered in the sunbeams, were gazing on us as we passed beneath them.

Weaving Oman

Mutrah is a considerable town, or rather a very large collection of huts, situated at the extremity of a cove, much frequented by the Imam's vessels, but seldom by those of others. Notwithstanding it is but a mile from the town, the road, leading over a range of hills is so rugged, that the communication between the two towns is maintained principally by boats. Its inhabitants are computed at twenty-thousand, and their principal employment is weaving cloth, or fabricating the woollen cloaks so generally worn in Arabia.

Scarcely a hut but contained its spinning wheel, with a female busily employed before it. All had their faces uncovered: their features were regular, and, in many cases, handsome, but the effect is, in a measure, destroyed by the absurd practice of dying the skin with henna. Their freedom of demeanour, when contrasted with that usually observed in Arab towns, gives no very flattering picture of their morals.

Camels had been provided for us, and, after a ride of two hours over a country wholly uninteresting, we arrived at the village of Ruwi (*Rooah*), which has some gardens and wells of water.

Camels and Ghaf trees west of Muscat

We passed several caravans of Bedouins, journeying to, or returning from Muscat. Their complexion is much fairer than that of any other Arabs that I have yet seen, and their stature, though short, is well proportioned. Their hair, which is permitted to flow in plaited folds as low as the waist, gives them a very striking and martial appearance when seated with their sword and shield, cross-legged, on their war camels.

They have dark, lively, expressive eyes; a well-formed nose and mouth; and their pearly white teeth offer a fine contrast to those of the town Arabs. They seem a laughing, good-humoured race, and chatted freely, as I rode at their side, of their country and its inhabitants. Now, and for some time afterwards, I found it difficult, without the aid of an interpreter, to maintain a conversation with the Omani Bedouins. The dialect which had served me in my communication with the tribes along the shores of the Red Sea was understood but very partially here. I am convinced, however, this could only occur to a person who had but a superficial knowledge of the language: one completely versed in it would find little difficulty in making himself understood in any part of the country.

After sunset we continued, occasionally, to pass groups of Bedouins, who had withdrawn some short distance from the road, and were seated with their camels round a fire. It seems customary on these occasions for neither party to proffer a salutation, which is contrary to the practice when they meet in the day, for then they exchange several sentences. About an hour before midnight, the loud and deep barking of some shepherd dogs denoted our approach to a village, which we entered a few minutes afterwards, and, after winding our way through several lanes, with large trees on either side, overhanging the path, we entered an extensive building erected for the use of travellers. The night air being cold, my guides soon prepared a fire, and a meal of rice and fish, of which we all partook most heartily. In the course of my several journeys, I have been never solicitous or particular about my place of repose, and I was much amused this night at the remarks of the Bedouins, when, instead of drawing near to the fire, as they were all anxiously doing, they saw me wrap myself up in a boat cloak, and lie down on a chunamed (*chinammed* lime-plastered) platform raised in the open air in the garden.

Early this morning, I visited the spring which was the object of my journey. The water gushes with much violence from an aperture at the base of a hill of clay ironstone. Veins of a crystallized quartz run in a diagonal direction through the rock, and large fragments have been dislodged from it.

Some faint indications of copper might be distinguished between the inner layers, but no traces of volcanic action were anywhere to be discovered. Close adjoining to the spot from whence the water issues a small square reservoir has been constructed for the convenience of those who come to bathe there. Immersed in this, a thermometer, Fahrenheit, indicated one hundred and ten degrees, which was two degrees less than at the rock. After repeated trials, I found it difficult to decide that it had any peculiarity of taste or smell. At one time I was induced to consider it slightly chalybeate [iron-rich], and at another to be in no higher degree saline; but, in neither instance, could I have given an opinion decidedly, and it may, therefore, be considered that, in both these respects, it differs but little from the water obtained in other parts of the country. Here the natives, after placing it to cool in porous pans, pronounce it excellent, drinking no other. It was evident that neither its heat nor any other quality which it may possess prevents its nourishing the surrounding vegetation. As a cure for cutaneous and other local disorders, these waters enjoy a great reputation amongst the Bedouins and town Arabs, the former frequently undertaking long and painful journeys from a great distance in the interior, that they may remain and use them for several days. Although the temperature was so high, yet I witnessed the submersion of several of the patients, who were kept under the surface by force for some time. One, an old man of eighty was so much exhausted by this rough treatment, that he appeared in a dying state: yet I was told that, if he lived, the operation would be repeated after an interval of two hours, for the natives believe if the waters fail in producing their desired effect, it is only because they have not been used sufficiently often. A few yards from the bath there is a small mosque, in which an old priest resides, who is ever ready to assist with his prayers to those who may require them.

Imam Ali pool

After leaving the reservoir, the water runs into a large shallow tank or basin, in which it cools ere it is permitted to reach the vegetation or trees, and numerous rills conduct it over the face of the country. The portion thus irrigated forms the seaward front or base of hills which extend, by a succession of yet higher ranges, into the interior of the country. The sun had just risen, and the cool temperature of the morning air felt delightfully refreshing. The smooth surface of the sea, at a distance of four or five miles, was receiving a rosy tint, which the Sawadi Island (Island of Barka/*Burka*), now before us, also shared, and so clear was the atmosphere that I was almost tempted to believe I saw the Persian shore.

Nearly all the fruits and vegetables cultivated in other parts of Oman seem to be found here, and in size and luxuriance of growth the trees equal those of India.

A small tribe, the Bani (*Beni*) Wahab, has held possession of these grounds for many ages; but in the hot weather, during the date harvest, the town Arabs arrive in great numbers. I was told as many as seven or eight thousand at that season of plenty and happiness take up their quarters here and sit all day under the trees, reciting verses from the Quran (*Koran*), or slumbering in repose beneath their shadowy branches, which at once afford them food and shelter.

At noon today our thermometer rose to ninety-four degrees in the shade, and some idea of the heat in the warm season may, from this fact, be estimated: yet shortly after the sun sinks behind the mountains, this parching heat was exchanged for a piercing cold. To the natives, this extraordinary fluctuation is not attended with any ill effects and they pronounce it at all seasons to be the most healthy spot in Oman; but it has proved fatal to one or more of almost every party of Europeans which has ever ventured to visit them.

CHAPTER 4
TRAVEL FROM MUSCAT TO BANI BU ALI

Departure for Sur - Devil's Gap - Timidity of Arab Mariners - Qalhat (Kilhat) - Ancient Gold Coins - Breakfast with a Sheikh - Account of Sur - Hospitable treatment - Market - Date Groves - Exports and Imports - Arab Shepherds - Anecdote of Arab Girls - Departure-Babel - The Bani bu Hassan (Beni-Abu-Hasan) Tribe - Their numbers - Interview with the Sheikh - Attempt to deter the Author from proceeding.

November 25th. A boat having been prepared for me, I left Muscat, with no small satisfaction, for Sur; for its climate, at all times unfavourable to the European constitution, was particularly insalubrious at this period, and the number of deaths which occurred daily, even among the natives, was very considerable. A poor Frenchman who had fled here, after escaping a hundred dangers subsequent to the defeat of the Turks in the Asir country, was dying in a vessel alongside of that which I had quitted, and a considerable number of the crew of an English ship lying there were seriously ill.

Off the Devil's Gap, a remarkable gorge or opening in the mountain range contiguous to the sea-shore, we experienced a heavy squall, during which I had a good opportunity of witnessing the timidity and irresolution of Arab mariners. We shipped a good deal of water and were really at one time in an awkward situation. The passage continued stormy, with occasional heavy showers of rain, to Qalhat, abreast of which we anchored for a few hours, while I went onshore to examine the ruins.

Qalhat is an ancient town, mentioned by several of the Arabian authors. Its ruins cover an extensive tract, but only one building remains in a state of tolerable preservation. This is a small mosque, which, judging from the writing on various parts of it, has been frequented by Indian Muslims. Its interior is covered with party-coloured glazed tiles, on which are inscribed, in relievo, sentences from the Quran. To the northward of these ruins, there is a small fishing village, the inhabitants of which also occasionally employ themselves in digging amidst the ruins for gold coins, the metal of which in Muscat is considered to be of the purest kind. Some of these bear the name of the Caliph Haroun Al Rashid.

Qalhat 'mosque' - Bibi Miriam Mausoleum

Quitting Qalhat with a pleasant breeze, we reached Sur shortly after sunset, and anchored in the inner harbour, within a few yards of the shore. From Muscat to this port the mountain ranges approach close to the sea, and are very elevated: they bear the name of Jabal Syenne and Rackee, and are intersected by several valleys, some of which are filled with streams of fresh water. Near to these are a few groves of the date palm, and, though the plain is cultivated, the hills are destitute of trees and verdure.

November 28th. I found the Sheikh this morning waiting on the beach to receive me, and, after breakfasting with him on dates and milk, we walked over the town.

Sur, the port of the district of Jaalan (*Jailan*), is situated on a low sandy shore, utterly destitute of vegetation or trees. It is merely a large collection of huts erected on either side a deep lagoon, which are separately occupied by different tribes. They are very compactly constructed with the branches of the date palm, are airy and spacious, and, as the streets are kept very clean, the whole wears a neat and pleasing appearance. There are no shops here, the Bazar being situated about a mile and a half from the beach, where a considerable number of the inhabitants reside. Thither, accompanied by its Sheikh, who had been sent for directly intelligence was received of my arrival, I set out and was much gratified at finding when I reached the village that my tent was pitched in a delightful spot, and that guards had been placed, and every precaution taken for the safety of my baggage. Here I was to remain until camels and guides could be collected for my journey.

Sur fort

A daily market is held on this spot, at which grain, fruit, and vegetables are exposed for sale. The houses, though small, are strongly built of stone and cement, and the largest and best are occupied by the Banians and people from Kutch (*Cutch*), who monopolise a considerable share of the trade. On the west quarter, there is a large fort, mounting a few old guns, but both it and they are in a very ruinous state.

The contiguous country is cultivated in patches of considerable extent, and the date groves are numerous and extensive. It is, however, to commercial pursuits that the people of Sur are principally devoted, possessing a good harbour. Belonging to the port they have about three hundred *baghlas* of different sizes, which trade, during the fair season, to and between the shores of India, Africa, and the Arabian and Persian Gulfs [Arabian Gulf here means Red Sea]. Its own exports and imports are trifling, the former being dates and salt fish, the latter grain, cloth, &c.; but the profit derived from the interchange of the various productions of the quarters I have named is sufficient to support them in affluence during the adverse period of the year. They acknowledge the authority but pay no tribute to Sayyid Said. Sur is thought to be of great antiquity - it is supposed to have been occupied by the Syrians.

December 1st. Early this morning I set out, accompanied by a guide, to visit the northern range of mountains. The road being impracticable for horses, we procured asses, which carried us at a brisk pace in two hours and a half to the foot of the hills. Here we dismounted and commenced our ascent on foot, by a rugged defile. After an hour's fagging, climbing in many places rather than walking, we breathed for a short space near to a small hamlet, and, after quenching our thirst at a stream of pure water, which rushes through the valley to the plains below, again set forward. Four hours more, during which we crossed several deep ravines, also well-watered, and interspersed with date trees and patches of cultivation, brought us to the summit; but, beyond the view we obtained of the surrounding country, and the delightful coolness of the atmosphere, there was little to repay us for our trouble. Bare tabular patches of limestone rock showed their bleak and wasted surface in all directions. A few sheep and numerous goats were browsing on the scanty herbage the other parts afforded, but, hitherto, we saw no human being to break the solitude of the scene. From this point, which forms the cape, or southeast extremity of the seaward range, to an extensive valley abreast of Qalhat, the mountainous tract is called Futlah. In the narrow ravines by which it is intersected there are said to be sixty villages, or rather hamlets, containing about one thousand five hundred inhabitants, who bear the general appellation of the Bani Khalid (*Beni Kaled*) and Bani (*Beni*) Daud. About six hundred of the former occupy a valley bearing the same name on the south-west side of the mountains, so very narrow and steep that one part in the line of its bed can only be crossed by means of ropes. Independent of the numerous streams and rills by which the several valleys are watered, rain is more frequently experienced here than on the plains, and a considerable quantity of grain and fruit is reared. One tenth of the produce of the soil goes to the Sheikh of Sur.

Proceeding for a short distance along this ridge we fell in with some shepherds, who testified at first no little surprise at our appearance, but a few words from my guide reassured them, and we accepted with much thankfulness an invitation to their mid-day meal of dates and milk. A huge rock, standing upright on the plain, sheltered them from the wind, which blew with much strength and keenness. In this group, beyond a somewhat fairer complexion and taller stature, I saw little to distinguish them from their neighbours of the plains. When we had finished our repast, our new acquaintances insisted on my visiting their huts. I found them situated in a small dell, near a stream of running water. They were of a circular form, the walls of loose stones, and the roofs neatly thatched with a description of reed which grows here in great abundance, but the interior exhibited neither space nor comfort. I had scarcely seated myself on a skin, spread on the ground in one of these dwellings, when some young and very pretty females entered, bringing with them a huge bowl of milk. Out of compliment to them I took a long draught; but no, this was insufficient. Was it bad? - try again, and again! In vain I extolled it to the skies; I was not permitted to desist until I had swelled almost to suffocation, and sworn by the beard of the Prophet that I could and would take no more. They were then delighted, and we became such excellent friends that, with the assistance of a few presents and some fair speeches, we parted with expressions of mutual regret.

Our return was by a path more steep and rugged, if possible, than that by which we ascended, and I did not, in consequence, arrive at the foot of the mountains until some time after sunset. No asses were to be found: the night was dark, with occasional showers of rain: we lost our path several times, and did not reach the tent until nearly midnight.

During my stay here, I received the following friendly and characteristic epistle from his Highness, the Imam:-

"In the name of God, most merciful, from Sayyid the Sultan to his Excellency, the esteemed, respected, beloved, the perfect Captain Wellsted, from the eastern government, peace be with you from the Most High God; and, after that your letter reached us, which was a proof of your love in remembering us, we greatly rejoiced at your arriving at Sur, and your departure for Jaalan, which is as we directed it, and from thence to Samad Al Shan (*Semmed*), and which was gratifying to you, and, therefore, pleasing to us; and, furthermore, anything which you require from us, whether little or much, it is only for you to request it, and it is on our part to grant it. Peace be to you, and farewell.

True,

"Sayyid Sultan."

December 2nd. My camels and guides were collected this morning, and I left Suq (*Suk*) Al Sur, where I had received every attention from its Sheikh. At 12:30, p.m., we were clear of the skirts of the village and entered a shallow valley. Rounded masses of limestone formed its bed, between which a few stunted acacia bushes, the only signs of vegetable life, forced their way. The hills on either hand were of a light red, or yellow sandstone, with an occasional streak of orange or purple. Although in October, November, and December, passing showers are here frequent, the natives say that heavy continued rain is only experienced once in three years and that the bed of this valley is then filled with a swollen and rapid stream, that renders it impassable for camels.

About two we arrived at the pass of Bab Al Rafsah (*Babel Rufsur*), where there is a small tower, and a piece of artillery. These and similar other buildings were erected by the Imam to check the incursions of the Wahhabis: they have now, however, been all permitted to fall to decay. Some streams of freshwater, with an occasional date grove, show themselves between this and the termination of the valley, which we reached at six, p.m. Hence we continued over a plain country, until eleven, P.M. when we halted near some hamlets, where the dogs kept up such a furious barking, and were withal so fierce, that my guides, although in want of food, were afraid to attempt to pass them. The night was clear and cold, and heavy dew was falling. The Bedouins slept in a circle, and placed the baggage in the centre.

Bab Al Rafsah

Thursday, December 3rd. Near to where we have encamped there are three-walled villages, Homaidah, Al Kamil, and Al Wafi (*Wafee*), severally containing about two hundred houses, and each having a small fort. Both within and without the walls, the country is well cultivated, and some streams of running water which cross their grounds afford abundant means of irrigation. The inhabitants evinced so much dislike at my looking over these fields, that I was obliged to quit them.

At 11:30 we continued our route over an extensive plain, where the soil was alternately either of very loose drift sand or a whitish indurated clay, covered with *sayel* bushes (male acacia). Parties of Bedouins, on their way to Sur, occasionally passed us, but, as the principal tribes were now at feud, a single individual was rarely met with beyond the precincts of the villages, nor was it without some precaution that our own party proceeded. Immediately that another *kafala* (كَفِلَة *kafilah*) was perceived our camels were brought together, the guards, as we approached nearer, advanced ahead, mutual inquiries ensued, and we then passed on. Any authority which Sayyid Said has acquired over this district, by the liberal distribution of presents to its Sheikhs, is more nominal than real. The Bedouins follow up their own quarrels, plundering, and not infrequently killing each other, with the same freedom as if they were on the Desert. Scarcely a day passed during my stay that I did not hear of some transaction of this nature.

Kamil Castle

At 3:30 we halted amidst the dwellings of the Bani bu Hassan Bedouins, which are mostly huts, erected beneath their date groves. They are very straggling, and we were three-quarters of an hour passing from one extremity to the other. As soon as the intelligence of our arrival had spread, they crowded around us in great numbers. Their curiosity was unbounded, and they expressed their astonishment at all in the most boisterous manner, leaping and yelling as if they were half crazy. My small tent (notwithstanding the presence, and repeated desire of their Sheikh) was soon completely filled, and I felt heartily glad when the approach of sunset sent them all to their houses.

The Bani bu Hassan Bedouins are estimated at one thousand two hundred men, exclusive of women and children, but they cannot muster more than seven hundred matchlocks. With no other employment than tending their date trees, which occupies but a small portion of their time, they lead an idle life and are constantly engaged in quarrels or disputes either amidst themselves or their neighbours. In appearance they are the wildest and most uncouth beings I have hitherto met with: they go almost naked, and their hair is worn long, reaching nearly to the girdle.

After sunset I saw no one but the Sheikh, who came alone for the purpose of dissuading me from visiting the Bani bu Ali Bedouins, whom he characterised as being disaffected to Sayyid Said, hating the English, and, in a word, "perfect devils;" but, as I knew the two tribes were at open variance, I evinced less disposition to follow his advice than he probably anticipated, and he took his leave, in consequence, somewhat coolly.

In truth, I was not without apprehensions as to the treatment I should receive from his neighbours, but my reasons will be understood when I state the circumstances which brought the English into collision with them.

CHAPTER 5
BANI BU ALI'S HISTORY AND ENVIRONS

T*he Bani bu Ali - Their origin - Sayyid Said's ineffectual efforts to subdue them - Obtains the assistance of British Troops - Disastrous expedition of Captain Thompson-Bravery of the Bent-Abu - Ali - Massacre of the British - Gallantry of the Imam - Expedition from Bombay - Attack upon the Bani bu Ali Fort - Fortitude of their Women - Final defeat and subjugation - The Author's reception at their Encampment - Deference paid to the British name-Hospitality - Oblivion of the past- Burckhardt - Visit from the young Sheikh - Discourse upon Women - European Customs - Tombs of the Vanquished - Contrast between the British and the Bedouin Soldier.*

The Bani bu Ali tribe came originally from a small district in Nejd, where a remnant of them is said still to exist. They accompanied those who separated from Ali's army during the struggle with Mowaiyah for the Caliphate and continued to follow the Ibadhi (*Beazi*) tenets until the invasion of [Saud bin] Abdulaziz [Al Saud], in 1811, when they became converts to the Wahhabis faith. From that period they have been an object of the most deadly hatred to the other tribes in Oman; and after Abdulaziz was beaten back at Bidiyyah (*Bediah*), their best efforts were necessary to prevent their total annihilation; but, continuing to temporise until they had erected a very strong fort, they, in return, became the aggressors, and, after carrying fire and sword into every part of the neighbouring district, became so formidable, that they were soon left in undisputed possession of their own and several of the neighbouring districts.

At a later period, several attempts were made by the Imam to dislodge or destroy them, but all his exertions proving ineffectual, in 1821 he made a requisition for assistance to Captain Thompson, who, after the fall of Ras Al

Khaimah, in the preceding year, had been left with a small force of eight hundred men, principally sepoys, at the Island of Qeshm (*Kishm*) [10]. Under an impression that some portion of the tribe had been engaged in extensive acts of piracy, that officer immediately dispatched a messenger with a letter of remonstrance to them, but he was massacred almost as soon as he landed. Captain Thompson, on the receipt of this intelligence, no longer hesitated to accompany a force which the Imam had already prepared to act against them, and, landing at Sur, he formed a junction, and they marched together against Bani bu Ali, which is situated about fifty miles, in a direct line, from their place of disembarkment. The Bedouins retreated before them, and occupied the date grove which surrounds the fort. After our troops had passed Bani bu Hassan and were sweeping round a hill, the greater part being in a line parallel to the trees, the whole tribe, who had hitherto lain concealed beneath them, suddenly rushed forth with loud cries and threw themselves headlong on the British force. Before the latter could be formed, or almost before the order could be given, the Bedouins were amidst them, the sepoys could not use their bayonets, but were hewn down by the long swords of their foes as they stood, and the whole soon became a mass of inextricable confusion. No quarter was given, and an officer, presenting his sword as a token of submission, was, at the same time, pierced through the back with a spear. They dragged the surgeon, who was sick, from his palanquin, and immediately butchered him; and the British force, leaving two-thirds of their number dead upon the field were compelled to retreat, and, after an undisturbed march of about eight days, Captain Thompson, two officers, and about one hundred and fifty men, the only survivors, succeeded in reaching Muscat [11].

Bani bu Ali - British graveyard from 1821

Intelligence of this disaster was soon carried to Bombay and a large force of three thousand men, under Sir Lionel Smith, again landed [12]. Nowise daunted by their superior numbers, the Bedouins, in concert with the Bani Janaba (*Beni Geneba*), planned a night attack, which, had it proved successful, would have placed the British force in a singular dilemma. The General and his staff were encamped at some distance from the army, and it was proposed by the Bedouins to cut off the whole of them.

But, either through mistake or treachery, the latter was not at the rendezvous at the appointed time, and the former proceeded alone. Having reached the General's camp, they hamstrung several of the horses, and committed other damages, besides cutting down several men. They then affected their escape without the loss of one of their own number.

When our force on their march had nearly reached the fort, the Arabs met them on a large plain. Their number did not exceed eight hundred: many of their women had now joined their ranks, and they rushed on with the same impetuosity as before, but were met at every point by the bayonet: they, nevertheless, fought with amazing obstinacy and courage, and did not give up the contest until nearly the whole of them were slain or desperately wounded [13]: amidst the latter was their Sheikh, who, with the few survivors, was taken prisoner to Bombay. After being confined there for almost two years they were released; much attention was then shown them, and they were sent back to their own country with presents and with money to rebuild their town, but since the period of their defeat, no European has entered their territory.

After my noon observation of the sun, a short journey of two hours brought me on to Bani bu Ali. A considerable crowd followed after me until I halted when I was soon joined by the young Sheikh and the principal men of the tribe. No sooner had I proclaimed myself an Englishman and expressed my intention of passing a few days amidst them, than the whole camp was in a tumult of acclamation; the few old guns they had were fired from the different towers, matchlocks were kept going till sunset, and both old and young, male and female, strove to do their best to entertain me: they pitched my tent, slaughtered sheep, and brought milk by gallons. A reception so truly warm and hospitable not a little surprised me.

The 'keep' Bani bu Ali Fort

Before us lay the ruins of the fort we had dismantled, - my tent was pitched on the very spot where we had nearly annihilated their tribe, reducing them from being the most powerful in Oman to their present petty state. All, however, in the confidence I had shown in thus throwing myself amidst them, was forgotten.

Sheikh Muhammed bin Nasir - early 20thc at Bani bu Ali

Although so near the sea-coast, the Bedouins of this and the neighbouring districts have remained uncontaminated by any intercourse with strangers, for they neither intermarry nor mix with them; and there is, therefore, reason to believe that they preserve, in its strictest forms, all the simplicity and purity of the interior tribes.

It is to be regretted that we know so little of the character and habits of the true Bedouins. Those on the frontiers of Syria and Mesopotamia have been vitiated by their intercourse with the Turks and other nations. The same remark applies to the only parts of Hijaz and Yemen which our travellers have visited. Burckhardt, though well aware of, and as well calculated to supply this deficiency, was prevented by sickness from doing so, otherwise, it was his intention to have passed a few months in the interior provinces. My object, therefore, while entering fully on what came under my observation during my stay amidst these tribes, now and on subsequent occasions, will be to furnish something towards this desideratum.

After their evening prayers, the young Sheikh, accompanied by about forty men, came to the tent and expressed his intention of remaining with me as a guard during the night. To ask the whole party in was impossible, and to invite a few only would have displeased others, so I took my carpet outside amidst them. It was one of those clear and beautiful nights which are only met with on or near the Desert: the atmosphere felt pleasantly cool, and we soon commenced an animated conversation. They were not wholly ignorant of our customs: some information on these points they had gathered from the men who had been prisoners of war in India; but their accounts were either so limited or exaggerated, that they served rather to increase than to allay the feelings of curiosity. The nature and observance of our religion formed, of course, their first subject of inquiry, and my opinion as to its comparative merits with the Muslim was demanded. It is generally a good maxim to allow yourself to be apparently beaten on questions of theology: I could not, however, at first, resist the temptation of leading to some of their least defensible doctrines, and stating the arguments which could be brought to bear against them, but they evinced so little prejudice or fanaticism on these points that I regretted having done so, and, to make amends, most willingly subscribed to the opinion of one of their old men, that either faith was best adapted for the country and people who practised it.

From this the conversation turned on our females. Was it true, they inquired, that those of high birth and condition danced in public, and went unveiled? Here they had me on the hip, as they fancied; and the rogues chuckled whilst awaiting my reply. I confessed it was, but we did not, like them, attach any indelicacy to it; that our females were never secluded, but were instructed in useful knowledge, and allowed equal liberty with the other sex, and that we found our advantage in doing so, for, instead of being objects of mere sensual desire, they then became companions. Here, however, I gained not a single convert. "Let them work," said they, "and attend to their household affairs. What business have they with reading and writing, which is only fit for *mullahs* (*Moolahs*)?" "The women to the distaff, the men to their swords," said a venerable old man, with a white beard, repeating a proverb which was echoed by all present. I wished some of their dames had been within hearing, they would have pitched their note in a minor key.

The females of this tribe possess a considerable share of influence in all their councils, and in the absence of their Sheikh, who had proceeded on the pilgrimage to Makkah, his wife and sister, at this moment, governed the tribe. Their remarks on some of our customs were highly amusing.

"We observed," said they, "that when you sat down to table each man had before him a small and a large glass; why apply to the small one so often when it would save so much trouble to fill the larger, and drink it off at once? Why did we send the ladies away before we had finished our wine, and yet rise up when they left?" &c., &c.,

One of the slaves kept pounding coffee from the time they first arrived. The pestle on these occasions is made to strike the sides and bottom of the mortar in such time and manner as to cause it to resemble the chiming of bells, and the slave usually accompanies it with a song. As we chatted away, although Wahhabis, they drank their coffee as fast as it was brought, and we did not separate until a very late hour [14].

Saturday, December 5th. When I awoke this morning I found a man kneeling by me with a bowl of milk in his hand. I drank it off, and, accompanied by my escort, walked over the plain where the British had been encamped, and visited the scene of Captain Thompson's defeat; but, on either spot, every trace of the fierce encounter had disappeared. Near the former, some rude graves were pointed out to me, but no " frail memorial " served to indicate whether their tenants were of the party 'of the victors or of the vanquished. It may serve to show the siccity, as well as purity of the atmosphere, to mention that the bodies of those slain on the first attack were found lying upon the sands untouched by worms, and showing not the slightest symptoms of decay.

The Bedouins evinced no disinclination to converse on the subject of the war, and their own defeat and losses they spoke of in the most perfect good humour. They were equally merry in their observations on the English during their stay in Jaalan: their mode of attack, the arms and accoutrements of the soldiers, &c., being severally criticised with much shrewdness. To an Arab, who goes to war with no greater burden than his camel can well approach or retreat with, seldom, indeed, carrying anything beyond his arms, a small bag of moistened flour, and a skin of water, the quantity of baggage which accompanied our troops must have been not a little surprising; but what excited their utmost astonishment was, that we should carry casks of liquor for the men. This circumstance was afterwards frequently mentioned in Oman.

CHAPTER 6
CULTURE OF JAALAN

Sultan - Visit to the Sheikh's Wife and Sister - Attachment to Ancient Customs - Admiration of the English - Peasants - Speech of Bedouin Ladies - Feast - War Dance - Camel Race - Arrival of a Janaba Chief - The Author proposes a visit to his Horde - Departure - Anecdote - Features of the Desert - Appearance of my Companion - Costume - Love of Song - Musical Instruments - Summer Tree - Tales of Love and War - Intense Cold - Game of Leap Frog - Sheikh's Wives - Interior of a Tent - Foliage of the Summer Tree - Description of the Bani Janaba - Singular substitute for a Canoe - Shark Fishing - Salubrious Climate - Modes of Punishment - Start for Beni-Abu Ali - A Bedouin Foray.

Towards noon I went, accompanied by his son Sultan, to visit the wife and sister of the old Sheikh, who was now absent on the pilgrimage to Makkah. We passed through a dirty courtyard filled with cattle into a small apartment, the doorway of which was crossed by a stile, to secure it from their intrusion. This, however, seemed insufficient, for several had managed to leap it, and were being ejected when we arrived. The Bedouins in the Desert find it necessary for better security to keep their cattle near to them and as they are the last people in the world to abandon old customs, they do the same in the towns when they reside there. Some months ago, when the Asir tribe occupied Mokha, they kept their sheep with them in the upper apartments of the very lofty houses of that town. The ladies received me seated on a platform, raised about two feet from the ground, and completely veiled from head to foot, not a finger during the whole of the interview was visible; but, in order to compensate, in some measure, for this disappointment, some very pretty Abyssinian females, who were not veiled, remained in the room to attend on them. They expressed themselves highly delighted that an Englishman had, at last, come among them, but spoke of Sayyid Said with contempt, and did not conceal their desire to throw off their present very slight connexion with him.

"It is the protection of the English we want," they observed, "and if your government would grant us that, and should afterwards require a port on the coast, by which they can open a trade with Oman, as well as the interior, we will gladly furnish them with one." As they grew more talkative, it was with difficulty I prevented them from sending forth amidst the mountains to collect the whole tribe.

A suite of tents, and several other articles, were pointed out to me, which had been sent by our government as presents to them. Notwithstanding we may, at present, entertain very different sentiments respecting our first attack on this people, and it is known that at least one high and influential member of the government did, yet the whole affair was quite to a Bedouin's taste, and both here and in every other quarter I heard nothing but praises of the English. "We have fought, - you have made us every compensation in your power for those who fell, - and we should now be friends," observed these ladies, when speaking of the transaction; but they never, it will be seen, have forgiven Sayyid Said.

A meal, consisting of camels' flesh, a sheep, boiled whole, and large bowls of rice, had, in the meantime, been preparing. Directly it was brought in the ladies retired, leaving Sultan and myself alone to partake of it. Upon my return to the tent I found there the whole of the tribe, at Bani bu Ali, consisting of about two hundred and fifty men, assembled for the purpose of exhibiting their war dance. They had formed a circle, within which five or six of their number now entered.

After walking leisurely round for some time, each challenged one of the spectators by striking him gently with the flat of his sword. His adversary immediately leaped forth, and a feigned combat ensued. They have but two cuts, one directly downwards at the head, and the other horizontally across the legs. They parry neither with the sword nor shield, but avoid the blows by leaping or bounding backwards. The blade of their sword is three feet in length, straight, thin, double-edged, and as sharp as a razor. As they carry it upright before them, by a peculiar motion of their wrist they cause it to vibrate in a very remarkable manner, which has a singularly striking effect when they are assembled in any considerable number. The shield is attached to the sword by a leathern thong; it measures about fourteen inches in diameter, and is generally used to parry the thrust of the spear, or *jambiya*. It was part of the entertainment to fire off their matchlocks under the legs of someone of the spectators, who appeared too intent on watching the game to observe their approach, and any signs of alarm which incautiously escaped the individual, added greatly to their mirth. Their only music consisted of a small drum, beaten by a slave.

Two Camels set off in a race

After exercising their skill in firing at a mark, during which some capital shots were made, they all dispersed. Towards evening a large party of Janaba Bedouins arrived, and two of their camels were matched to run against the same number belonging to the Bani bu Ali. As I had never before witnessed a camel race, I felt much interest in the spectacle. They rode them with nose strings as well as bridles, but the animals did not appear to take an equal relish in the sport with their masters, for they could not be set going without much trouble, and were afterwards very untractable. Their speed, when at full gallop, I did not think very great, perhaps a third less than that of a horse, and when they are urged to this pace their gait and movement appear excessively awkward.

Finding the Sheikh who accompanied the party was a lively intelligent fellow, I proposed to take a run for a few days with him in his own country. After inquiring my motives, and finding that it was merely to live amongst them for that time, he gave a hearty consent. In the evening I was visited, as usual, by a large party, and we had some singing in the Bedouin style.

December 6th. I found the Sheikh and his followers, consisting of fifty Bedouins, mounted on camels, this morning all ready for starting, and we were soon clear of the skirts of the town, and away at a full trot over the Desert. The air was cold and pure, the sun just sufficiently high to render its warmth agreeable, while the wild appearance and movements of my Bedouin friends gave an exhilarating novelty to my sensations: even the very solitude of the scene rendered it more pleasing. While sweeping across these solitary and boundless wastes, although destitute of trees, mountains, and water, or any of the features common to softer regions, there is something in their severely simple features, their nakedness and immensity, which reminds me of the trackless ocean, and impresses the soul with a feeling of sublimity. The aspect of my companion is in perfect keeping with the peculiar attributes of his native land. His sinewy form, and clean and compact limbs, are revealed by the scantiness of his garments: his dark and ruddy countenance is lighted up by the kindling of his resolute eye: his demeanour is honest and frank, and his whole appearance breathes a manly contempt of hardships.

Simr Acacia/Vachellia nilotica

"You wished," said the Sheikh, "to see the country of the Bedouins - *this*," he continued, striking his spear into the firm sand, "*this* is the country of the Bedouins." Neither he nor his companions wore more than a single cloth around their waist, all the rest of the body being left bare. Their hair, which is permitted to flow unconfined as low as their waist, and is usually kept loaded with grease, protects them, in a measure, from the intensity of the sun's rays, but they adopt no other covering. For a short time after leaving the town they kept together, but now they were away in all directions, chasing each other with loud shouts across the plains. In this manner we continued over a level country, intersected by traces of numerous torrents, for about four hours, and then crossed a narrow ridge of low, calcareous hills: in two hours more we entered amidst some mounds, thickly interspersed with the *Simr* (*summer*) or gum-Arabic tree (*Acacia vera* - probably the modern *Acacia/Vachellia nilotica*). Very little of the gum is collected by the Bedouins, who complain that the price it brings in Muscat does not repay them for their trouble. At 4:30, we halted near some wells of brackish water. Our course hitherto has been south-south-west, and the distance we have travelled is forty-two miles. A party of the natives, who joined us directly we halted, were sent on for rice and dates; we, in the meantime, had lighted a fire under a large tree, and lost no time, as soon as they returned, which was not till sunset, in cooking what they brought, when I with the rest, made a very hearty meal. I had with me neither servant nor baggage, conceiving that, even for the short time I should remain amongst them, the objects of my journey would be best attained by adopting their mode of living; and the result did not disappoint me. Among all these tribes there appears to exist a considerable portion of traditionary lore, of which the details of the wars and predatory excursions of themselves and ancestors form the greatest and most attractive portion. The exploits of a favourite horse or camel are dwelt on with equal enthusiasm. I sat up drinking coffee, and listening to their recitation of these events, until a very late hour. Several watch-dogs kept guard round our encampment during the night [15].

Sunday, December 7th. Towards midnight we had hard rain, which continued without intermission until sunrise. It was piercingly cold, and, as we could obtain no shelter, we were thoroughly drenched. To the Bedouins it afforded infinite pleasure, as they were now sure of pasturage for some time. At daylight, to divest our limbs of their numbness, we jumped and ran races, until I bethought myself of our English game of leap frog, Very great was the diversion this afforded them, until our breakfast of milk and dates was announced, after which we packed up, and resumed our journey, At eight, a.m., we continued to thread our way to the west - south-west, between the same sandy mounds as yesterday, until four, p.m., when we arrived at a small encampment, in which dwelt the Sheikh's wives: shortly afterwards, the good dames sent for me. I found them in a small hut of a conical form, constructed of poles, fastened to the upper part with leathern thongs, and covered with skins. It was so very small, that two persons lying down would fill its whole area. The women were seated on an old carpet near a good fire, and I was invited to place myself between them. They were unveiled, and entered freely into conversation with me. After answering a hundred questions connected with the English and their country, coffee, and then milk, were introduced. They brought the latter in a bowl wove from the husk of the cocoa-nut, but its texture was so close that none escaped. I saw no other furniture except a few skins, for holding dates or water; an earthen pot for boiling coffee; and two or three copper vessels for rice; together with a few ragged blankets (*kamalines*), mats or skins, on which they sleep. A heap of salt fish lay in one corner. After making them a few trifling presents, with which they were highly delighted, I took my leave, and walked out with the Sheikh to seek for botanical specimens, of which I found a great abundance.

I remark both here and in other parts of Arabia, that the trees which are at all umbrageous, have the ground immediately beneath them, even in the most sultry weather, damp with moisture, and generally covered with a thin sprinkling of grass, on which the cattle feed with much avidity. This appears owing to some peculiar property which their foliage possesses of retaining the falling dew, which is usually more copious in the Desert than elsewhere, for I have frequently in the morning observed the leaves of the *Simr* (*sumr*) tree (*Acacia nilotica*) to be slightly curved upwards, with a drop or two of water in them. These, as the sun exerts its influence, assume their natural form, and the moisture is deposited on the ground beneath. Under their shade, the more vigorous vegetation which springs up after rain derives nourishment for some time after that which is more exposed appears dried up and withered. Nevertheless, it is very remarkable that the most succulent plants are found in those spots which receive the full force of the sun's rays. The Bani Janaba, or "Wandering Children," are a scattered race of about three thousand five hundred men, the greater number of whom are found occupying the country south from Bani bu Ali to Ras Madrakah (*Cape Isolette*); but there are several families who live intermixed with other Bedouins on the intermediate wastes between the Great Desert to the westward, as well as on the Oasis of Oman, together with some few who reside with their principal Sheikh at Sur. To this individual all grave offences are referred, and he is responsible to the Imam for the general conduct of the tribe. The Bani Janaba present some peculiarities which render them, in a measure, distinct from other Bedouins, Although, as I have noticed, their numerical superiority is not great, yet they spread over a large extent of country, and are divided into two distinct classes; those who subsist by fishing, and such as follow pastoral pursuits. We will first consider the former.

It is a remarkable fact that a race in many respects similar is found in almost every part of the coast of Arabia, and even along the north-east shore of India and Macrau. In some districts, as those, for instance, which lie to the northward of Jeddah in the Red Sea, they are considered as a separate and degraded race, with whom the Bedouins will neither eat, intermarry, nor associate; but with this and several other tribes, so degrading a distinction does not exist. The whole coast abounds with fish, and, as the natives have but few canoes, they generally substitute a single inflated skin, or two of these, having a flat board across them. On this frail contrivance the fisher seats himself, and either casts his small hand-net, or plays his hook and line. Some capital sport must arise occasionally when the sharks, which are here very numerous and large, gorge the bait; for whenever this occurs, unless the angler cuts his line, and that, as the shark is more valued than any other fish, he is often unwilling to do, nothing can prevent his rude machine from following their track, and the fisherman is sometimes, in consequence, carried out a great distance to sea. It requires considerable dexterity to secure these monsters, for when they are hauled up near to the skins they struggle a good deal, and if they happen to jerk the fisherman from his seat, the infuriate monster is said to dash at once at him. Many accidents, I learn, arise in this manner, but if they succeed in getting him quickly alongside they soon despatch him by a few blows on the snout. After the fish is brought to the shore it is either dried or salted, and that portion not required for their own consumption, is conveyed into the interior and exchanged for dates and cloth. In the cool season the pastoral Arabs of this tribe reside, for the sake of more plentiful herbage, at or near the sea-coast, living, as those I have already noticed, in small tents, constructed with poles, and covered with skins; but, upon the approach of the southwest monsoon, they retreat to the hills, and become regular Troglodytes. They then occupy, with their flocks, the most secluded valleys, where the pasturage is usually better than on the plains. The whole of this tribe are in bad repute with their neighbours, and it is said that they make no scruple of plundering boats which may be unfortunate enough to fall into their clutches. It was the Bani Janaba that approached the American sloop Peacock, when aground near Masirah (*Mazura*), in 1835, with the intention, it was supposed, of plundering her: this intention, however, they stoutly deny. Milk, dates, and fish form their principal food, and, as the water is indifferent, they drink large quantities of the former. Their dates are obtained principally from the extensive groves at Bani bu Ali, with the people of which they are intimately connected by the ties of blood.

Their country boasts a very salubrious climate. Invalids from Muscat frequently reside here for two or three months, partaking of the simple food of its inhabitants, and they are said, even in the most obstinate cases, to derive great benefit from it. As to their modes of punishment, for stealing a camel, sheep, &c., provided it is the first offence, simple restitution only, is insisted on; for the second, they impose a fine; and for the third, the offender is manacled and imprisoned. Fines are also inflicted for abusive language: murder or manslaughter, as with other tribes, is revenged on the offender by the relations of the deceased.

Tuesday, December 8th. At ten, a.m, we decamped to return to Bani bu Ali by another route, more to the westward. Very much did I regret being compelled to do so, since I might, with my present escort, without the slightest fear of interruption, have proceeded to the confines of the Mahara Bedouins; but Oman, "metal more attractive," was before me. Until 1:30, the face of the country continued the same as I have before described it, but afterwards we crossed some arid plains, exhibiting neither trees nor bushes, and displaying alternately either a pebbly surface, or extensive saline incrustations. At sunset we halted for a short time to feed the camels, and then, as the night was fine, resumed our journey. At 12:45, after a long ride, at a hard pace, of fourteen hours, we arrived at a small Bedouin encampment, where we put up for the night. What an enviable attainment is that of being able to sleep on a camel! By the time I reached our halting-place I was fairly tired out, but, with the exception of the Sheikh, who rode alongside of, and was chatting with me, every other individual of the party had fallen into a sound slumber.

December 9th. Early this morning we again set forward, and, after a pleasant ride, at a good round pace, arrived at Bani bu Ali. I found the greater number of the tribe assembled around the tent, and, upon inquiry, discovered that some Bedouins of the neighbouring tribe, of Bani bu Hassan, had approached during the night, and purloined a goat which had been sent by the Sheikh of Kamil the day before as a present for me.

My servants having made the head man of the tribe acquainted with it, were waiting for my arrival to retaliate upon the plunderers by seizing some of their cattle, and it was not without difficulty that I dissuaded them from this intention. Among these warlike tribes the most trifling incident is sufficient to set them by the ears, and I am told scarcely a year passes that the Imam is not compelled to send some influential individual to adjust their broils.

CHAPTER 7
TRAVEL THROUGH BIDIYYAH

Departure - Hospitable Invitation - Copious Dews - Dreary Prospect - Inroads of the Sand - How arrested Scarcity of Water - Melancholy fate of a Bedouin Family - Wadi Batha (Betha) - Abundance of Water in Oman - Water Skins - Anecdote - Bidiyyah - Its low situation - Subterraneous Watercourse - Magnificent Trees - Abundance and Excellence of the Fruit - Amazing Fertility - Accident - Medical Patients - Anecdote - Encamp at Ibra (Ibrah) - Presents - Description of the Town - Market - Inquisitiveness of Bedouin Ladies - An alarm.

Thursday, December 10th. I quitted Bani bu Ali this morning shortly before noon. The old men begged I would come again, and pass a month with them, in which case they promised to build a house "like those in India," and keep me in great state. The ladies were equally pressing in their entreaties, and the whole tribe accompanied me to the skirts of the village of Bani bu Hassan. "If you will visit us next year," said young Sultan, "my father will have returned from Makkah, and I will accompany you with a party of our own and the Janaba Bedouins as far as the limits of the Maharas." This I promised, if circumstances permitted, and, after shaking hands with all present, which they had learnt was our custom, we parted with mutual expressions of regret. I cannot forget the unaffected kindness which I experienced from this simple people, and shall ever recall the week spent with them and their neighbours as the most agreeable in my travels.

At 1:30 we passed the extremity of the Bani bu Hassan village. There are very few houses either here or at Bani bu Ali, and those few are small and rudely constructed. The natives occupy huts of various forms, built of the branches of the date palm. We now entered a shallow valley, called Wadi Batha, with large *Ghaf* (*gaff*) (*Acacia Arabica - Prosopis cineraria*), and *Simr* trees, on either hand; from the latter the gum Arabic is produced. *Sidr* (*Nebek*) trees (*Lotus Nebea - Ziziphus spina-christi*) in the bed of the valley are also numerous. A Bedouin hut occasionally peeps forth from beneath the trees, and some few cattle are browsing on the grass which grows beneath them.

Bedouin woman spinning goats wool - with a date palm hut behind

At 4:30, we passed Kamil, and at seven halted for the night amidst some sand downs about fifty feet in height. The night was clear, and the atmosphere of such uncommon purity that, not even in Egypt, do the stars shine forth with greater brilliancy. This I observed to be generally the case in extensive sandy tracts. But why are the dews so heavy, and the nights so cool on the Desert? The former are often so copious that they leave on the ground all the effects of a smart shower; and however torrid and parching may be the heat of the day, yet it is always succeeded by cool, and even cold nights.

Friday, December 11th. I rose this morning at an early hour, and scrambled to the summit of one of the highest of the sand hills, in order to obtain a view of the surrounding country. In the bleak and desolate expanse before me I discerned, as far as the eye could reach, nothing but hillocks of sand, rolled in from the Desert like the waves of the sea, until their course had been arrested by the barrier on which I stood. Upon inquiry I could not learn that this was progressing, and my own observation induced me to think it was not, for, upon examination, I found that the hillocks which formed such an impediment to their encroachments, were covered with *miswak* (*rak*) [*Salvadora persica*] [16] and other Desert bushes, the roots of which sink deep into the sand, and there become matted, producing the same effects as the Bent Star in England. A single bush, from this peculiarity, arrests the progress of the sand, and collects it into a mound: other bushes spring forth on its surface, and they thus continue receiving alternately separate layers of sand and increased vegetation, until they attain considerable magnitude. Was it not for this happy provision, a flood of sand must long ago have overwhelmed the country to the very base of the seaward range of mountains. As there is but little water beyond this barrier, the wells being many days apart, the Bedouins rarely venture to cross it, for the hillocks are said to alter their outline, and even shift their position with every strong breeze that blows: they consequently lose their marks, and very distressing accidents frequently occur. Last night, Hamed related to me that when a young man, he, his father, and about twenty of their tribe, encountered near this spot a party of Wahhabis, by whom they were defeated, and compelled to fly with their wives, who accompanied them. Several of their tribe had occasionally crossed the Desert to some wells about three days' journey from the barrier, in the vicinity of which there was water and good pasturage. Here it was their intention to have remained until the hostile party had passed on, and left the road open for their return. But on the second day they were overtaken by a strong gale from the westward, which obliterated every trace of the path, and so filled the air with dust that they were unable to discern objects beyond a few yards. In this emergency they crowded together near a tree, where they had no alternative but to remain until there should be a change for the better; but the gale continued unabated for three days. On the third day from their leaving the barrier, (their small stock of water being consumed on the first) they killed the only two of their camels which could be spared, but the quantity thus obtained was soon exhausted amidst so many; and on the fifth morning two of their females and a young man, Hamed's brother, died. On the sixth day they reached the wells, but their horror may be conceived when they found them filled nearly to the surface with sand [17]. "We knew of no other,' said Hamed, ' nearer than three days, but, being then too weak to proceed further, we quietly laid ourselves down to die. I recollect nothing after that night, until I found myself lashed on a camel, and my father alongside of me driving it. From him I learnt that we were discovered on the following morning by another party of our own tribe, who had just filled their skins at a well not half a mile from us, and that we were now on our way with them to our own hamlet."

At seven hours we left our encampment, and resumed our journey along Wadi Batha, which still continues shallow, exhibiting on its surface a few dwarfish bushes. At ten hours we passed a halting place called Roocsat, where there is water, and from thence crossed over a plain and desert country, the face of which is furrowed by numerous shallow ravines. When rain falls on the mountains these serve as channels to feed the mainstream, which flows along the bed of the valley with much impetuosity, and finally discharges itself into the sea at Bar Al Hikman (*Ras Mazura*), As the chain where they originate is, however, of primitive formation, and the country through which they subsequently pass of an arid and sandy description, they bring no fertilising principle: yet the water, filtering through the channel during their brief course, affords, by means of wells, a plentiful supply at other seasons of the year.

At four, p.m., we halted at the frontier village of the Bidiyyah district. From Bani bu Ali to this point I count sixteen hours slow travelling, or forty-two miles; and, as the road winds very little, this may be considered the correct distance, as I found from its agreeing with the observations. The Arabs call all the portion of the country from Bani bu Ali to this point, Jaalan.

Wadi Batha and edge of desert

Bidiyyah is a collection of seven hamlets, situated in as many oases, each containing from two to three hundred houses. The Suq, or market, is held on that which is the most centrical. For their relative position I must refer the reader to the map, which, being originally constructed on a large scale, enabled me, as I proceeded, to fill up a description of the face of the country on it. One striking feature in the appearance of these towns is their low situation. They are erected in artificial hollows, which have been excavated to the depth of six or eight feet, and the soil thus removed is left in hillocks around their margins. These were the first oases I had hitherto met with, and my attention was consequently forcibly drawn to them. I found that these, and nearly all the towns in the interior of Oman, owe their fertility to the happy manner in which the inhabitants have availed themselves of a mode of conducting water to them, a mode, as far as I know, peculiar to this country, and at an expense of labour and skill more Chinese than Arabian. The greater part of the face of the country being destitute of running streams on the surface, the Arabs have sought in elevated places for springs or fountains beneath it; by what mode they discover these I know not; but it seems confined to a peculiar class of men, who go about the country for the purpose but I saw several which had been sunk to the depth of forty feet. A channel from this fountain-head is then, with a very slight descent, bored in the direction in which it is to be conveyed, leaving apertures at regular distances, to afford light and air to those who are occasionally sent to keep it clean. In this manner water is frequently conducted from a distance of six or eight miles, and an unlimited supply is thus obtained. These channels are usually about four feet broad, and two feet deep, and contain a clear rapid stream. Few of the large towns or oases but had four or five of these rivulets or *falaj (falj)* running into them. The isolated spots to which water is thus conveyed possess a soil so fertile, that nearly every grain, fruit, or vegetable, common to India, Arabia, or Persia, is produced almost spontaneously; and the tales of the oases will be no longer regarded as an exaggeration, since a single step conveys the traveller from the glare and sand of the Desert, into a fertile tract, watered by a hundred rills, teeming with the most luxuriant vegetation, and embowered by lofty and stately trees whose umbrageous foliage the fiercest rays of a noontide sun cannot penetrate. The almond, fig, and walnut trees are of enormous size, and the fruit clusters so thickly on the orange and lime trees, that I do not believe a tenth part can be gathered. Above all, towers the date-palm, adding its shade to the sombre picture. Some idea may be formed of the density of this shade by the effect it produces in lessening the terrestrial radiation. A Fahrenheit's thermometer, which within the house stood at 55°, six inches from the ground, fell to 45°, From this cause, and an abundance of water, they are always saturated with damp, and even in the heat of the day possess a clammy coldness. Such spots present, indeed, a singular and peculiar scene, unequalled perhaps in any part of the world. Of this, nothing can furnish a more striking idea than the list of their productions, all of which are frequently reared in a plot of ground not more than three hundred yards in diameter; and I am confident no equal space, in any part of the world, will afford a catalogue more numerous and varied, more luxuriant in growth, or more perfect in form.

Bidiyyah sand dunes with date palms and dates drying in the sun

SATURDAY, DECEMBER 12TH. THE PEOPLE HERE ARE LESS CURIOUS than might have been expected, considering it is doubtful if they have seen a European before. They pass with a single gaze, and then leave me to the undisturbed enjoyment of my pursuits. I discovered to-day, to my great mortification, that the jolting of the camels had rendered my chronometer useless, although it was packed with the utmost care. I am consequently obliged to have recourse to the occultation of the stars by the moon, as a means of obtaining the longitude. To a person who is stationary, this presents a very facile mode; but to the traveller, many circumstances constantly arise, which render the possibility of its adoption less frequent than could be wished. I found the latitude of the place by a meridional observation and the mean of several stars, to be 22° 27'; the variation by morning and evening observation, was 2.7 westerly.*Sunday, 13th*. I had several applications made to me this evening for medicine. Fevers, and ulcers on the legs, were the most prevalent complaints: both seem to arise from the cold and damp of their dwellings, which are erected in the neighbourhood of grounds continually saturated with moisture. At eight, a.m. we proceeded N.W. ¼ W., along Wadi Betha, and passed several hamlets on either side the road. At nine hours forty-five, we arrived at the Suq, or market. This place is celebrated for two defeats of the Wahhabis, one in 1811, when their force was under the direction of Abdulaziz [18], and the other a few months after my visit. On the former occasion, among others, there fell a chief named Sheikh Mutlak, whose son, Saad bin Mutlaq, then but a boy, was with him on the field. With much of that vindictive feeling which forms so prominent a feature in the character of the Arab, the young Sheikh from that moment continued to cherish the most deadly hatred to the tribe and when, this year, he was appointed to the command of the Wahhabi frontier force at Buraymi (*Bireimah*), although the Wahhabis were at peace with the Imam, he suddenly marched with three thousand men direct to Bidiyyah. But the tribe he had destined to destruction, receiving intelligence of this movement two hours before he made his appearance, they collected eight hundred men, all who were then present, to oppose him. These were well armed, and the Sheikh's threats that he would afford no quarter urged them to their best efforts.

Notwithstanding their unequal numbers, they attacked the Wahhabis so unexpectedly, and with such fury, that they drove them from the field, and after slaying a great many, compelled the others to seek for safety in flight. The Sheikh, almost maddened at his defeat, was foremost in every danger, and, but for the devotion of a few who hurried him from the field, he too would, on the same spot, have probably shared the fate of his father. After halting a short time at this village, waiting for our camels, we continued N.N.W. until twelve, when we arrived at Qabil (*Cawbil*), which is walled round and has several forts.

The Sheikh met me at one of the gates, and accompanied me on foot through the town; he appeared very anxious I should halt here, but I was desirous to push on to Ibra. The tops of the houses and the windows were crowded with people assembled to see us. At one hour we passed Dariz (*Dereeza*), and at 1:30, Mudhairib (*Moderak*); both small oases with villages within them. At two hours, the country, which had hitherto presented a succession of plains, now alters its character. Low hills of limestone formation, about one hundred and fifty feet in height, intersect it. Jackals and hyenas occupy the numerous caverns which its surface presents. At 5:30, winding from N.N.W. to W.N.W., still along Wadi *Batha* (Betha), we arrived at the town of Ibra.

I pitched my tent in the dry bed of a torrent, within a few yards of the Date Grove. A clear and sparkling stream flowed around its margin, and on its banks were seated several females, who had been bathing, and were then, notwithstanding my approach, nearly in a state of nudity. Others were washing linen, or cleansing their bright copper cooking-pots; and all laughed and chatted with much volubility. Halting immediately after, I received the usual offering of a sheep and several bowls of milk; but during the evening I was troubled with but few visitors.

Monday, 14th. Accompanied by old Saaf I visited the town, formerly a place of some note, but now greatly fallen to decay. The instant you step from the Desert within the Grove, a most sensible change of the atmosphere is experienced. The air feels cold and damp; the ground in every direction is saturated with moisture; and, from the density of the shade, the whole appears dark and gloomy. There are still some handsome houses at Ibra; but the style of building is quite peculiar to this part of Arabia. To avoid the damp, and catch an occasional beam of the sun above the trees, they are usually very lofty. A parapet encircling the upper part is turreted;

and on some of the largest houses guns are mounted. The windows and doors have the Saracenic arch, and every part of the building is profusely decorated with ornaments of stucco in bas relief, some in very good taste. The doors are also cased with brass, and have rings and other massive ornaments of the same metal.

Qabil fort

A daily market for the sale of grain, fruit, and vegetables is held here, to which the Bedouins and inhabitants of the neighbouring villages resort in considerable numbers. The stalls at which the vendors take their stand are only occupied during the hours of business. They are small square buildings, surrounded by a low wall, roofed over, open in front, and have a floor raised about two feet from the level of the street. Adjoining to Ibra, within about two hundred yards, there is another small town, but the inhabitants are at feud with each other, and a crowd which followed us from the former would not enter within the precincts of the latter. On the rugged and pinnacled heights in the vicinity of this and the neighbouring towns there are perched several round towers, which serve as strongholds in intestine feuds or against foreign invasion. In many of them there are wells, and they are usually sufficiently stored with provisions; so that in a country where artillery is seldom used, they would be capable of holding out for a long time. Ibra is justly renowned for the beauty and fairness of its females. Those we met in the streets evinced but little shyness, and on my return to the tent I found it filled with them. They were in high glee at all they saw; every box I had was turned over for their inspection, and whenever I attempted to remonstrate against their proceedings, they stopped my mouth with their hands. With such damsels there was nothing left but to laugh and look on. Saaf, a sober, staid personage, seated himself in a corner, where he remained silent, and, to appearance, perfectly horrified at the passing scene. On one occasion, however, their mischievous pranks got the better of his philosophy, and arming himself with a horsewhip, he would have dispersed the party by no very gentle means if I had not prevented him. Towards evening these good dames took their departure, and their place was filled with far less entertaining visitors - some senseless and bigoted old *mullahs*, and a few rude and troublesome young men. I got rid of the former, who had come for the purpose of disputation, by subscribing to all they asserted, and Saaf's influence rid me of the latter.

After obtaining a meridian observation for the latitude, which I made 22:41, we left our encampment. In passing through the town a crowd of vagabonds (aided by all the children) rose up and fairly hooted us through it. A few stones were also thrown, one of which struck me on the arm. I then turned to a group of old men, and inquired if it were possible that this could be a town of Sayyid Said's? They made an attempt at interference; but it was very plainly to be perceived that they were rather pleased than dissatisfied at the riot. At last, feeling seriously apprehensive for my servants, who were following at some distance, I faced about to join them, and the inhabitants seeing I had firearms, and thinking I was about to use them, scampered off in all directions. We availed ourselves of this panic, and got through the gate, after which they did not attempt to follow us. It is disturbances of this nature which a traveller has most to fear, for a mob in an Eastern town, when once raised, quickly proceeds to acts of violence; but I must remark, that this was the only part of the Imam's dominions where I was not received with the utmost attention, and it is not probable we should have been thus insulted had the Sheikh himself been present.

CHAPTER 8
MEETING LIEUTENANT WHITELOCK IN SAMAD AL SHAN

Mountain Scenery - Sagacity of the Camel - Climate of Oman - A Thief - Gum Arabic - Attachment to the Camel, laughable Anecdote - Lieutenant Whitelock - Breakfast with the Sheikh of Samad Al Shan - Interior of his Fortress- Hospitality - Gravity of Bedouin youth - Anecdote - Sheikh Nasser - Bedouin robbers - Anecdote - Manah (Minna) - Beautiful Scenery - Honesty of the women - Nizwa (Neswah) - Sheikh - Visit to the Fort - Trade - Dress and habits of the Natives.

At 1:30, from an elevated ridge, I caught a glimpse of the mountains over Sur, bearing E. by ½ S. Our course here has been W. by S., and from hence it was N.W. Small hills of limestone formation, of a pyramidal form and rugged outline, their blackened surface exhibiting no traces of bushes or desert shrubs, extend on either hand. The intermediate valleys and plains are sprinkled with grassy knolls, and towards sunset we again entered a woody tract. Shortly after dark we lost the path: the camels, immediately this falls out, discover it instinctively, and then seem to be possessed with a spirit of devilry. They erect their tails, run here and there, and against each other; and generally conclude, as they did with us this evening, by two or three scampering away and capsizing their baggage. After this I thought it better to halt, and our Bedouins having discovered a hollow, which they always select in preference to other spots, because sheltered from the wind and serving to conceal their fires, we collected our camels and unloaded them for the night. Fahrenheit's thermometer stood this evening at 56°, and we found a fire not only comfortable but necessary. The Bedouins have a singular mode of sleeping; they strip themselves of all their clothes, and having dug a hole in the sand, pile these, and whatever they can get in addition, over them; the sword, shield, and matchlock are placed by their side, and so disposed as to be ready for immediate use.

Although equally cool, the atmosphere is not so clear and pure as that which we have left. The air of Oman (I use this word in the restricted sense I have attached to it in the map) is considered to be proverbially unhealthy in the cold season; especially within the oases. Bedouins from the Desert rarely reside there three or four days without being attacked with violent fevers, and my own sufferings subsequently, unfortunately verified the correctness of this opinion. The climate of Batinah (*Batna*) and Bidiyyah is said to be salubrious; but in this respect Nejd is considered superior to all Arabia. The approach of some Bedouins being this night discovered by the neighing of my horse, in an instant every individual was upon his feet with his matchlock ready. The party, which consisted of five or six, finding themselves discovered, were now stealing off, and I had some difficulty in preventing our party from firing on them. Having set a guard, we slept undisturbed until the following morning. To pilfer some article from the baggage was the object our visitors had in view, but at daylight we discovered nothing to be missing.

Tuesday, December 15th. At 7:45 we continued across the same woody track as before. The *Simr* trees here are of great size, and the gum exudes in considerable quantities. I was chatting with Hamed, who rode alongside of me, respecting his camels. He related many singular cases of the attachment which the Bedouins bear towards these useful animals. In order to draw further information from him I professed my incredulity on certain points which he had mentioned. A party at this moment happened to be approaching from an opposite direction, and Hamed, somewhat nettled, proposed to test the truth of his statements by what I should witness. The parties approached: "May God Almighty break the leg of your camel!" bawled out Hamed to the foremost of the party, who was riding somewhat in advance of the others. Without a moment's hesitation the stranger threw himself from his beast, and advanced sword in hand on Hamed, who would probably have had but little reason to congratulate himself on his experiment, if several of our party had not thrown themselves before him, and explained the story. But the Arab still appeared deeply offended, and replied to all that was brought forward in explanation by asking 'Why he abused his camel, and in what manner it had harmed him?' The matter was adjusted by a few presents, and I passed on, determined in my own mind not to trust again to an Arab's delicacy in settling a question of this nature.

At 9:45 we arrived at Wadi Ethelee, where there are some wells of good water. Antelopes, partridges, and other games are numerous. Here old Saaf and I were very successful, and when we left, the dogs had a famous course after an antelope, which they picked up in a run of ten minutes. At one hour we arrived at the S. E. extremity of the grove and town of Samad Al Shan (*Seemed*), and at 1:30 pitched our tent alongside a beautiful stream of running water, a few yards from the trees.

Wednesday, 16th. Samad Al Shan is of greater extent than many of the other oases, but there are no more than four hundred inhabitants at present on the spot. This is the native city of my old guide and companion, Saaf, and I found, to my great regret, that he was to leave me here. In the evening I was joined, most unexpectedly, by Lieutenant Whitelock, who was travelling with leave of absence, in order to acquire a knowledge of Arabic. As it suited both our views, it was agreed that we should proceed together. He has assumed the native dress, but I still retain that of England [19].

Samad Al Shan Fort

Thursday, December 17th. We visited the Sheikh's dwelling, on an invitation to breakfast. It was a large fort, very strongly built with the same material as the houses. The rooms are spacious and lofty, but destitute of any furniture. Suspended on pegs, protruding about two feet from the wall, are the saddles, cloths, and trappings of their horses and camels. The ceilings are painted in various devices, but the floors are of mud, and only partially covered with mats. The windows, in place of the usual ornamental wood-work, are crossed by transversed iron bars; and at night, in order to protect the inmates from the keenness of the winds, they are wholly closed by wooden shutters. Lamps formed of shells, a species of murex, are suspended by lines from the ceiling, and the whole was essentially different from what I have seen in other parts of Arabia. Our meal, after the usual style, was sumptuous and plentiful; but so strictly do the Arabs regard the laws of hospitality, that it required much entreaty to induce our host, a man of high birth, to seat himself with us. This originates in a prevalent belief that if he partakes of the meal he will neither have leisure nor opportunity to look after his guests, and he, therefore, insisted upon waiting on us in the capacity of an attendant. It was not until I told him that we would not commence unless he did so, that he could be prevailed on to join in, and then we perceived he could play his part as well as the best of us. On returning to the tent I found, as usual, a great crowd collected there, but they were kept in tolerable order by a little urchin about twelve years of age, whose father, a man of great influence in these parts, had, a few years before, been killed by the Bedouins. He had taken complete possession of our tent, and allowed none of his countrymen to enter but with his permission. He carried a sword longer than himself, and also a stick, with which he occasionally laid about him. I was excessively amused at the gravity and self-importance of this youngster, who appeared perfectly well acquainted with the numbers, resources, and distribution of the native tribes, and his conversation on these and other subjects was free and unembarrassed, and, at the same time, highly entertaining. It may be observed, generally, of the Arabs, and particularly of the Bedouins, that their boys share the confidence and the councils of the men at a very early age; and on several other occasions I have seen their youths exert their influence in a manner that to us would appear preposterous. But it is a part of their system of education to cease treating them as children at a very early period, and they acquire, therefore, the gravity and demeanour of men at an age when our youth are yet following frivolous pursuits, and being birched into propriety of conduct and manners.

I amused the whole assembled party this evening with Bruce's experiment of firing a candle through two parts of an inch deal plank. When I proposed it they declared the thing impossible, and in this opinion they were staunchly supported by our young friend; but we may pardon their unbelief, as well as surprise, after the feat was performed, when we reflect that it was not many years since in "all enlightened England" that the possibility of the act was very gravely questioned, and Bruce's narration of a similar exploit very charitably attributed to his "love of the marvellous."

Saturday, 19th. We struck the tent, and, after I had obtained a latitude, left at one, p.m., accompanied by the Sheikh and a guard of about twenty men, mounted on asses. Continuing our course along the valley, in forty minutes we arrived at Muyasar (*Omaseer*), where there is a fort and a few houses.

At three hours we came to a pass called Urif, which has a descent down a narrow ravine of about two hundred feet. The rock here contains an astonishing quantity of iron pyrites, the glistening of which is perceived from a considerable distance.

At four hours we passed a town called Gaza, bearing S. S. W., and at 5:45 arrived at Khadra (*Kothra*), where we halted. Two miles from this, in a S.S.E. direction, there are some copper mines, but our guides would not conduct us to them. They are still worked, but the quantity of ore obtained is very small, and scarcely covers the expense. Khadra is a small hamlet with 'an abundance of water in its vicinity: the night was cloudy, with light drizzling rain; but within our tent we passed the time very pleasantly, chatting with Sheikh Nasser and his Bedouins to a very late hour.

Sunday, December 20th. Having taken leave of Sheikh Nasser, who is the most intelligent Arab I have yet met with, at 11:30 we continued our journey, with a guard of about seventy men, for the road between this place and Nizwa is said to be infested with robbers, who plunder small parties in open day. Our course was W. ½ N., and we passed a great number of villages, which appear on our map. At 2:20, we halted 45 minutes at Aqil (*Okahil*), in order to obtain a fresh guard; the men collected for this purpose were apparently volunteers, who seemed to enjoy the fun a good deal, although in some places they proceeded with their matches lighted, and under every preparation for an attack. The robbers who frequent the Jaalan district arrive from the Western Desert in parties of fifty to one hundred, being generally mounted on swift camels. No warning is of course given of their approach; and after a foray they retreat with equal celerity. They often possess themselves of the African slaves belonging to the town Arabs, which they bring up in the same habits as themselves, and not unfrequently marry their daughters to them. Life is seldom taken in these affrays; though I saw a great number of people suffering from sword and gun-shot wounds; the latter, it occurs to me, are not unfrequently occasioned by their own or their friends' carelessness.Everybody on a journey carries a match lighted, and no more care is taken of their matchlock then, than when unloaded; so that when these men clustered round upon our approach to any suspicious spot, I always thought there was more reason to dread danger from my friends than foes. At 4:25 we arrived at Tulhat, where there are two small forts erected on the pinnacles of a hill rising over the town. The town itself is walled round; the date groves in its vicinity are very extensive, and a noble stream of water passes through it. Hitherto I have avoided sleeping in these groves, but here we were compelled to do so, and the consequence was what I anticipated, two of my servants being next day attacked with severe fever. Fahrenheit's thermometer 58°.Monday, 21st. We started at ten, and at twelve, crossing a desert country, passed a town at the base of the Green Mountains, called Birkat Al Mawz (*Birket el Moge*), bearing north, and distant about eight miles. At 12:30, we arrived at Mahyoul (*Mayul*), on the south side of which there are two round forts; and at 1:30 we entered the precincts of the town of Manah.

Manah differs from the other towns in having its cultivation in the open fields. As we crossed these, with lofty almond, citron, and orange-trees, yielding a delicious fragrance on either hand, exclamations of astonishment and admiration burst from us. "Is this Arabia," we said; "this the country we have looked on heretofore as a desert?" Verdant fields of grain and sugar-cane stretching along for miles are before us; streams of water flowing in all directions, intersect our path; and the happy and contented appearance of the peasants, agreeably helps to fill up the smiling picture; the atmosphere was delightfully clear and pure; and, as we trotted joyously along, giving or returning the salutation of peace or welcome, I could almost fancy we had at last reached that "Araby the blessed," which I have been accustomed to regard as existing only in the fictions of our poets.

Upon entering the town, I was met by some relations of Sayyid Said, who conducted me to an open spot, where we pitched our tent. These chiefs are at feud with the neighbouring tribe of Ghafiri (*Ghafari*), who possess an extensive fort contiguous to the town, and do not acknowledge the authority of the Imam.

The Ghafiri are among the noblest of the tribes of Oman, and, with the Yarubi, have at different periods respectively furnished an Imam. Their power is now limited to the possession of a few castles, from which they occasionally sally and annoy the surrounding country. The Sheikh of Manah informed me that, wearied with the constant broils which his unruly neighbours thrust on him, he, a short time before, had undermined their fort, which was but a few yards beyond the walls of his town, and that upon any return of disturbance, he would destroy the whole nest of them. I should have been incredulous to the truth of a statement so entirely at variance with their usual mode of warfare, if, on condition that I would instruct them how to lay and fire the train, which they were afraid of doing themselves, he had not offered to conduct me to the spot; but, of course, I declined any interference.

Manah is an old town, said to have been erected at the period of Khosrow I Anushirvan's (*Nushirvan's*) invasion; but it bears, in common with the others, no indications of antiquity: its houses are lofty, but do not differ from those I have described at Samad Al Shan and Ibra. There are two square towers, about one hundred and seventy feet in height, nearly in the centre of the town; at their bases, the breadth of the wall is not more than two feet, and neither side exceeds in length eight yards. It is therefore astonishing, considering the rudeness of the materials, (they have nothing but unhewn stones and a coarse, but apparently strong cement) that, with proportions so meagre, they should have been able to carry them to the elevation they have. The guards, who are constantly on the look-out, ascend by means of a rude ladder, formed by placing bars of wood in a diagonal direction in one of the side angles, within the interior of the building. The country in every direction around this town is flat and even; and the commanding view they obtain from their summit enables them to perceive from a long distance the approach of an enemy. A telescope which I presented to the Sheikh was most thankfully received, and it promises to be of every service to them.

Manah

The females here are equally bold, and more numerous than those of Ibra. Yet, notwithstanding my tent was constantly crowded with them, and a temptation to pilfer must have been presented in a hundred seducing and facile forms, I did not miss the most trifling article. I hope their other virtues may be commensurate with their honesty. More frolicsome, laughter loving dames I never beheld: they were never for an instant quiet, and, as for their chattering! - he must be a bold man, and worthy of his destiny with such damsels, who, availing himself, in point of plurality, to the full extent of Mohammed's permission, finds no reason to repent having done so.

Tuesday 22nd. At 9:40 we left the skirts of the town, and, continuing north, over much cultivated ground, at length arrived at the base of a low ridge of hills, which forms the roots of the Jabal Akhdar range. At 10:30 we continued rounding a cape of the hills, and at 1:30, arriving at the small fort and villages of Rawḍah (*Rhodda*) and Firq (*Furk*), we crossed over much marshy ground, filled with the high reeds of which the Arabian pens are made; and at 3:30 reached Nizwa. I proceeded at once to the residence of the Sheikh, who possesses great influence in these parts. We found him seated before the castle gate, with an armed guard of about fifty men, who were standing on either side. The whole town had followed us thus far; but directly Sayyid Said's letter was produced, and it was discovered who we were, they immediately dispersed, and the Sheikh expressed his regret that I had not sent him an intimation of my intended visit, in order that he might have met me on the road with a proper escort. We accompanied him to his audience-room, within the fort, which was lofty and well furnished. A house was soon procured, and here, for the first time since leaving Muscat, I enjoyed the luxury of being alone, and remaining with our every motion unwatched, for, at the different other towns on our route, the Sheikhs and principal men thought they honoured us in proportion to the time they passed in our society. During the evening, the Sheikh, accompanied by a few of his friends, paid us a visit. To my surprise the latter applied to us for brandy, and drank as much as was given them without scruple; nor did the Sheikh express any disapprobation of such an indulgence. I found they had been in the habit of procuring spirits from Muscat, where, though they are contraband, a considerable quantity is smuggled on shore from the Indian ships. When they first made their appearance there was a mullah with them, but he took his departure very soon, in consequence of some fumes of tobacco passing over his person.

We spent the day in looking over the town and the surrounding gardens, and towards evening went to visit the fort, which, in the estimation of all the surrounding country, is impregnable. We were admitted, after much ceremony, by an iron door of great strength, and, ascending by a vaulted passage, passed through six others equally massive before we reached the summit. In order to render appearances more imposing, a janitor behind each inquired the purport of our visit; and, being told we were servants of the Sultan, he removed several locked bars and chains, and we then passed on. The form of the fort is circular, its diameter being nearly one hundred yards, and to the height of about ninety feet it has been filled up by a solid mass of earth and stones: seven or eight wells have been bored through this, from several of which they obtain a plentiful supply of water, and those which are dry serve as magazines for their shot and ammunition.

We found a few old guns here, one bearing the name of Imam Saaf, and another that of Kouli Khan, the Persian general who took Muscat. A wall forty feet high surrounds the summit, making the whole height of the tower one hundred and fifty feet. It is certainly a work of extraordinary labour, and, from its appearance, most probably of considerable antiquity; but, on this point, I could gain no certain intelligence. The natives have not overrated its strength; neither artillery nor shells could make much impression: it would be too high to scale, even if the upper wall was breached; and the only practicable way which I can conceive, would be either starving out the garrison, or mining it. Even the latter operation would be tedious.

The dry bed of an extensive stream passes its base. Within this several houses have been erected, but, about three years ago, after some heavy falls of rain on the mountains, it filled its bed so suddenly that the whole of these, as well as a considerable part of the town, were washed away. It had not been known to rise to such a height for thirty years before.

Nizwa in extent resembles Manah, but the groves are more numerous. A great quantity of sugar-cane is grown, and its produce manufactured here by a process similar to that adopted in India, from whence they appear at a very late period to have borrowed it, as none was made at Muscat in 1760, when Niebuhr visited it. The best halwa (*ulwah*) in Arabia is obtained at this town. They also make a few copper pots, and there are some workers in gold and silver, but not having many artisans of any description, all their other manufactured commodities arrive from Muscat. I must not, however, omit to mention that a considerable quantity of cloth and some good mats are fabricated from the rushes which grow on the borders of the streams. Preparing cotton in the yarn is the principal occupation of the females. In the cool season they may be perceived coming out from beneath the groves with their spindles after breakfast, to enjoy the warmth of the sun's rays. The men alone attend the looms. Besides mats the females manufacture some pretty baskets from the rushes. The former serve them to sleep on, and the latter they carry with them to market to deposit their purchases in. A great many *bishts* (*kamalines - cloaks*) are fabricated here, and also brought from Nejd. The best, worn by the Sheikhs are of a light-brown, or cream colour, and sell for forty or fifty Dollars; the black *bisht*, and those striped in alternate vertical bars of brown and white, eight or ten Dollars. The *bisht* forms the most important article of their dress, and its quality denotes the condition and rank of the wearer.

Nizwa Fort

CHAPTER 9
ASCENT FROM NIZWA TO JABAL AKHDAR

R*evenue of Nizwa - Currency - Author lodges in a Mosque - Tanuf - Mountain Scenery - Perilous Descent - Sayq (Seyk) - Amiable character of its Inhabitants - Romantic Landscape - Hodin - Pomegranate Wine - Shirayjah (Shirazi) - A Termagant - Bedouin Curiosity - Country of the Franks - Description of Shirayjah - Excursions - The Almond - Figs, &c. - Altitude of the Mountains - Wild Animals.*

Nizwa is the only town in Oman from whence the Imam derives any revenue, and even here it is scarcely more than nominal, for not more than one thousand dollars a year are remitted to him. The following are the coins in current use amidst the towns in the interior. They were nearly all coined during the reign of Imam Saaf, and differ from those now in use at Muscat and on the sea coast. All have inscriptions, but nothing bearing a likeness to any object in animated nature.

New coinage at Muscat.

20 copper coins make a ghazi (*gazi*). Spanish dollar 200 *pice* or *ghazi*,

20 *ghazi* a *mahmudi* (*mahmidi*). A baisa (*basi*) 40 ""

15 *mahmudi* a dollar, *mahmudi* 20 ""

shuk or 5 ""

The following were the principal articles exposed for sale, with their prices, both of which are nearly the same at all the other interior towns :

Rice 12 *pice* per lb.

Wheat 12 ""

Barley 11 ""

Beans 10 ""

Camel's flesh 16 ""

Beef 20 ""

Mutton 16""
Kid 14""
Sweet oil 50 ""
Ghee 56""

Friday, December 25th. At 11 a.m. we left the town on a visit to the celebrated Jabal Akhdar, or Green Mountains.

Jabal Akhdar rises from near Birkat Al Mawz

Following the skirts of the hills to our left, we passed several sterile plains which present nothing worthy of observation, and at three hours arrived at Tanuf, where the Sheikh resides, whose authority is paramount on the mountains. After halting we were at first lodged in the mosque, which, strange as it may appear, is generally used in Oman as *caravansarai*; but fearing they might not relish our walking about with our shoes on, and it being rather too cool to go without them, I procured another house. Here I was soon joined by the Sheikh, who came with several others to dissuade me from my intention of visiting the mountains. Most frightful pictures were drawn of the passes; and I believe they thought that we, like many of their worthy countrymen, who pass their lives on the plains, had never visited a mountain district.

Tanuf

The natives were also described as being little better than savages, and especially hostile to the visits of strangers; but finding all their arguments ineffectual in changing our intention, they took their departure, evidently somewhat disappointed.

Tanuf has two small forts, which serve to command the entrance of the valley; in other respects it is an insignificant hamlet, surrounded by considerable cultivation.

Saturday, December 26th. In the early part of the day, every obstacle on the part of the Sheikh and the inhabitants was thrown in the way of our proceeding, and matters were at length only settled by my threatening to ride back to Nizwa, and bring the Sheikh with me.After we had fairly started, a few dollars to those who were to accompany us acted like magic in removing objections, and at 1:30 we commenced our ascent, about a mile from the village. The mountain asses with which we were furnished are of a large size; and by constantly traversing these acclivities, acquire a firmness of step equal to that of mules. They proceed at a very quick pace for about sixty or eighty yards, and then halt to obtain breath and push on again. At this rate we ascended very rapidly along the southern ridge, in some places approaching to within a few paces of a ravine, which sunk down perpendicularly to a tremendous depth. On our left, in one part, where the dangers of a smooth narrow track were further increased by a slight slope towards the precipice, our off feet were swinging over it, and I then became conscious that the representations we had received from the natives below were not so much exaggerated as we were at first inclined to believe. At two hours we quitted the ridge to ascend the face of the mountain, and our track then lay over tabular masses of limestone, until 3:30, when we halted in a narrow ravine near some wells of water. Hitherto the hills are wholly destitute of trees or herbage. Some scanty tufts appear at intervals, but the ravines by which they are intersected, notwithstanding their rocky bed, nourish several lofty *athel* (*tarfa*) or tamarisk trees (*Tamarix aphylla - Hedysarum Alhaghi*) [20].

The mountaineers who accompany us, appear neither social nor good-humoured. After dark I noticed five different fires; the Bedouins of a single party always club around one.

December 27th. At 5:30, the thermometer stood at 53°; but it was not until seven hours, when the sun had risen sufficiently high to warm them, that our guides would proceed. We then continued our ascent over the same country as yesterday. The bushes become more stunted and scarce as we proceed, and all other vegetation entirely disappears. At 9:30 we arrived at the summit of the ridge, and from thence obtained a good view of the general outlines of the hills which form the most elevated portion of the range. They present without deviation the usual character of the limestone formation, ascending with a steep slope at an angle of about 30° with the horizon, and terminating to the southward in mural precipices of great depth. Along the face of one of these our route continued for some distance; the path was a stair-like projection, jutting out from the face of the cliff, and overhung by threatening masses of rock, while below, it sunk perpendicularly to the depth of 700 or 800 feet. As this path was too narrow to admit of the asses proceeding with their baggage in the usual manner, what could not be packed on their backs was carried by the drivers.

We now commenced our descent by a path so steep and slippery, that we were compelled to take off our shoes; yet the asses proceeded at a quick pace without making a single false step. Shortly before this, one of the men separated himself from the party, and called on me to follow him. I did so, and after scrambling for some distance down the precipice, holding on by the branches and roots of the trees, we suddenly turned an angle of the rock, and found that the track led along a narrow ledge for about two hundred yards. It appeared as smooth as glass, and in many places not more than a foot in breadth, with a steep precipice on either hand above and below. I know not whether he expected me to imitate his example in taking a shorter route, or if it was only to exhibit his own fearlessness and dexterity; but directly we opened upon the scene, he stopped, and inquiring, with a smile, if I would follow further, tripped carefully along, supporting himself by his hands in those places where the rock projected and compelled him to bend his body over the precipice, and in the course of a few minutes, was safely seated at the opposite extremity, beckoning and calling on me to proceed. But it was a feat beyond my performance, and I returned to accompany the others by the safer path.

Shirayjah and the hill of a pyramidal shape

At 2:30 we passed some straggling hamlets, of which the huts were constructed of loose stones, and at 3, arrived at the valley and town of Sayq. Hitherto since leaving Tanuf, we had not met with any individual; but the inhabitants now crowded out in great numbers to welcome us as we passed along. Several entreated us to remain for the night at their village; but I was anxious to pass on to Shirayjah, which is described as being the most extensive and plentiful of all the valleys. Our reception there, however, led me subsequently to regret that I did not take advantage of the kind offer of these villagers; for a wilder, more romantic, or more singular spot than was now before us, can scarcely be imagined. By means of steps we descended the steep side of a narrow glen, about four hundred feet in depth, passing in our progress several houses perched on crags or other acclivities, their walls built up in some places so as to appear but a continuation of the precipice.

These small, snug, compact-looking dwellings have been erected by the natives one above the other, so that their appearance from the bottom of the glen, hanging as it were in mid air, affords to the spectator a most novel and interesting picture. Here we found, amidst a great variety of fruits and trees, pomegranates, citrons, almonds, nutmegs, and walnuts, with coffee bushes and vines. In the summer, these together, must yield a delicious fragrance, and produce a picturesque, verdant, and beautiful landscape. It was now, however, winter, and the whole were denuded of their leaves, and had a cheerless appearance. Water flows in many places from the upper part of the hills, and is received at the lower in small reservoirs, from whence it is distributed over all the face of the country. It is however so cold, that although very thirsty from the length of our walk, we were not able to partake of more than a sparing draught. From the narrowness of this glen and the steepness of its sides, only the lower part of it receives the warmth of the sun's rays but for a short period during the day; and even at the time of our arrival, we found it so chilly that, after a short halt, we were very happy to continue our journey. Ascending therefore on the opposite side of the valley also by steps, and passing over much rugged and uneven ground, we crossed a level tract of country, overgrown with brambles and thistles, and at 4:30 arrived at a small town called Hodin, where we found the cultivation on the open plains. The gardens and fields of grain in these spots, present a strong and pleasing contrast to the bleak and barren appearance of the general surface of the range. Water seems plentiful; and some of the fruit-trees are very large. The natives make incisions in several of the pomegranate fruit, which cluster together on the same branch, and place under them large *calabashes [Lagenaria siceraria]*, into which the juice for some time continues to flow. It is afterwards mixed with that of the grape, for making wine.

Housing Jabal Akhdar

After descending another pass of about seven hundred feet, we arrived at a third town called Shirayjah. But the ground in its neighbourhood was so uneven and rugged, that we found no place where our small tent could be pitched; and as the nights at this elevation are excessively cold, I was very desirous to obtain the shelter of a house. After being led from one to the other, the inmates of all refusing to admit us, on the plea of having no room, we were at length shown into a low, confined, filthy apartment, and our baggage lodged with us. We had not been seated here very long, before an old woman made her appearance with a flock of sheep and goats, to whose tenement we now discovered that the inhabitants, from a desire of amusing themselves with the wrath of its irascible owner, had conducted us. Nor were they disappointed; for the old lady no sooner caught a glimpse of the intruders than she raised such an outrageous clamour, that we were but too happy to effect a safe retreat. Although completely fagged (for we had been walking nearly the whole of the day), and somewhat displeased at our unceremonious ejection, still we had no sooner seated ourselves beneath a rock, which sheltered us in a measure from the keenness of the wind, and had lighted a good fire to cook our evening meal, than the whole affair appeared so amusing that we indulged a hearty laugh. Not so the Arab who accompanied us as a guide; with our situation it was very evident he had marvellous little sympathy, notwithstanding his professions to the contrary. But that a true believer, and a Sheikh of fifty followers, should meet with so little consideration and hospitality, was beyond endurance; and dire and manifold, as he sat shivering in the cold, were the imprecations which he heaped on the heads of the "wine-bibbing *kafirs*."

How long he amused himself in this way, I know not; for after collecting all the clothes we had with us, and selecting the softest piece of ground we could discover, we were soon asleep.

Early this morning, the natives assembled to inquire how we had passed the night, and finding we made no complaint either of our lodgings or the keenness of the air, they applied to Ali for information, as to who we were, and from what country we came; but he was indignantly silent. It was evident that they expected we should suffer in an equal degree with those of the lowlands who had visited them; their surprise, therefore, was very great when they next applied to my servant, a shrewd fellow, who spoke Arabic with considerable fluency, and learnt that we came from a climate far colder than their own; "where, instead of having ice and snow but a very few days in the year, as you have here, it is found for six months together." After listening to this explanation they went away for a short time, and prepared a small shed, which had formerly been used as a cowhouse, for our reception; thither we were conducted, and they then supplied us with a hearty meal of dates, milk, and dried fruits.

Shirayjah contains about two hundred small houses, built around the commencement or head of a valley, which extends thence in a south south-east direction to the plains below. They are small, square, solid-looking edifices, and built expressly to withstand the showers and tempests which in those regions occasionally sweep over them. Narrow loopholes in the walls serve as windows, and the door also is very diminutive. None of these edifices have more than one story; and although for warmth and culinary purposes they are compelled constantly to have a fire within them, there is no chimney, nor any outlet for the smoke except by the door or window. The inconvenience is not however so great as might be imagined, since they manufacture large quantities of charcoal, which is most commonly used, together with a kind of peat, procured from some morasses in the lower part of the valleys. Whether it is owing to any peculiarity in their mode of preparing the former, I know not, but I could never learn that any accidents arise from its use, although the rooms in which it is constantly burnt are low and confined, and the doors and windows all closed at night.

The subsequent three days were passed by us in traversing the country in various directions, and I shall now give the result of our observations on the figure and general productions of the range. The Jabal Akhdar occupy from east to west, which is their greatest length, a distance of thirty miles. At right angles to this they are intersected by narrow deep valleys, along which, during the rainy season, on either side, the torrents descend, and lose themselves, either in the sandy soil which crosses the plains, or pour their waters into the ocean. The maximum breadth of the chain is fourteen miles, and the northern and southern declivities are very rapid. Taken generally, it will be seen by my narrative of our route, that the range by no means deserves the appellation it has received, "Green," for a great proportion of its surface is bare limestone rock, which presents in some places naked tabular masses, and in others, the shallow, earthy deposit lodged in the hollows is as poor as the worst part of the plains; but the valleys with several hollows are extensively cultivated, and supply such an abundance of fruit, &c., that many writers have considered them as common to the whole range, and hence is derived its present appellation. The most important of these productions are the vines, which extend along the valley for miles. They are chiefly grown on terraced grounds, and entwine themselves around poles about six feet in height. They are abundantly watered by artificial rills, and the soil appears rich and fertile. Their fruit is of several kinds; wine being made principally from the white, while the large black grape is used for drying into raisins.

Hyena (Hyaena hyaena) Oman

The Arabs consider the almond-tree to be a native of Oman. It attains a greater size here than in the plains below, and some were shown to me from thirty to forty feet in height. We found both the sweet and bitter kinds; and while the latter are considered very appetising, the former enter largely into the composition of all their made dishes, whether of grain, sweetmeats, or animal food. They also have walnuts, figs, and nutmegs. The last are smaller than those brought from the Eastern Islands, but in richness of flavour, are fully equal to them. The figs (*Ficus Carica* of Linnaeus) taste sweet and pleasant, but are very small, being inferior both in size and flavour to those brought from Turkey. They are dried and sold in large quantities in all the towns. A small quantity of coffee is grown; but owing, in all probability, to the little care bestowed on its culture, it is considered to be of inferior quality to that brought from Yemen. In addition to these, all the fruits and grain common to the plains below, are produced in large quantities. Muscat and other ports on the sea-coast of Oman, together with Ras Al Khaimah, Sharjah, and many others on the southern shores of the Persian Gulf, receive their supplies from this range.

By a tried thermometer, I found that water boiled at Shirayjah at 200 ¾ °, which gives an altitude of about six thousand one hundred and eighty-seven feet. This I ascertained by several other observations to be from eight hundred to one thousand feet below the level of the summit of the greater part of the chain. After rain at this season, they have not unfrequently ice and snow, but the latter rarely remains on the ground longer than a few hours. As far as inquiries enabled me to judge, the climate in the summer season must be very temperate, the natives say, not warmer than in the plains below; and at present, the hot and parching winds, which are there of such frequent occurrence, seem wholly unknown here. I could not, therefore, but conclude this must be a delightful residence when everything was in bloom. Water, which gushes from numerous springs, never fails them. At Shirayjah they have a copious stream, which, after being led into a deep and capacious reservoir, in sufficient quantities to irrigate the whole of the cultivated part of the valley, flows down in a yet considerable body, and supplies the small village of Birkat Al Mawz at its extremity.

In some of the valleys on the south-east side of the range, where brambles and dense thickets are very numerous, wild boars, foxes, and hyenas are said to abound. The two latter we saw, but were never sufficiently fortunate to obtain a glimpse of the former.

CHAPTER 10

DESCENT FROM MOUNTAINS TO NIZWA

T*he Bani Riyam - Use of Wine - Description - Arms - Manners - Author's disappointment - Women - Return to Nizwa - Desertion of the Guides - Ruined Town - Mountain Pass - Magnificent Precipice - Perilous Descent - Anecdote - Geological Structure - Birkat Al Mawz - Salubrious Climate - Bedouin Chief - Anecdote - Love of the Desert - Cheerful temperament of the Bedouin - Robber Hordes - Domestic Manners and Customs - Contradictions of Character - Games - Talismans - Necromancy - Story-tellers.*

The Bani Riyam, who inhabit this range of mountains, occupied the principal share of my attention during our stay. I think there is every reason to believe their own assertion that they have never known a master, and, as they never venture below but in small parties, for the purpose of disposing of their various articles of merchandise, and do not proceed beyond the foot of the mountains, where regular markets are established, they may be still regarded as an isolated race, removed from, and unconnected with, the several tribes in the plains below. The steep, rugged, and dangerous nature of their passes, which frequently lead through defiles, where a few resolute men might make the way good against a thousand, and also the strong positions which they have chosen for the erection of their villages, are alone sufficient to secure their independence.

Their number does not amount to more than a thousand souls, and a consciousness of this numerical weakness has made them aware that a strong bond of union is necessary to their preservation. They boast, therefore, that, while the low country has, at different periods, suffered from foreign invasion, or been involved in the anarchy and confusion consequent to intestine broils, they have cultivated their vines and grain in peace, without fear or interruption; and, although they bear the reputation of being affluent, yet the Imams have never been able to exact a duty from them. In their persons, although more athletic and robust than their neighbours of the plains, they have not the usual healthy and hardy look of mountaineers, but, on the contrary, their faces are wrinkled and haggard, and appear as if suffering from premature decay. I have little doubt but this is owing to an immoderate use of wine, which they distil from their grapes in large quantities, and partake of openly and freely at their several meals. They defend the practice by asserting that the cold renders it necessary.

Their wine, in flavour and appearance, bears a close resemblance to that brought from Shiraz. Large quantities are taken in skins to the surrounding countries and to the sea-coast, and is there sold publicly. In the winter season the men leave the culture of their vines to the females, and, having nothing to do themselves, pass the time within their houses, until the sun is sufficiently high to warm them, and then they crawl forth and bask in it. While amidst their mountains, few go armed with more than the common *jambiya* or dagger, which also serves them on many occasions as a knife; but those who resort with their fruit, &c., to the plains below, carry with them their matchlock and sword, and that they well understand their use, is but too frequently demonstrated in their brawls with their Arab customers, by whom they are considered an irascible, slothful, and immoral race.

"They neglect their prayers, break the fast of the Ramadan, and openly indulge in the forbidden pleasures of wine," was my friend, the Sheikh's, summary of their character.

Wanting, at least in their estimation, the Bedouin virtues of frankness and hospitality, which at once convert the person they meet with into an open foe or a cherished guest, they have invested the inhabitants of Jabal Akhdar with the heaviest charge which can be brought against them, that of being niggard and sullen in the exercise of their hospitality: certainly what came under my observation during our short stay among them, produces little which could be advanced in contradiction of it. There was none of that freshness and vivacity which we usually meet with amongst mountaineers. Their manners, indeed, are far more rude than those of the wild tribes who inhabit the Desert below. They displayed no feeling of curiosity, nor did they seek either to amuse, or evince any desire to be amused. I had, from the very first moment that these mountains were mentioned to me, permitted my imagination to dwell with delight on the rich treat which I anticipated their investigation would afford; I had, with a too simple belief in the exaggerated tales of the Arabs, pictured to myself a range of verdant hills, clothed with the richest vegetation, crowned with lofty forests, and peopled by a simple and interesting race, whose habits, usages, and condition would present an ample field of inquiry: the result of such expectations are before the reader.

Birkat Al Mawz with its date palm oasis

Their women go unveiled, and the men appear by no means jealous. Whenever we fell in with them, they were either employed tending their vines, or in other occupations connected with husbandry, or were carrying water on their heads from the fountain, in the same manner, and in vessels similar to those used in India. Constant exercise in the open air gives an elasticity and freedom to their gait, as well as a ruddiness and clearness of complexion which we do not meet with in the females below: these, combined with a disposition equally lively, and a form, although somewhat taller, yet possessing outlines by no means inferior, render them a far more interesting subject for consideration than their worthy helpmates. I have more than once regretted it when in conversation with them, that, with such faces and forms, fate had not assigned them a less rude lot. Yet are they, in common with those who, from local and other causes, rank lower in the scale of human condition, apparently content with the station which has been assigned them, and we may question if any change would increase the sum of their general happiness.

Thursday, December 31st. It now became necessary for us to return to Nizwa, where I expected letters connected with my further progress were awaiting me, but an unforeseen obstacle presented itself, which at first gave me no small trouble. The men we brought from Tanuf complained much of the cold, and had been desirous to return immediately after our arrival at Shirayjah, and in this feeling they were supported and encouraged by our Arab guide. Yesterday morning they grew more than usually importunate, but finding I paid little attention, they took advantage of our absence from the house, and threw everything out of the bags in which our baggage had been placed, breaking several of the articles, and then took their departure. We were consequently, on our return, left without any means of quitting, and being aware of the share the villagers had in the fracas, I was anxious to leave before they should be excited to any further mischief. I accordingly went this morning to the Sheikh, who at first evinced no inclination to assist us, but after two hours' talking, (for the Arabs never perform the most trifling undertaking or engagement without an enormous expenditure of words) he agreed, upon the promise of a present, not only to furnish us with asses, but also to accompany us himself to Birkat Al Mawz. All was prepared by 8:30, and we then commenced our descent to Nizwa by another road, called Darb Muaydin (*Durbh Moidien*): its general direction being S. 13° E. it is unnecessary for me to detail the windings of our route. Before us, there rose from the centre of the valley a hill of a pyramidal form, on whose summit stood a ruined tower of large dimensions and massive architecture. This building is said, in latter years, to have served the purpose of a mosque; the date of its erection I could not ascertain, but tradition asserts that it was also frequented as a place of worship by their Pagan ancestors. However, if it be true that such, in either instance, was the purport to which it was applied, the mountaineers, considering the steepness and ruggedness of the path to the summit, must have been actuated by a more fervent spirit of religious zeal than they possess at present, if they ever troubled themselves with a single, instead of the requisite five daily visits to it.

Following the direction of the western brow of the valley, though sometimes this path led over several hills and much uneven ground to a considerable distance beyond it, and at others approached close to its verge, at 10:30 we arrived at the summit of a pass, and from thence obtained a full view of the wild and savage glen beneath. Vines and terraced grounds extended for three or four miles from Shirayjah, and below that, patches of cultivated ground occur at intervals throughout its whole extent. There was also a chain of capacious pools of water, and the lively green of one, joined to the glistening of the other, continued to form a striking contrast with the sombre and shadowy line of the magnificent wall or sheet of rock, which rose perpendicularly on either hand. It took us until twelve, quick travelling, to reach the bottom of this pass. No consideration would have induced me to ride down, and I should have thought no human being in his senses would have attempted it; but our old guide, the Sheikh, after accomplishing half the descent, was so fagged that, notwithstanding every remonstrance of ours, he mounted his ass, and thus safely accomplished the remainder of the pass. "Friend Sayyid," observed I, "if you make the attempt you will most assuredly break your neck." "It may be so," he replied, "but *Allah Akbar* (God is great), and I am tired."

Wadi Muaydin

The steps, formed of unhewn stones, about three feet in width, are ranged along a sloping ledge, jutting out from the face of an almost vertical precipice; and in those places where its width was found insufficient, the rock has been scarped away. Considering these, together with many other difficulties which have been overcome with equal perseverance, it is impossible but to conclude that the mind which could have conceived and executed a work of such enormous labour, must, in a country like Arabia, where public works of any magnitude are almost unknown, have been of no common order. We are now on our descent through Wadi Muaydin (*Wadi Moidien*), which preserving the same name, extends from Shirayjah to Birkat Al Mawz. In no part we are traversing does its breadth exceed one hundred paces; and the hills, which rise perpendicularly in some places, were overhung to the height of from 2000 to 3000 feet. It consequently resembles an enormous cliff, and we have a good opportunity of investigating the geological structure of the range. The whole appears to consist of -

1. Alpine limestone;
2. Old red sandstone, with an occasional micaceous vein;
3. Alternately mica slate and granite.

Large masses have been splintered from the sides of these, blocking up the bed of the valley, and compelling us to wind our way over or between them. A large stream of water traverses the centre; small hamlets, date groves, and patches of cultivated ground occur occasionally, until we arrived, at five hours, at the village of Birkat Al Mawz, situated at the gorge of the pass, where it opens out into the plain.

Birkat Al Mawz fort

As we here partook of our evening meal, we could not but congratulate ourselves upon our return from a journey, which the reiterated assurance of the Arabs to whom we mentioned it, would have led us to believe could only be performed with much labour and considerable peril. Birka, or Birkat Al Mawz, has a fort, with a very capacious and good-looking castle, belonging to the Sheikh of Suwayq (*Suweik*), within its walls. Around these are several large groves and plantations; the plantain trees are numerous, and hence its name. A very large rivulet, or *falaj*, furnishes an ample supply of water, and from its situation, Birkat enjoys a delightfully cool atmosphere from the Jabal Akhdar, and bears the reputation of being very salubrious.

January 1st. Having remunerated the Sheikh with the promised present, at which he was well pleased, we procured a fresh supply of asses, and set out for Nizwa. Shortly after leaving, we were met by the Sheikh of that place, with a guard of fifty men, mounted on camels. Although somewhat more haughty in his manners to those around him, and more showy than other chiefs in his dress, while within the town, yet here, in common with his followers, he had nothing more than a plain turban on his head, and a cloth around his waist: the reason he gave for this, when I inquired of him, was, that if an individual were to dress himself out more conspicuously than the rest, he would at once be selected by the Bedouin marksmen as the leader, and would most probably be the first to fall. This was very plausible; but I am induced to refer the custom of stripping themselves when on the Desert to another cause. Those cooped up in the towns and oases, which are interspersed throughout the Desert, lose, in consequence of their frequent journeyings from one to the other, but little of a Bedouin's real attachment for a residence on, or a journey across it, and they appear beyond measure delighted when any event renders it necessary for them to do so. Their actions, as I have often witnessed on these occasions, are all directed to assimilating their party as nearly as possible in dress and manners to the Bedouins. The change in point of appearance, from the staid, sober demeanour of a resident Arab to all the buoyancy, laughter, and wild freaks of the former, is most amusing.

Seeing our party so well mounted, I could not help inquiring of the Sheikh his reason for not adopting some active measures for putting down the robber hordes which infest this district. "Our camels are, as you observe, very fine animals," said Abin Arish, "and I have no reason to doubt the courage of my followers; but the robbers approach in parties of thirty or forty, bringing with them several led camels, on which, frequently before any force can be raised to oppose them, the plunder is placed, and they are away in full retreat to their Desert. Thither, from our total unacquaintance with their haunts, we are unable to follow, and moreover, whenever we do give chase, it is soon found that our camels are no match in point of fleetness to theirs; but with a troop of thirty horse, I would engage in six months to insure the safe passage of gold through any part of the adjoining country."

During my progress in this country, with a view to initiate myself into their manners and domestic life, I mixed much with the Bedouins, frequently living and sleeping in their huts and tents. On all occasions I was received with kindness, and often with a degree of hospitality above, rather than below, the means of those who were called upon to exercise it. The medical character which I assumed proved then of much service to me, although, it must be acknowledged, that I was often teased for assistance where it was not required, or where it was wholly unavailing. The Arabs have singular ideas with respect to medicine - medicine, in its most comprehensive sense, it certainly is to them,-since they look for no peculiar results from the use of one kind more than another, but will swallow with avidity all which is given them under that denomination. One morning I had thrown without the door, as wholly useless, some damaged papers of magnesia and rhubarb; but the Arabs, who had seen me remove them from the small case I always carried with me, formed a different opinion, and, after an eager scramble, in which some of their females joined, they were collected and greedily devoured. In addition to human, I had not unfrequently other patients to prescribe for - horses, camels, asses, and sometimes cats. It is a mistake which Europeans, who have adopted this character, have fallen into, not to do so, for an Arab will never understand why, when you cheerfully attend a slave, whose loss he can supply for thirty or forty dollars, you should not do so to animals which are of greater value to them. It is all well enough with European ideas, to speak of the superiority of the human race over the brute species; but an Asiatic will not understand why, if you oblige him in one point, you should not do so in the other. My practice proved very extensive, and, if not travelling, the early part of the day was thus occupied. I always carried with me a large quantity of pills made of ambergris mixed with opium, and found, on 'account of the stimulating property which the former is supposed to possess, that I could not, to an Arab, make a more acceptable present. Towards noon I walked out alone with my gun, when I made my notes, or otherwise, and was accompanied by a group of Bedouin boys, who collected flowers and Desert shrubs: - to avoid suspicion, I ascribed medicinal properties to what they brought, - and the Arabs were then in no manner surprised at my solicitude for them.

All orientals are early risers: the Arabs go to bed about ten, and their first sleep is over shortly after midnight. The poorer classes repose upon mats on the ground: those in better condition on rude bedsteads with four legs, having the frame crossed by ropes. Although I have known a Bedouin on a Desert journey travel three days and as many nights without any other slumber than that obtained on his camel, yet within a town or encampment they will sleep during the greater part of the day, without finding it any interruption to their usual repose at night, and they often expressed surprise that I did not thus indulge. As soon as it is light, an Arab commences his religious exercise by saying, "*La ilaha illa Allah, Muhammad rasul Allah*" [21]; he then awakens those around him (for in the Desert, as on board ship, they usually sleep in groups), and invites them to join in his prayers, which he most commonly begins with a verse from the Quran, intimating that prayer should be preferred to sleep. Their first repast, called *futur* (*el moza*) is taken shortly afterwards. If with a Sheikh, our breakfast consisted of coffee, boiled rice, fish, and vegetables: but the poorer classes are content with dates and coarse bread. The former have also a mid-day meal, called *ghada* (*el sady*) consisting of meat dressed in a variety of ways, and fruit: but the principal meal, with all classes, is that at sunset, called *asha* (*asshar*) with those who can afford it. Our dinner consisted of a lamb or sheep boiled whole, and stuffed with rice and spices, dishes full of ribs of mutton, soups and curries. Neither chairs nor tables are in request here; the several articles being brought in, and placed on circular mats upon the floor. Around these the company seat themselves cross-legged, without regard to any rules of precedence: some one is invited to begin; then, after "*Bismillah* [22]," which is echoed by all present, a dozen hands are thrust at once into the dish. No beverage is called for during the meal, and a single draught of water concludes it: then, *al ḥamdu lillah* ("*Al hum'd Allah)* [23]," the guests rise, and the remains of the meal are abandoned to the servants and slaves.

The character of the Bedouin presents some singular contradictions. With a soul capable of the greatest exertions, he is naturally indolent. He will remain within his encampment for weeks, eating, drinking coffee, and smoking his *nargile* (*nargyl*), and then mount his camel, and away off to the Desert, on a journey of two or three hundred miles: whatever there may be his fatigues or privations, not a murmur escapes his lips. In excuse for their slothful habits at other periods, it may, however, be observed that the Quran prohibits all games of chance, and that their own rude and simple manners completely relieve them from the artificial pleasures and cares of more civilized life. In the account of my stay with the Bani bu Ali Bedouins, I have given a description of their war-dance, which is graceful and impressive; but their other amusements are trifling, and utterly at variance with the usual gravity of their deportment. One is the game of blind man's buff, played by children in England: in another they conceal a ring, or some other ornament, under one of several inverted cups, and in discovering that, consists of the art of the game. Professed story-tellers were also in great request, and I have often felt a high degree of interest in witnessing the effect of their tales on the listeners. They have-little action, are seldom over-loud or vehement, but a choice selection of words, which flow apparently without effort, a peculiar, energetic, and even graceful delivery, and an invention or memory which appears never to flag, produce effects of which the most accomplished orator would feel proud: every feeling which he could hope for or desire was exhibited on these occasions.

In the absence of amusements of a higher interest than these, without arts or literature, and debarred, by the nature of their government and country, from any opportunity of mental improvement, it is not surprising that the same species of credulity and superstition, but a few centuries ago so universal in Europe, should still hold its ground in Arabia. With many, a firm belief exists as to the power of enchanters and sorcerers; and their diabolical agency is thought to be principally exercised in transforming men into goats. It is even pretended that there are marks by which such unfortunates may be recognised; and a Bedouin, about to become a purchaser of a goat, may often be observed looking with much gravity and earnestness for them. I could never, however, prevail on them to explain of what nature they were. Many other tales of a similar nature were related to me, but, as they possess no higher interest, I forbear from narrating them. A talismanic power is also attributed to certain words, and, as with other Muslims, amulets and charms are worn, but their use is not so general as with the town Arabs.

CHAPTER II
VIOLENT FEVER GRIPS THE PARTY

E xpectations of reaching the Wahhabi Capital - Unexpected obstacles - Lieutenant Whitelock - British Agent at Muscat - Refusal to honour the Authors Bills - Munificence of the Imam - Dangerous attack of Sickness - Compelled to return to the Sea-coast - Imti (Maty) - Date Groves - Obstinacy of the Guides - Affecting incident - Samail (Temayel) - Wadi Khor - Heat - Fortitude of the Bedouins - Wahhabi irruption into Oman - Presents of Persian Fruit - Grateful recollection of the Imam's kindness.

From what I had hitherto seen of the country, and gathered from several Arabs and Sheikhs who had repeatedly traversed the road, I saw no reason to doubt but that I should be able, after completing the investigation of the northern portion of Oman, to proceed on to Diriyah, the Wahhabi capital; and it was therefore arranged that, while I occupied myself with filling up the map of my route from Sur, Lieutenant Whitelock should proceed to Muscat, in order to procure the necessary funds for our journey, as well as to seek some influential individual to accompany us, for which purpose he left early in the morning of the 3rd of January. From this period until the 12th of the same month I was fully occupied with the map, and in making excursions into the surrounding country. On my return from one of these on the morning of the 8th, I found unexpected intelligence awaiting me.

In my application to government for leave to undertake my present journey, I had requested that the British agent at Muscat, Ruben ben Aslan, a Jew, should be directed to advance me such sums as I might, from time to time, find it necessary to draw on him; but, by some inadvertence, consequent to a press of business when my letter passed Council, no reply was made to that particular paragraph; but, upon referring to the Secretary's office, it was thought that, as I was furnished with a certificate, stating I was travelling under the direction of the British government, and requiring every assistance to be rendered to me, by those who were desirous of maintaining its friendship, that it was of little moment, and I had already drawn, when in Muscat, a considerable sum from the agent. My surprise was, therefore, very great to learn from Whitelock this morning that he had refused to honour my bills, unless they previously obtained the sanction of Commander S. B. Haines (*Acting Commander J. B. Aines*), in charge of the Hon. Company's brig *Palinurus*, then lying in the harbour, who, I had been given to understand in Bombay, was also instructed to afford me every possible assistance, but who, from motives to me inexplicable, did not, in this case, think proper to concur.

The several other merchants of Muscat, instigated, as I have reason to believe, by the former of these gentlemen, also declined to supply me with money. In this unpleasing and unlooked-for dilemma, I should have scarcely known how to proceed, had I not received by the same opportunity a communication from the Imam, stating that, having accidentally learnt how I was situated, he had given orders for my accommodation to any extent, by drafts upon his own treasury. The opposition I had encountered in quarters so unexpected (which was of course immediately published abroad), not only created suspicions as to the honesty of my views, but even rendered it questionable if I was in reality the accredited person I had described myself to be. It was, therefore, with no ordinary feelings of gratitude that I found myself relieved from the probable consequences of these surmises by the generosity of the prince. The detention, however, to which this occurrence subjected me, was productive of consequences even more serious, and which for a time completely obstructed the objects of the expedition.

Several days elapsed before my letters could reach Lieutenant Whitelock, and during this period I was repeatedly warned by the Sheikh that I was risking my health by staying so long at Nizwa; that strangers from any part in Oman rarely remained more than three or four days without being attacked with dangerous fevers. Confiding, however, in my general health, which was then excellent, I was heedless enough to pay but little attention to their advice.

On the 10th all my servants fell sick, and on the 13th I was added to the number. The fever was of the most violent and singular character, the paroxysms frequently coming on twice in the twenty-four hours, and sometimes never leaving the patient for double that period. It attacked my head, and produced delirium forty-eight hours after its first appearance. Without attendants, my situation was lonely and cheerless; and until the morning of the 18th I was insensible to all which was passing. I believe some Arabs, sent by the Sheikh, took charge of me for a part of the time. The fever on the previous evening had reached its height, and a favourable change now took place; the cool blood again traversed my veins, I regained possession of my faculties, and gradually became better, though dreadfully reduced and debilitated.

On the 20th I was joined by Lieut. Whitelock, who had not been more fortunate than ourselves. He too was suffering from a fever caught at Muscat, which had left him so weak, that he could neither walk nor stand without assistance. He had procured the necessary funds, and entered into an engagement with a Sheikh, in the Imam's presence, to convey us, when we reached Buraymi, with one hundred of his followers, to Al Ahsa (*El Hassa*), and from thence to Diriyah; but for the present it was necessary all our plans should be abandoned.

To proceed in our present state of health was impossible; to remain at Nizwa was to destroy the only chance of recovery for the other patients, who were now sinking fast; and not without a severe pang of vexation, I turned from all my former splendid visions, to a determination of proceeding at once to Seeb (*Sib*), on the seacoast, in which spot, renowned for its salubrity, I hoped in a short time to recover the health of all.

On the 22nd January, accompanied by the Sheikh and about fifty of his followers, we left Nizwa [24] in circumstances somewhat different from those under which we had first entered it. We were then full of health, and joyous at the idea of visiting unknown districts; but now, worn down and somewhat despondent from sickness, the appearance and condition of our party was far less enviable : one of the servants fell repeatedly from the ass on which he was mounted, and the Bedouins at last were compelled to lash him on a camel.

After four hours we reached Birkat Al Mawz, which I have already noticed as enjoying a good climate; and here, finding it impossible, from the state of the party, to proceed, I pitched the tent, and determined to remain for a few days. My own health and spirits continued to improve at Birkat, but that of the rest of the party received a small amendment. The Arabs were very attentive, and supplied us with every necessary, and on the 26th January, there being a general belief that the party was strong enough to proceed once more, we struck the tent and continued our journey.

Quitting Birkat at eleven hours, a.m., we continued for forty minutes through a date grove, and over cultivated ground, and then entered a shallow stony valley, with a few dwarfish mimosas scattered over its surface. At 1:30 we passed the village and date grove of Izki (*Zikki*), which is romantically situated in a hollow, under some hills, on which also there are several towns. At two hours we passed the small hamlet and grove of Qarut (*Karrut*), and at 3 p.m., arrived at the northern termination of the town of Imti, where we halted for the night.

Wednesday 27th. At 11 a.m. we left Imti, which contains about three hundred houses. Contiguous to it is another village, nearly equal in size, named Tihama. From hence our route continued along a stony valley, called Wadi Bani Rawaha (*Wadi Roweyha*), with hills about five hundred feet in height on either hand. We passed several villages and date groves, which appear on the map; and water, with much cultivation, was seen throughout the day. Several q*a*fila (قافلة *kafilahs*) (caravans) of from thirty to forty camels passed us laden with fresh fish, principally sharks, for the interior towns. The approach of a long train of camels, as they move slowly along in these narrow and rugged glens, has a most picturesque and striking effect. Before emerging from some cape of the hills, we first hear the voice of the camel-leader breaking the overheated sultriness of the atmosphere-now chanting to the utmost extent of his voice some traditionary song, or in reproachful accents chiding for tardiness or wanderings his docile, patient charge. Each animal has its separate rider, and as the whole train becomes exposed to view, the ever-ready matchlock and sword denote the general insecurity of the country, while the gay trappings of the camels, their lighter colour, the long woollen tufts suspended from the party-coloured saddles, and almost sweeping along the ground, stand out in bold relief from the dark and frowning crags around. We had a strong breeze, with dark cloudy weather, throughout the whole of the day. At four hours we halted at the hamlet of Byah.

Thursday 28th. The camel-men this morning were very clamorous, and from some whim of their own, after packing, they again removed everything from the camels, refusing to proceed, and at 11 a.m. were about to return to Nizwa, leaving us to shift for ourselves. An old man, despatched by the Sheikh of Nizwa, on a supposition that something of this kind might occur, arrived at the moment, and soon brought them to order, and at twelve hours we quitted Byah. The country we are passing over continues along a valley, and is nearly the same as that described yesterday. The hamlets, fresh water, &c., are equally numerous; they all appear on the map, and a mere insertion of their names, when no other distinction marks them, would answer no useful purpose. The hills on either hand are of a micaceous schist, of nearly equal height; they have usually a pyramidal outline, are rugged, and of a dark colour, crossed by veins and patches of a lighter grey. There is, however, a considerable change in the appearance of the soil; as we approach the coast it becomes more sandy and of a lighter colour.

Instead of occurring in open plains, as within the oases, the groves are now found in narrow valleys, and in place of a *falaj*, all the streams leading to them are above the surface [25]. Fruit and grain become more scarce, and the date palm forms the principal object in sight.

At five hours we halted at the south-east termination of the town of Samail (*Semayel*), which is considered the half-way station between Muscat and Nizwa, and took up our quarters in a very small but neat *cadjan* hut. A beautiful stream of water glided along before the door. Weary and faint from the fatigue of our day's journey, in order to enjoy the freshness of the evening breeze, I had spread my carpet beneath a tree. An Arab passing by, paused to gaze upon me, and touched by my condition and the melancholy which was depicted in my countenance, he proffered the salutation of peace, pointed to the crystal stream which, sparkling, held its course at my feet, and said, "Look, friend; for running water maketh the heart glad." With his hands folded over his breast, that mute but most graceful of Eastern salutations, he bowed and passed on. I was in a situation to estimate sympathy; and so much of that feeling was exhibited in the manner of this son of the Desert, that I have never since recurred to the incident, trifling as it is, without emotion. From the Sheikh of this town we received much attention and civility; he expressed the most lively concern at witnessing the state of our health, and most confidently predicted a speedy recovery at Seeb: he even offered to allow two of his own slaves to accompany us to the coast, which was in a high degree liberal, for few Muslims are fond of lending their slaves to Christians.

Samail Fort

Friday 29th. At 10:50 we left our comfortable quarters, and did not arrive at the opposite termination of Samail until 12:50. Throughout the whole distance an abundance of water is found. On the heights on either side of the valley, which is about a quarter of a mile in width, watch-towers have been erected at various distances, and their appearance, perched on the summit of some craggy pinnacle, is very picturesque. At the termination of the Samail grove, another nearly equally extensive, crosses it in a transverse direction; beyond this, with the exception of a small hamlet, the valley continues desert and barren, until we arrive at 5:20 at Furza, where there is a small fort erected on a neighbouring hill, around which are several neatly constructed houses. We suffered much in our present weak state from the heat of the weather, which in these narrow valleys was at times truly oppressive. I have often, on such occasions, admired the patience of the Bedouins, who, with a pair of tattered sandals on their feet, which but partially protect them from the hot sand, and with heads bared to the scorching heat of the sun, will walk all day alongside their camels, without uttering a murmur of complaint or impatience, and in the evening will make their supper on dates and a draught of water in perfect contentment. In attacks of pain or disease they exhibit the same inherent spirit of resignation and fortitude. An old man we had with us on this occasion suffered so much from an internal complaint, that he frequently dismounted from his camel, and writhed in uncontrollable agony in the sand; yet when the paroxysm was over, not a syllable of discontent escaped him. Their children are also taught at an early age to suppress all outward signs of emotion; and whatever may be the extent of their misfortunes in after life, "*Allah Akbar*" (God is great) is all that escapes from them.

Saturday, 30th. At 10:30 we again proceeded, the face of the country having the same barren appearance as yesterday, until 12:30, when we entered Wadi Khor, through which a very large stream flows towards the sea. It was beautifully clear, and in some places twenty feet across, with an irregular chain of pools six or eight feet in depth, and a line of date groves extending on either hand. We next ascended a small eminence, and beheld the sea; and continuing our journey over the maritime plain, at 3:50 arrived at Seeb, where we took up our quarters in a small round fort, near the sea-beach. This rude tenement was, however, so infested with cats, rats, and other vermin, that I shifted our quarters to my tent, which, in order to enjoy the delicious coolness and freshness of the sea-breeze, we pitched beneath some trees near the beach. The climate of Seeb had not been exaggerated, for after recovering from the immediate fatigue of the journey, the whole of the party rapidly recovered. To insure ourselves against the possibility of a relapse, which in these fevers is more to be dreaded than the original disease, I delayed my intention of moving until the 20th; and finding we were all then sufficiently recovered, wrote to the Imam at Muscat, requesting he would furnish a guide to conduct me to Buraymi, the frontier station of the Wahhabis. From hence, though the season was far advanced, I had but little reason to doubt being able, with some *kafala*, yet to reach Diriyah. My disappointment was therefore very great on learning from his Highness in reply, that the Wahhabis had but a few days before made a sudden irruption into the northern parts of Oman; that they had seized, plundered, and burnt several towns near to Sohar; that the inhabitants of Ibri (*Obri*), on the road to Buraymi, were engaged in hostilities against their neighbours; and that his Highness would most strongly recommend, in the present unsettled state of affairs, that I should not continue my journey. I never contemplated being able to complete the duty on which I was employed without risk; and this was an occasion involving in itself the examination of nearly half the province, which appeared to justify my undergoing it to the fullest extent; nor did I as yet despair, if I could reach Buraymi, of being able to pass on to Diriyah. With many acknowledgments, therefore, for his kindness, I communicated my wishes to the Imam, and I was highly pleased on the morning of the 24th to find at my tent a most respectable old man, well known throughout the country, in perfect readiness to accompany us.

The houses at Seeb stand separately, and in groups of two or three, amidst the date groves. Fresh meat, fruit, and vegetables may be obtained, and the bazaar, considering the small number of inhabitants, is well supplied. When the Imam heard of our arrival here, instructions were immediately despatched to the Sheikh to furnish us with whatever we should require, and he certainly acted up to the spirit of the order. Small presents of fruit, brought from Persia, preserves, and other articles which it was thought might be agreeable or of service to us in our weak state, arrived occasionally from the Prince; and I have little doubt but that our speedy recovery was in a great measure owing to the unremitting attention we received.

I would here rather subject myself to the imputation of egotism, than omit the following anecdote, because it displays the generous feelings I have elsewhere attributed to this great prince, in a very favourable point of view. It has been previously noticed that during my stay at Muscat, a Frenchman was, to appearance, dying, in a vessel alongside of that in which I was. Unwilling, however, to forego the chance which still remained of his recovery by change of air, I hired a boat to convey him to Seeb, a situation possessing a more salubrious atmosphere than Muscat, and gave those to whose care he was entrusted a few Dollars to defray his expenses in case he survived, or inter him should he not. When this circumstance was mentioned to the Prince, he struck the crooked staff [26] (which he carries, in common with all other Arabs) forcibly on the ground, and said, with much energy, "That's a man."

When we reflect that the custom of giving presents, so general throughout the East, is in most cases directed by ostentatious rather than generous motives, and that his Highness was not ignorant of the national enmity existing between France and England, it required (at least in Asia) that nicety of feeling with which he is so eminently gifted to have enabled him to appreciate the motives in which, according to his judgment, the mere act of humanity I have briefly alluded to must have originated. Hitherto too little has been known in Europe respecting this enlightened Prince. His recent appropriate present to our Sailor King of a large vessel of war completely equipped, and his desire to form a more intimate alliance with Great Britain, has brought him into some political notice, while his munificent encouragement of science and the arts, has attracted the attention of an influential learned society, which lately nominated him one of its honorary members.

These occurrences are but trifling, and I must solicit some indulgence for their insertion. Indeed, were I to record every act of consideration and kindness which we received from the Prince during our stay in Oman, there are few of the pages of this journal in which they might not be made to appear. To say that they were accepted with different and higher feelings than those with which we are usually disposed to view the favours of the great, expresses faintly my sense and recollection of them; but that they should have awakened a feeling of this nature, may convey an idea to others of the mode and spirit in which they were bestowed.

CHAPTER 12
MOVING FROM BURKA TO SUWAYQ

How to avoid being plundered - Bedouin Fort - Intense cold - Crossing Torrents - Rapid Vegetation - Barka (Burka) - Population, - Trade, Revenue, &c. - Arab Law suits - The Bazaar - Fishery - Musannah (Mesnah) - Interview with the Sheikh - Dissimulation - Dates - Distillation of Arak - Superb Shells - Suwayq - The Sheikh's Wife - Sayyid Hilal - Personal Appearance and Generosity - Energy and Influence of Arab Females.

February 25th. At 2:10 we left our encampment. Our life here had been so dull and monotonous, that none of the party were sorry to quit it. In order to hold out as little temptation as possible for plunder to the wild tribes with which we were about to mix, we had reduced our baggage to a single trunk and the inner part of the tent: so that the number of camels was reduced to five, the same number as the party.

After leaving the skirts of the village, we continued, until 4:30, to pass a succession of gardens and the richest vegetation. Fields of wheat and barley continually presented themselves springing from a dark and loamy soil.

At 5:30, being overtaken by a violent squall, we were happy to obtain shelter in a wretched building called a Bedouin fort. The rain fell in torrents, and the thunder and lightning were truly awful: at times it blew a hurricane, and the camels grew so alarmed that, though turned adrift to browse on the herbage around, they crowded about the door whenever it was opened, and endeavoured to effect an entrance. Some females, who had followed the party from Seeb, were crying all night with fright and cold, for the roof of the small space in which we had crowded, admitted the water in every direction, and all were completely drenched. I was most happy when the dawn of day permitted us to crawl out of our den, and warm our cramped limbs in the sun.

Friday, 26th February. Last night's heavy rain has filled the hitherto dry beds of all the streams, and now, having overflown their banks, they are rushing with much impetuosity towards the sea. We easily crossed all these on our camels, but in several places the poor asses, driven before us, lost their footing in the violence of the current, and were in imminent danger of perishing. Every part of the road being flooded, we, in consequence, soon lost all traces of the track, and, after floundering about until we were all covered with mud, I prevailed on old Ali Ibn Megati to cross over to the sea-beach. The peasants we met were all, however, in high glee at the prospect of a plentiful harvest, and the abundant pasturage which would now very shortly be afforded to their flocks. It is, indeed, most astonishing to witness the change a single shower produces on the face of this country. The most arid and sandy districts become, with others more promising, completely clothed with a light grass, which, for a time, wholly changes the appearance of the country; but this, unfortunately, is of brief duration. The dews at night afford nourishment for a time, but the heat of the sun's rays soon predominates, and, in a week or ten days, all becomes parched and arid as before. Barka was formerly the summer residence of the Imam, and here he rid himself, by stratagem, of his formidable uncle, Badr bin Saif (*Saif Ibn Buddu*).

At present Barka is principally remarkable for its fort, which, owing to its great height and size, is very conspicuous from seaward. It mounts thirty pieces of artillery; but so little attention is paid to them or their carriages, that not one half could be fired; yet is it deemed by the Arabs impregnable; nor, probably, so far as they themselves are concerned, are they mistaken. An almost total ignorance in such affairs is common to both the attacking party and the besieged, and the means and appliances of the former would be insufficient to overcome the advantages possessed by the latter. Sayyid Hilal's harem was confined here at the period of my visit, and we were not, in consequence, admitted beyond one of the towers near the entrance. From the summit of this I, however, obtained a good set of theodolite bearings, and also a tolerable view of the town and its neighbourhood. Surrounding the fort, at a distance of two hundred yards from either side, there is a turreted wall, and, within the intermediate space, some neat and substantial houses. I noticed, as a peculiarity, several that had pillars in front, supporting a rude portico: this I never observed in any other part of Arabia. The other habitations are merely *cadjan* [palm leaf] huts, containing by far the greatest number of inhabitants.

Barka Fort - canon

Including women and children, the population of Barka may be estimated at four thousand. A considerable portion of these, as on other parts of the coast, are employed in fishing, and the remainder attend the date trees. The bazaar is very extensive, and the Bedouins flock in from the surrounding country to make purchases of grain, cloth, &c., and almost every article procurable in Muscat may be obtained here. The anchorage at Barka is an open roadstead, affording no protection against the prevailing breezes. The same remark applies to nearly every town on the coast, and they have, in consequence, but few *baghlas* of any burthen trading along it. Merchandize is brought from or conveyed to Muscat in small boats, of from thirty to fifty tons burthen. Vessels of this size upon the approach of bad weather are hauled up on shore beyond the action of the sea with little difficulty.

Baghla under sail

A revenue of from three to four hundred Dollars is annually drawn from Barka. It arises principally from dates, on which, as well as on all other exports or imports, a duty of ten percent. is levied. The Imam maintains a small force of about two hundred men here: their wages are partly paid out of this impost.

Sunday, 28th. We passed the morning in listening to some law cases, mostly relative to debts and trifling offences, which were decided by the *qadi*. It rained hard all day, and we were unable to leave, but derived considerable amusement from watching the busy scenes passing in the bazar. The seller disposes his several articles in a heap before him, and seats himself quietly on his haunches beside it. A buyer approaches, and the affair is settled, probably, after not more than half a dozen words have been spoken. But mark the contrast: at the distance of a few yards is also seated a female, who sells grain; one of her own sex approaches for the purpose of buying;-that war of words has lasted now nearly an hour, and yet appears no nearer a conclusion than at first. Here there is a boy with a basket of dates on his head, bawling forth, as he totters under the weight of his load, the superiority of his commodity and its price. There, a man parading to and fro with a turban and a pair of sandals. At a distance are some butchers' stalls, and beef, mutton, &c., are doled out to those who crowd around it, by means of a very rude pair of wooden scales, having stones as a substitute for weights.

Monday, February 29th. Quitting Barka, at eight hours, we passed in succession the various villages and towns which appear on the map. The fishery is here conducted on a grand scale, by means of nets many hundred fathoms in length, which are carried out by boats. The upper part is supported by small blocks of wood, formed from the light and buoyant branches of the date palm, while the lower part is loaded with lead. To either extremity of this a rope is attached, by which, when the whole of the net is laid out, about thirty or forty men drag it towards the shore. The quantity thus secured is enormous, and what they do not require for their own consumption is salted and carried into the interior. When, as is very generally the case, the nets are the common property of the whole village, they divide the produce into equal shares; but if they belong to a private individual, or a company, those only who assist receive a share proportionate to their degree of labour.

Upon our first arrival at Musannah, I went to the Sheikh's house, and, after waiting upwards of an hour in a court-yard, amidst his slaves, and without any protection from the sun, I became somewhat angry, and passed on to a small date grove, about a mile from the town, where we pitched our tent.

February 30th. At daylight on the following morning I received a visit from the Sheikh, who came to seek an explanation for my leaving his town without seeing him. He exhibited as much state as his means enabled him to assume, walking alone at a pace or two before his followers, who were about thirty in number. After he had seated himself, and made known the purport of his visit, I simply stated, that it was not our custom to stand at any man's door for the length of time I had waited at his, and if he had been aware of it, I was sorry he so lightly considered the character of a British officer as to suppose he would put up with such treatment, and that if his slaves were our servants, they would be severely punished for their neglect. He expressed the utmost surprise at all this, which he pretended to have heard for the first time, observing that he was at prayers, and hoped I would think no more of the matter. He then took his leave, swearing vengeance against his attendants, - all which was, however, feigned, -the very men being at that time standing around him. It is but fair to confess that such behaviour is by no means common, excepting, as in this instance, with petty Sheikhs, who strive to enhance their dignity in the eyes of their followers, by keeping persons of any consideration waiting when they call upon them.

The date trees on this coast form a continuous grove to Khor Fakkan (*Khorfakan*), a distance of one hundred and fifty miles, and the Arabs have a saying that a traveller may proceed the whole distance without ever losing their shade. Dates form the principal export from Oman, large quantities being taken to India, where a considerable share is consumed in making the government Arak. The middle classes of the Muslim and Hindu (Hindoo) population are very partial to them. The best are brought from Basrah and Bahrain (*Bahrein*), those from Oman being classed next in excellence. There are several methods of preserving them; some are simply dried, and then strung on lines; others, which is the usual plan, are packed in baskets. Notwithstanding their great number, every tree has its separate owner, and disputes between the relations of those who die intestate are, in consequence, very frequent. Towards noon we left our encampment, and continued along the beach, passing numerous hamlets and villages. Firewood seems very plentiful here; it is packed in large stacks, ranged along the beach, so that boats in passing run in, purchase, and load at once. From thence we passed the skeleton of a whale, a large quantity of roots of trees, and other driftwood, several varieties of sea-weed, of which the *Sargassum vulgare* and the *Gongolaria barbata (Fucus barbatus)* were most commonly met with. The beach was almost entirely composed of fragments of most superb shells, and I picked up several very beautiful specimens.

At 3:30 we arrived at Suwayq, and found the Sheikh absent, looking for the Wahhabis, who, it had been reported, were then in the neighbourhood; but we were most hospitably received by the Sheikh's wife, who had a house and every other accommodation very soon prepared for us. The orders of this lady (of whom more anon) were much to the point. "You will please those gentlemen," said she to her slaves who were sent to attend us, "and let them want nothing, or look to your heads." We accordingly received every luxury which the Sheikh's kitchen could afford.

Suwayq castle, courtyard

In the course of the evening the Sheikh returned from an unsuccessful search. I had procured a letter for this individual from the Bombay government, as he was considered to possess considerable influence over the Bedouins in Northern Oman. Probably nothing could have afforded him more satisfaction than this mark of our notice, and he was, partly from this, and partly from his own natural hospitality, most attentive to me during my stay.

Sayyid Hilal, a cousin of Sayyid Said's, is about thirty-five years of age, and in point of character, he stands of all the chiefs of Oman next to that prince: his figure is tall and commanding; he excels in all warlike exercises; is passionately attached to hunting and other field sports; and though somewhat spare in figure, is considered, in addition to his extraordinary agility, the strongest man of his nation: he is generous to profusion. I have heard the Arabs in Muscat relate that when upon a visit to the Imam, he has received from him a present of eight hundred or a thousand Dollars; in the course of a couple of hours afterwards, he has bestowed the whole of it in presents to his followers.

When the surveying vessels visited this coast in 1828, a large portion of the surrounding country, including the extensive groves of Khadra, and many towns on the sea-coast, were tributary to this chief; but shortly after the Sheikh of Sohar possessed himself of his own territory he, with a view of increasing the number of his forces, so as to enable him to act with greater efficiency against the Imam, made an offer to the several petty Sheikhs and their followers, if they would enlist under his banners, and quit those of Sayyid Hilal, to remit the whole of the imposts which had been by that chief formerly exacted from them. The bait was too tempting to be resisted, and in the course of a few days Sayyid Hilal, from possessing an influence which had rendered him formidable even to the Imam, found himself stripped of his territory, his revenue, and his power, and eventually became a mere pensionary to him.

Connected with this struggle, two events occurred, which display the energy and influence of the Arab females in so strong a light, that I shall give insertion to them.

A few years ago, Sayyid Hilal was induced, under promise of protection, to proceed to Muscat. Some accusations were brought against him of endeavouring to subvert the authority of the Imam, by instigating the Bedouins to rebellion. Immediately that the Sheikh's wife, a sister of Sayyid Said's, heard the intelligence, and she sent messengers to collect the various Bedouin tribes who were in the interest of her husband, and made other preparations to march in person against the dominions of the Imam; but before any succours could arrive, the latter had despatched a force to Suwayq, in order to take possession of the fort, with an assurance, that unless it was given up, the Sheikh should be put to death. "Go back," said this spirited female, when the message was delivered to her; "Go back to those who sent you, and tell them that I will defend the fort to the utmost of my power; and if they choose to cut him to pieces before me, they will find it make no alteration in my resolution." She accordingly defended it with so much bravery and skill, that the Imam's force, after losing several men and wasting considerable time, were compelled to raise the siege and proceed to Muscat. Some months afterwards, the Imam became convinced of the falsehood of the charges exhibited against the Sheikh, and permitted him to return to his own government.

The Sheikh's sister distinguished herself in a similar manner while in charge of the same fort, against an unexpected attack made by the Sheikh of Sohar. The latter was passing on his road to Rustaq, with a body of about two hundred men, without any apparent intention of acting against it, when he suddenly turned, and brought the whole of his force before the walls.

Though the Sheikh was absent, his place was well supplied by this lady, who closed the gates, collected the garrison, harangued them, and finally made such good use of the guns, which are mounted on the towers, that after a stay of three days, and several ineffectual attempts to lead his troops again to the assault, the Sheikh was obliged to abandon his enterprise.

Report says that Sayyid Hilal feels the greatest respect for, and stands in some awe of this dame, without whose advice and concurrence he undertakes nothing of moment.

CHAPTER 13
FROM THE COAST TO THE MOUNTAINS

Household of Sayyid Hilal - A Professed Story-teller - Arabian Nights - Arab Artillery - Anecdote - Manufactures, &c. of Suwayq - Arab Horsemanship - Weapons - Hire Horses - Bid adieu to the Sheikh - Shepherds - Khadra - Irruption of the Wahhabis - El abu Shied - Cultivation - Alarm - Desertion of the Guard - Falaj Bani Rabiah (Feletch), Romantic situation of - A ragged Regiment - Mountain Torrent - Cheerful Encampment - Dangerous Ford - Miskin (Muskin) - Progress of Vegetation.

Sayyid Hilal lives in more state than any other chief I have met in Oman. The number of his household slaves is said to exceed a hundred, and of these twenty or thirty, attached to his person, wear a neat uniform. A huge meal, consisting of a great variety of dishes, sufficient for thirty or forty people, was prepared in his kitchen, and brought to us on large copper dishes, twice a day during the time we remained. They were all dressed according to the most approved Persian style, and we soon became warm converts to their culinary process. On these occasions, there was a great profusion of blue and gilt China ware, cut glass dishes, and decanters, containing not wine but sherbet, with several other costly articles. The Sheikh, after his evening meal, usually passed several hours with us. I was fond of leading him to various topics connected with the tribes in northern Oman, and his conversation afforded me much interesting and valuable intelligence.

On one occasion he was accompanied by a professed story-teller, who appeared to be a great favourite with him. "Whenever I feel melancholy or out of order," said the Sheikh, "I send for this individual, who very soon restores me to my wonted spirit." From the falsetto tone in which the story was chanted, I could not follow the thread of the tale, and upon my mentioning this to him, the Sheikh very kindly sent me the manuscript, of which the reciter had availed himself. With little variation, I found it to be the identical Sinbad the Sailor, so familiar to the readers of the Arabian Nights. I little thought, when first I perused these fascinating tales in my own language, that it would ever be my lot to listen to the original, in a spot so congenial and so remote.

Suwayq is a small walled town containing about seven hundred houses. The fort, situated nearly in the centre, and garrisoned by the Sheikh's household slaves, is a large strong building, mounting a few guns on its towers. The Arabs have a singular practice of keeping two or three pieces of artillery just without the entrance of their forts. As I passed these one day with the Sheikh, I inquired of him if it would not prove somewhat awkward if the castle should be surprised, and the attacking party get possession of these, so that they could at once, by blowing open the gates, obtain a fair entrance. He Laughed and said, "Our warfare differs somewhat from yours, as I had reason to witness at Bani bu Ali. In the first place, the Arabs, in all probability, would not think of such an act, and even if they did, as you know we do not carry guns when we go to war, I question whether they could muster sufficient powder, or if so, know how to load them afterwards."

The greater number of people belonging to Suwayq live in small huts without the walls. They fabricate turbans and *lungis* here, but the greater number, as in most other parts of the coast, are employed in fishing or agricultural pursuits.

The population is a good deal mixed, but the same toleration is exercised as in Muscat. Even the Shias (*Shiahs*) have a mosque here.

Horses Oman

Friday, March 4th. At 10:45, accompanied by the Sheikh and about 40 horsemen, we left the town. Having emerged from the groves upon the open plains, they amused us with a display of their mode of attack in battle. In wheeling and pulling up at full gallop, they display on these occasions great command over their horses, and the bit they use is certainly a very severe instrument. They have no stirrups, and in place of a saddle, throw a quilt, stuffed with cotton, across the animal's back.

Their principal and most formidable weapon is a spear about fifteen feet in length ornamented near the extremity with a tuft of red and black feathers. This is never thrown, but carried in nearly the same manner as was usual with the ancient chivalry of Europe. Their loose, gay dresses, and splendid steeds of the purest Nejd breed, as they scoured at full gallop across the plain from various directions, were exhibited to great advantage. They have, on these occasions, a favourite manoeuvre by which individuals clasp each other by the thigh, and thus, side by side, urge their steeds to the utmost fleetness. Accompanied by this gay party, all in the highest degree animated and excited, we pursued our course for five or six miles. Sayyid Hilal, who rode a beautiful horse, the value of which was estimated at three thousand Dollars, and who had been foremost, in every exercise, then dismounted, and with many cautions as to our future line of action amidst his unruly neighbours, bid us a very kind farewell. We shook hands with all his followers, and then, as John Bunyan says, "went on our way."

The groves and cultivated ground extend about three miles from the beach. Beyond that, the plains are crossed by many shallow streams, which have originated amidst the hills during the late rains. Very large *Ghaf* and *Simr* trees, dot the surface of the landscape; and seated beneath their scanty and feathery shade, might frequently be seen an Arab shepherd, with several enormous dogs to aid him in his charge of the flock grazing around; but his pipe and crook are wanting: their place is supplied by the matchlock and spear.

At one hour we arrived (our course from Suwayq being W ½ N.) at the straggling and extensive Bedouin encampment of Khadra. Their huts are constructed of *cadjans*, and in order to shelter the inmates from occasional showers, are mostly shaped like the roof of an English barn.

I was told by our guide, that about four years ago, the Wahhabis, under Saad bin Mutlaq, in a predatory excursion, approached Khadra by night, as was their usual custom, with a view to burn it. However, partly owing to their constant broils, and partly to the expectation of an attack from another quarter on the same evening, its inhabitants were well prepared; and it was not until they had beaten off the enemy with considerable loss, that they discovered who their real adversaries were. Such is the dread inspired by the ravages of these fanatics, that upon any rumour of their approach private feuds are forgotten, and the several tribes forthwith unite together for mutual protection, These inroads are not, therefore, without their use; they frequently prove, as in this case, the means of bringing together two tribes who for many years before had been at feud. Intermarriages then take place, and they become fixed in permanent alliance.

El Abu Sheid, El Sad, and El Hilal, are the principal tribes now confederated together, whose aggregate number is estimated at three thousand men. They have numerous date groves, fields of grain, and plantations of sugar, cotton, and indigo. Within their groves are several forts, for they are an intractable race, caring nothing for Sayyid Said, or the Sheikh of Sohar. Although they formerly paid the *zakat* (*zireat*) or tithe to the Sheikh of Suwayq, they now are frequently at feud with him.

It being anticipated that something at issue at this period would lead to a disturbance, our party fetched a long circuit to avoid their encampment: this was settled before my return, for we then passed without molestation through the centre of it. At four hours the country alters its appearance; we have small hills intersected by deep narrow ravines, at the bottom of which there is a rich grass, on which numerous sheep were feeding. At 5:45 we arrived at the village of Falaj Bani Rabiah.

The whole country seems in a state of great alarm, owing to an anticipated visit from the Wahhabis. Ali ibn Negati was constantly inquiring for intelligence of all we met; while, on the other hand, the unexpected appearance of our party created a most amusing scene of alarm and confusion. Girls and boys screamed; men ran for their arms; their dogs barked incessantly; while mothers were seen flying with their children under their arms, and adding by the shrillness of their voices, a delightful tenor to the Babel of sounds with which we were saluted. In vain Ali lifted up his voice to proclaim who we were; it only increased the confusion. I then suggested that the party should halt when we reached a small eminence, and send a single slave to quiet them and explain matters. This produced the desired effect. In a few minutes they were all, male and female, chatting and laughing around us with a vivacity and pleasure proportionate to their former alarm. They then very obligingly sent a meal of boiled mutton and rice, sufficient for the whole party.

Saturday, March 5th. We found this morning that our guard, notwithstanding the positive directions they received from Sayyid Hilal at Suwayq, to accompany us to Ibri, had decamped during the night with the camels, camel-men, and old Ali's ass. I was so much amused at the ire he displayed, and the curses he bestowed on them, their fathers, and forefathers, that I forgot our own helpless situation and detention. However, after breakfast, we prevailed on the Sheikh to ride over to a small town in the neighbourhood, where, as a *qafila* had passed yesterday, it was thought that others might be procured, and about noon he returned with as many as we required.

Falaj Bani Rabiah is most romantically situated in a hollow, and consists of not more than two hundred houses interspersed amidst the trees, which frequently fling their bright green foliage over or around them, so as to render but a small portion visible. It is not easy for mere description to convey an idea of the singular effect produced by the verdant appearance of this hollow, when contrasted with the light brown or chalky appearance of the hills which bound it. At 1:10 we left Falaj Bani Rabiah , with a ragged guard of six individuals, which the Sheikh insisted upon our taking. Our New friends certainly appeared, as far as clothing went, in somewhat indifferent trim. Their matchlocks too were rusted more than half through; and otherwise, both as regards equipment and variety of figure and age, they really formed no bad prototypes of Falstaff's recruits. Moreover, they rode on asses, which here are somewhat diminutive, and the contrast they presented to those mounted on the magnificent animals they were sent to protect, was too amusing to pass unnoticed even by the sedate and sober Ali, for, directly it appeared that he would have to travel in their company, he quitted the ass procured for him in lieu of the one he had lost, and mounted a camel. Our route lay for some time along the margin of a valley called Wadi Gabir, whose bed was but just moistened in the centre by a stream, which, however, formed at the sides a few shallow pools. We passed several colocynth shrubs to-day, and also a kind of dwarfish bush, bearing a small red fruit, in size and flavour resembling a cranberry, of which the Bedouins are very fond. At four hours, descending a pass, we entered the valley of Russut el Kuroos, and at 5:15 halted at the hamlet of Sidan: we were delighted with our resting-place, which was just at the gorge of the pass, where it emerges from amidst a pile of mountains of great height. The rugged and pinnacled summits of these shadowy masses, as they rose abruptly in quick succession before us, were now receiving the last bright and gorgeous tints of a setting sun; but the lower ranges were already lost in the evening's gloom. We could just perceive a mountain torrent about fifty yards in width, which takes its rise amidst the chain, and was now chafing or forming its way along the valley, over and between the rocks and other obstructions which line its bed. We soon lighted a large fire on its banks, by which we prepared our evening meal. Enjoying all our former health and wanted spirits, we indulged, whilst seated around its cheerful flames, in those gay and sanguine anticipations of the future, which involuntarily arise when the mind, warped for a time by sickness, recovers its former tone and elasticity. I believe that, whilst under the influence of this peculiar reaction, any incident or adventure, however perilous and wild, provided it afforded an ample portion of excitement, would have been far from disagreeable to us.

March 6th. After taking a hasty sketch of the entrance to this pass and the contiguous mountains, at 10:30 I continued my journey through the valley. There was no track except along the bed of the stream, which in some places was so deep and rapid that it nearly swept my horse from his legs. A few date groves, and an occasional cluster of huts, show themselves on either hand. At 2 p.m. we struck off a minor branch of the stream, along Wadi Thilah, to the westward. We had now penetrated beyond the lower ridges to the main branch of the mountains, which rose in steep precipices to the height of from three thousand to four thousand feet, terminating in abrupt and pointed forms. Mica, slate, and felspar enters largely into their composition, and I spent a considerable time in examining the singular contortions of the former. A few aloes, dwarfish bushes and aromatic shrubs, on which some sheep browsed, are the only signs of vegetable life we met with, and at 5:30 we halted on the summit of a small hill. Old Ali's apprehensions respecting the Wahhabis were evidently increasing, for he stationed a guard with loaded matchlocks to look out during the night. I learnt, from casually questioning him on the subject, that his fears arose from the circumstance of the tract we were now crossing not being in the possession of Sayyid Said, but in that of his rival Mohammed of Sohar.

Monday, 7th. At 11:30 we continued our journey along Wadi Thilah, passing the mouths of several lateral valleys. Our course now became so devious that I found it impossible to keep any account of it. At 2:30 we ascended a hill about eight hundred feet in height, but I could obtain no other view from its summit than a vast wilderness of bare, bleak rocks and hills. After crossing this ridge, we gained the territory of the Bani Kalban, whose acknowledgment of the Imam's authority so delighted old Saaf, that on dismounting at the hour of prayer, he expressed his satisfaction by giving his camel more than half his supply of dates. We continued journeying for three hours along the valley, which is called Wadi Kalban, the name of its inhabitants, and passed large clustering patches of aloes, bearing a greater resemblance to those of India than to the *Aloe perryi (Aloe Socotrina).*

At 5:50 we halted, in the neighbourhood of Miskin, near some enclosures of wheat, which were secured from the intrusions of cattle by means of a rude fence constructed with the thorny branches of the *Sidr*. Miskin is a small village, and appears to have derived its name from its peculiar situation amidst the hills. I was highly delighted to observe within these groves the whole process of vegetation exhibited in various stages of advancement, by each particular species of tree. The date-palms were shedding the last year's leaves; the mango, the plantain, the *Sidr*, and the fig had renewed their foliage; the branches of the vine are still denuded; while in their immediate vicinity the peasant is engaged reaping his corn: thus we see before us the peculiar attributes of each season produced from different causes, at one and the same time.

CHAPTER 14

BARRIERS TO FARTHER TRAVEL

Tedious progress - Arab Bargains - Anecdote - Attempts at imposition - Remedy - Honesty - Reflections - Mode of obtaining a proper insight into Character - Quit Miskin - Ophthalmia - Sheikh Nasser - Attempts to dissuade the Author from proceeding - Maqniyat (Makiniyat) - Arab Funerals - Green Mountains - Solar Heat - Dariz (Derese) - Shady Groves - General appearance of the Sheikhs of Oman - A Contrast-Inhospitable Treatment - The Wahhabis - Expectation of an affray - Prepare to quit Ibri.

Wednesday, March 9th. Our progress through this part of the country is rendered slow and tedious, in consequence of its being divided into separate districts, all in a manner independent of each other, and acknowledging but slightly the power of any general authority. As those who furnish camels for their own district will not, nor would they be permitted, to proceed further, it results that on entering the frontier of another, we are delayed to bargain for a fresh supply. This business, which sometimes lasted for two or three hours in one uninterrupted war of words, I was too happy to resign to old Ali, who entered with all an Arab's eagerness and talents for disputation into its full spirit. The patience of an Englishman (I advance the remark advisedly), however extensive his travels, would assuredly fail him on such occasions in a few minutes, and the wily Arab wishes no better advantage. Not so my friend Ali, who, confident of his own consummate address, appeared perfectly in his element. Their bargains usually commence in a low tone, by one party naming a price, ten times greater than what he intends to take, or expects the other to give: a sneer, or stare of well-feigned astonishment, is the only answer : the debate gradually becomes warmer, and the parties shift their seats from one spot to the other. At one time old Ali's voice could be heard shouting high above that of his opponent; at another time, huddled together in some hollow, as if afraid the very winds might bear away some part of their counsels, I could just catch the sound of his voice, exerted in tones of pathos, reproach, expostulation, or entreaty. At length he would start up and retire, breathing maledictions against their unheard-of rapacity, but followed by one or two of the by-standers who bring him back, when a repetition of the same scenes occurs, until the affair is settled. I must again repeat that no human being, save an Arab, could endure the trial to which his patience is subjected whilst adjusting these interminable bargains. Even when the affair, to all appearance, has been settled, something still remains to furnish a plea for new exactions; a further supply of dates for themselves, or fodder for their cattle, I found to be the favourite plea. Very often in the course of this journey I have been delayed for hours, rather than yield up a quarter of a dollar more than Ali informed me was the customary demand. When in Jaalan I had tried at first a contrary plan; but got tired of giving long before they were of asking; indeed, the experience of a few days convinced me that any concession was, in proportion to the amount conceded, made the plea for further exactions. In general, professed carriers, among the Bedouins, are a cheating, lying, avaricious race; yet have they good qualities, among which may be noticed a thorough detestation of petty theft. I never lost the most trifling article of my baggage, but have frequently known them seek for any missing article with far more anxiety than I felt respecting it; and in fetching wood, water, and other similar duties, when we halted, they were usually very obliging.

There is a class of travellers who proceed through a country with a determination to shut their eyes against all which does not accord with their peculiar views. They either entirely omit or only touch slightly on unfavourable points of character and manners, and are, generally speaking, more pleasing companions than men who pursue an opposite course. Yet it can scarcely admit of a question, that a perfect estimate of the character of any people can only be acquired from a thorough knowledge of their vices as well as virtues; and the result of the examination will be, that both are more equally distributed than does at first sight appear. Viewing the matter in this light, and aware how illiberal it is to generalise upon any topic, I have always endeavoured to record faithfully my impressions of those amongst whom I have been thrown, whether for good or evil. It has never occurred to me that the reader would consider their merits and demerits otherwise than abstractedly, and not as furnishing a national portraiture, which, in the instance I have just given, would be as unjust as if an estimate of the English character were formed from its hackney or stage coachmen.

March 10th. At 12:30 we left Miskin for Maqniyat, and at five hours halted near the castle, where the chief of the Beni Kalban, Sheikh Wasser, resides. In the course of a few minutes, though he appeared to be suffering from ophthalmia, he made his appearance to welcome us; but when I presented Sayyid Said's letters, which were very strongly worded, and contained an urgent request that he would pass us on, he seemed sorely troubled. "Almost daily," said he, "are individuals proceeding alone to Ibri robbed for the sake of the tattered clothes on their backs; and I am required to conduct you in safety, where the very name of an Englishman will be sufficient to attract a host of plunderers." I told him that, having been made aware of the risks to be encountered long before we left, we should endeavour to bear any misfortune of that nature with good grace; and here indeed we were perfectly sincere, having taken good care to bring nothing of value with us. This evening in the greater part of the following day were consumed in negotiating with the Sheikh; but finding we were not to be driven from our purpose, he agreed on the morrow to furnish us with the best and largest guard his situation would admit of.

Maqniyat castle

Though once a large city, Maqniyat has dwindled down to its present insignificant state, having never, as I was given to understand, recovered from a visit which the Wahhabis paid to it in 1800. They then took the castle, burnt the houses, and destroyed the greater number of trees. By a noon observation, and several meridional transits of the stars, I fixed the latitude of Maqniyat at 23° 21' 25" north. Here, as with many other towns in Oman, I was surprised at the little care which they bestow in the burial of their dead. The corpse, after being washed, is covered with a cloth and interred with very little ceremony. The grave is usually not more than three feet in depth, and after interment, a rude stone, without inscription of any kind, is placed at the head and feet.

During my stay here a female died who was related to the Sheikh, and he, with all the male relations, followed the corpse to the grave. There are no hired mourners in these towns, but the females from the neighbourhood of the deceased assemble, and continue for eight days, from sunrise to sunset, to utter loud and mournful lamentations.

March 11th. The body of the Green Mountains bore this morning E. by S.½ S., and were distant about thirty-five miles. I found the Sheikh had assembled a guard of seventy men, scarcely more respectable in appearance, though somewhat better mounted than those supplied us from Miskin. At 10:30 we left the skirts of the town, and proceeded west, at a rapid pace, over the plains. Our escort sent forth scouts to the right and left, and an advanced party a-head: notwithstanding all their apprehensions, we reached the village of Ayal at 1:30 without meeting with a single individual. Our route ran along a broad valley, on either side of which the hills run in a table-topped range, with sloping sides, or are broken into detached chains, presenting isolated pyramidal hills, somewhat truncated at the upper part, but of the same uniform level and direction as the continuous ridges. Quitting Ayal, where we obtained a second guard, we entered another broad valley, in the centre of which there ran a narrow rivulet, and at 5:30 put up for the night at the small village of Arudh.

March 12th, At ten hours our guard, who had passed the night right joyously within the walls of the village, being collected, we left, and crossed a succession of sandy, barren plains, similar to those of yesterday. Not a breath of wind was stirring, and as we occasionally passed through the narrow valleys which intersected our path, the concentration of the solar heat within them was almost overpowering.

At 12:50 we passed the extensive grove and town of Dariz, with the people of which our party were at feud, and, in consequence, we gave it a wide berth. At 1:50 we arrived at the town of AynAyn (*Inan*), here the Sheikh of the tribe resides. A few years ago he was possessed of considerable influence, not only in his immediate vicinity, but also with the most powerful tribes in Nejd; but his power is now confined to AynAyn, where he usually shuts himself up in its fort. Our path conducted us through the centre of the town, and I observed that cultivation was carried on in enclosures to an extent equal to any spot I have seen in Oman: some of the trees are also very lofty, and, again, an imagination at all alive to passing scenes must have been forcibly struck by the contrast which the shade and gloom, upon which we were now entering, presented to the dust and heat of the parched and sandy track we had just quitted.

After passing another town, somewhat similar, at 3:50 we arrived at Ibri. Passing the bazar, they conducted us to an open space before the Sheikh's house, where we were left with our baggage to await his appearance. Towards sunset he paid us a visit, and I thought I could perceive at a glance the character of the being we had to deal with. It will apply as a general remark, that the Sheikhs of the towns in Oman are very personable men, with a dignified deportment and pleasing manners; but this was a sneaking, greasy-looking animal, who had more the appearance of a butcher than a Sheikh. Upon my producing the Imam's letters he read them, and, without returning any answer, took his leave. About an hour afterwards he sent a verbal message to request that I should lose no time in quitting his town, as he begged to inform me, what he supposed I could not have been aware of, that it was then filled with nearly two thousand Wahhabis. This was, indeed, news to us: it was somewhat earlier than we anticipated falling in with them, - but we put a good face on the matter, and behaved as coolly as we well could. In the mean time we prepared to pitch our tent, and, having done so, sent a messenger to the Sheikh to intimate that I wished to see him. About nine, A.M., he came, accompanied by some cut-throat looking ruffians, whom he styled his relations. I then led the conversation at once to the subject, and inquired what number of men he could furnish to conduct me to Buraymi. This roused him, and he swore by the beard of the Prophet, such was now the danger of the road, that he neither could nor would furnish me with a man. I was unprepared for his refusal, but, as we should never take an Arab at his first word, I strove, by every argument I could think of, to shake his resolution. I stated that the dangers of the road were well known to Sayyid Said at the time he addressed the letters, and his certain anger when he should learn that he had been disobeyed. I hinted that I would myself amply reward him, provided he would comply; but he remained unmoved. Then, as a last resource, told him that I could not think of going back, unless he furnished me with a letter to the Imam, containing the substance of his present communication, which he very readily promised to do. I inquired if it was true he had sent a verbal message to request I should leave his town: this of course he denied, but ten minutes afterwards indirectly repeated it, and then left. We experienced none of those offers of assistance, provisions, or other accommodations, which we had been always in the habit of receiving from the other Sheikhs in Oman, his object without doubt being to drive us out of the town as soon as he could; and all I saw and heard gave me little reason to delay obliging him in that respect. The Wahhabis had been crowding around us in great numbers, and seemed only waiting for some pretext to commence an affray. On these emergencies I always adopt one plan, which is, to remove every weapon from the reach of those who were with me. Whitelock and myself alone were armed, and we knew too well the consequences that would accrue from any rash use of weapons, to encounter such a risk. The men were in general small, and had no other clothes than a cloth round their waist. Their complexion was very dark, and they wore their hair long. It was not until some time afterwards that I discovered they were a party under Saad bin Mutlaq, whose future proceedings and subsequent defeat I have given in my account of Bidiyyah. Our situation was therefore very precarious, the only chance of escape depending on our firmness and conduct, for they were then marching to attack a part of the Imam's dominions, and he was the only protection we had.

Old Ali, who had an awful opinion of our new acquaintances, declared that he could not sleep; that they were prowling about the tent, and we should inevitably be robbed or murdered before the morning. My interpreter, a Persian, six feet high, and stout in proportion, was so perfectly unmanned by his fears, that he went into fits. There was some ground for his fears, as I believe the Wahhabis have a more thorough detestation of the Persians, as secretaries of Ali, than any other class of Muslims. When the Sheikh came and presented me with the letter for the Imam, I knew it would be vain to make any further effort to shake his resolution, and therefore did not attempt it; in the mean time news having spread far and near that two Englishmen, with a box "of Dollars," but in reality containing only the few clothes that we carried with us, had halted in the town. The Wahhabis and other tribes had met in deliberation, while the lower classes of the townsfolk were creating noise and confusion. The Sheikh either had not the shadow of any influence, or was afraid to exercise it, and his followers evidently wished to share in the plunder. It was time to act. I called Ali on one side, told him to make neither noise nor confusion, but to collect the camels without delay. In the meantime we had packed up the tent, the crowd increasing every minute; the camels were ready, and we mounted on them. A leader, or some trifling incident, was now only wanting to furnish them with a pretext for an onset. They followed us with hisses and various other noises, until we got sufficiently clear to push briskly forward; and, beyond a few stones being thrown, we reached the outskirts of the town without further molestation. I had often before heard of the inhospitable character of the inhabitants of this place. The neighbouring Arabs observe that to enter Ibri a man must either go armed to the teeth, or as a beggar with a cloth, and that not of decent quality, round his waist. Thus for a second time end our hopes of reaching Diriyah from this quarter; I did not however yet despair, but determined to push on for Seeb, embark there, and endeavour, from the port of Shinas (*Schinas*), to cross over to Buraymi. I had letters to the Wahhabi chief, and if I could only reach him, I had little doubt but that I might in safety continue on to the former town.

Ibri is one of the largest and most populous towns in Oman. Few of its inhabitants, who are of the Yaknah tribe, engage in mercantile pursuits of any kind, confining their bartering to the mere necessaries of life, and living on the produce of their date groves and corn fields. Agricultural pursuits have in other parts of the world a tendency to humanize and soften the character of a people. There they produce no such effects, and where the husbandman endeavours, by an assumed ferocity, to stifle or suppress any softer feeling. I imagine they are urged to this by a desire, when they mix with their Bedouin neighbours, to make up by such display, for the low estimation in which people not unfrequently regard all those who follow occupations more peaceful than their own.

Indigo, dates, and sugar are their exports, and rice; spices, and white cotton cloth, sent to be dyed blue, the imports. We passed several enclosures of barley, and towards evening halted near our former encampment at the village of Ayal.

Contrary to Ali's expectations, we got through the night minus only a few trifling articles, which we deserved to lose, because they were left without the tent.

March 14th. Nearly the whole of the village, at the instigation of Ali, watched around us last night. I had killed three or four sheep for them, and, either from being too intent on their supper, or from some other cause, a gun, sword, and a few other things were purloined. In our present mode of travelling we could ill spare those articles, and I accordingly represented the matter to the Sheikh, and he to the elders of the town. After making a great noise, and a furious debate, it was decided the articles should be restored.

When this was resolved on, in order, it would appear, to avert the disgrace and consequent punishment of the offender, who, I have reason to suppose, was a near relation of the Sheikh's, the latter issued directions that the articles stolen should be deposited, in the space of half an hour, in a certain obscure part of the grove; and there they were found at the expiration of the appointed time.

CHAPTER 15
DESCRIPTION OF NORTHERN OMAN

A*dvice to travellers - Honesty of the Bedouins - Sayyid Hilal - Advises the Author to abandon his enterprise - Sohar - Its commercial importance - Population - Trade - Hamud bin Azzan [Al Said] (Ahmed ibn Aisan) - Defeated by the Wahhabis - His character - Revenue - Harbours of Oman - Asses - Shinas - Villages - Date Groves - Dibba (Dibbah) - Description of the Country - Buraymi - Water - Milk Bush - Goats - Inhabitants.*

In a country where the natives are disposed to be hostile, a traveller, if he can possibly avoid it, will do well not to return by his former road. In the first instance he will most probably have passed before they recover from the effects of their surprise, but afterwards he naturally becomes the subject of much conversation and inquiry, and on his return, if disposed for mischief, they look out for him. The events of to-day and yesterday, in addition to many others which occurred previously, convince me of the propriety of these remarks.

On our way to Ibri we passed through AynAyn without exciting more attention than a gaze of astonishment; but the intelligence of our return had preceded us, and, in consequence, we were received at the entrance of, and followed through the town, by a mob of young men and children, who hooted and pelted us through it. The Sheikh too, who was formerly all civility, now would not suffer us to proceed without a present, in addition to the one I had already given him for his trouble; nor had I any other alternative, much to my annoyance, than to submit. It is, however, worthy of remark that, with the exception of the few articles at Ibri, this was the first and only time I have lost anything by petty theft or open extortion in Oman.

On the afternoon of March 19th we again reached Suwayq, where Sayyid Hilal received us with all his former kindness. He was much amused, but no way surprised to hear of our reception at Ibri, and his only astonishment appeared to be that we escaped so well. I found, that having received intelligence of the forward movement of the Wahhabis, he had sent a messenger to recall us, but who missed, and passed us on the road.

The Sheikh gave me no encouragement to persevere in my attempt to reach Buraymi.

"However," said he, "if you are desirous of trying the only remaining chance, I will furnish a good boat to convey you to Shinas, and instruct the Sheikh there to forward you on, with a guard, to Buraymi."

On the 22nd we therefore embarked for that port, and reached it on the afternoon of the 25th. The coast between these two points presents such a number of towns and villages (all of which will be seen on the map), that I question if it is not among the most populous in the world. The principal, and by far the largest of these is Sohar.

In point of commercial importance, Sohar ranks next to Muscat. It has about forty large *baghlas* belonging to it, and maintains a considerable trade with Persia on the one hand, and India on the other. The number of inhabitants is estimated at nine thousand; but some of these, residing in contiguous hamlets, are included in the estimate. Sohar is an ancient town: from its ports the Arabian ships formerly took their departure for China. I find mention made of it in several early authors.

'To the Portuguese, under the name of Soar, it was well known. In 1829, during the minority of Hamud bin Azzan [Al Said], the present Sheikh of this town, the Imam possessed himself of the government of his district, and, as it is generally thought, intended to retain it, but his design was defeated by the young Sheikh, who, by stratagem, obtained possession of the fort, and has since successfully held it against several attempts of the Imam to dislodge him. Peace has been subsequently declared between them; but as the territories of this chief are prolonged in a narrow strip, in a south-east direction, from Sohar to Rustaq, through the very heart of the Imam's dominions, Sayyid Said, it is thought, still views him with a jealous eye, and would seize with avidity any opportunity which might present itself to dispossess him. The government of this district is mild and regular, and similar in its elements to that of Muscat; but the character of its ruler is bold, reckless, and inconsistent. The Imam, in speaking of him, always styles him the Madman.

There are about twenty families of Jews at Sohar, who have a small synagogue. They are of the same class as those of Yemen, and, like them, subsist by lending money at interest to the people. The Arabs call them "Vad Sarah," the "Children of Sarah," but hold them in great abhorrence. Limes are dried here, and exported in large quantities to the Persian Gulf.

At the period of my visit the Sheikh was engaged in hostilities with the Wahhabis, who plundered several of his towns, and even compelled him to shut himself up in his fort at Sohar. The Imam, desirous of seeing his power humbled, would neither interfere nor render any assistance; but had his followers possessed resolution equal to that of their chief, the contest would very soon have been decided. The inhabitants of the sea-coast constitute very indifferent warriors, and having made a dash, on their first appearance, into the very centre of the enemy's forces, he found himself deserted by the greater number of his troops, who were principally composed of this class, and only succeeded in making his escape by the most reckless gallantry: this has since taught him more caution.

It is thought Sheikh Hilal aspires to the sovereignty of Oman. Many of the Ibadhi sect, for reasons which I have given in another place, are disposed to regard their present Imam as one who has fallen away from the true faith, and Hamud bin Azzan Al Said trims his sails accordingly. He affects great sanctity, and being endued with the gift of tears, is seen to remain without speaking to any one, weeping for hours. He also aspires to the spirit of prophecy; and flimsy enough as is the veil, has succeeded in creating among many with whom I have conversed the precise feeling he has been desirous to create.

Hamud bin Azzan Al Said's revenue is derived from the port of Sohar, which yields him annually ten thousand Dollars. He also exacts a duty of five thousand Dollars from the town of Rustaq; but this is not more than one half of the aggregate sum collected by Sayyid Said, when in possession of the country, because Ahmed remitted a moiety as a consideration for their acknowledging his authority.

British Attack against Shinas 1810 John Heaviside Clark

From Muscat to Shinas the coast of Oman is remarkably destitute of harbours, the only shelter the whole line affords being some narrow salt water creeks, or *khors*, as they are styled by the Arabs, which have only a sufficient depth of water to admit vessels of two feet draught. The inhabitants in consequence possess few boats of larger size than can be accommodated within them, or hauled upon the beach, which, upon the appearance of a north-wester, they most commonly do. In the date season they follow the same plan until they are freighted, and again launched for the purpose of proceeding to their destination. But the communication with the different ports seems more general by land than by water. For this purpose asses and camels are put in requisition; more generally the former. The price of a good ass is from fifteen to thirty Dollars: their pace is considerably faster than that of a camel's, the latter being two miles and three quarters, and the former three miles and a half an hour: it is a short, quick trot, which they maintain throughout the greater part of the day. The asses of Oman are nearly equal to those of Bahrain, and a considerable number are annually shipped off to the Mauritius.

Shinas is but a small town, with a fort and a shallow lagoon, affording anchorage for small boats. It is said to yield to the Imam an annual revenue of three thousand Dollars; but that is not more than is sufficient to defray its expenses. During the expedition to Ras Al Khaimah, in 1809, our force, in an attack on the fort, lost several men. Its inhabitants that year had thrown off the Imam's yoke, and, connected with the pirates, infested the entrance of the Gulf for some months.

But soon after Ras Al Khaimah fell they returned to his rule, and its fort admitted a party of Balouchis soldiers, whom he retains in his pay. I found the Sheikh absent, and from those he left in charge we could obtain neither answers to our questions nor common civility. However, upon my threatening to leave their port, and represent our reception to the Imam, they became alarmed, and towards the evening I was enabled, by their assistance, to forward the Imam's letter to Saad bin Mutlaq, the Wahhabi chief, who, I had every reason to believe, was still at Buraymi: with it I also sent a note, requesting that, if he were willing to receive me, he would, as the intermediate country was in a very unsettled state, send a small force to conduct the party from the sea-coast to his encampment. I employed the time which elapsed after the despatch of our letters in collecting information of, and examining, as far as my means enabled me, the surrounding country, of which I shall now give some description.

There is such an universal sameness in the common features of this part of Oman, that it would be unnecessary and tedious to enter on minute details; 1 shall therefore give a general outline of the country and its inhabitants, commencing with the sea-coast.

From Shinas to Ras Musandam, the north-east extremity of Arabia, the Maceto and Acabo of the Greeks, and the Ras Al Jabal, or cape of the hills of the Arabs, the general direction of the coast is N. ½ E.; and throughout the whole distance it is indented with deep bays, coves, and inlets, which become more numerous and more irregular in their outline as they approach the Cape. This indentation is also continued on the western side of the promontory, and a narrow ridge, five hundred yards in width, is all that separates Khasab (*Kasab*) Bay on one side, and Goobut

Gureiyah on the other. There are probably few parts of the world presenting an outline so tortuous and irregular as the space included between this isthmus and the Cape.

A succession of villages and date-groves extend from Shinas to Dibba, where the maritime plain Batinah (Batna of the Map) commences. At Dibba the Imam has a fort, and he formerly drew from the village a small annual revenue of four thousand Dollars. Water, vegetables, and cattle, all good in their several kinds, may be obtained here. It has a few boats, which are employed in bringing grain from the Persian shore. The intermediate parts of Khor Fakkan and Khor Kalba (*Kulba*) are similar in size and in the productions they afford to Dibba.

From Dibba to the northward, a range of mountains rise up directly from the sea, exhibiting in many places the most romantic aspect. The only beach met with is at the extremity of the coves, where a small portion of sand or shing, composed of broken coral or shells, is occasionally found, thrown up by the force of the wind and waves, From the main ridge of mountains, the average height of which is about two thousand five hundred feet, nearly midway between the eastern and western shore of the promontory, several lateral valleys extend towards the sea.

Buraymi may be approached from Shinas by two of these, Wadi Khor and Wadi Uttar. From Fujairah (*Fidgira*) another road leads across the ridge to Sharjah, which is two and a half days distant. A few date-groves are reared near the banks of the rivulets, which wind along their beds; but little else is cultivated, and the line of oases, extending from Ibri to Buraymi, forms the boundary of the cultivation in that part of Oman. From thence to the shores of the Persian Gulf the whole is an arid and sandy waste. Two days' journey from Shinas, a few miles to the southward of Wadi Uttar, on the road to Buraymi, there is a collection of thirty hamlets, called Beldan Beni Chab, from the name of the tribe who occupy them. They are in number about one thousand five hundred, and though Wahhabis, are remarkable for the protection which is afforded by them to all who flee there, be their crimes or their faith what they may.

Bearing south from this small district stands the town of Buraymi, similar in its extent and general features to Bidiyyah: it possesses several hamlets, and is watered by as many streams. There is a fort here, mounting a few small guns, belonging to the Ghafiri tribe, who profess the Wahhabi tenets, and refuse to acknowledge the authority of the Imam. The usual number of inhabitants is estimated at two thousand, but, owing to the late influx of the Wahhabis, there were at this season nearly treble that number collected within its precincts. The inhabitants bear the character of being equally wild, and averse to the visits of strangers with those of Ibri. Although the heat of the summer season is very great, the climate of Buraymi is considered far superior to any part of Oman, and almost equal to that of Nejd, which is everywhere extolled as the finest in Arabia.

From Dibba to Ras Musandam, together with that extent of hilly country included within the bifurcation of the main range and the sea, the whole space appears to be barren, and generally destitute of water. That obtained near the sea-coast is indifferent and brackish; and the lonely clumps of palms, which occasionally peep forth from some secluded nook or hollow, when contrasted with the bleak and sombre appearance of the hills, afford, by their verdant hue, a pleasing contrast. A scanty sprinkling of grass in the sandy beds of the valleys, and a few aromatic herbs and shrubs peculiar to the Desert, furnish but indifferent pasturage to the numerous flocks of goats which are everywhere met with.

The *Euphorbia tirucalli* (*Euphorbia Tiruecalla*), or milk bush, is also found here, growing out of the fissures of the rock. Notwithstanding the peculiarly acrid nature of the juice of its leaves, which is sufficient to excoriate any part of the skin on which it may be placed, the goats and camels feed thereon with impunity. Sheep are scarce. Both roam over the rocks without an attendant, yet they are taught to come at call, when it is necessary to milk them. The distance to which their owners will make themselves heard on these occasions is very great, and they can maintain, without difficulty, a distinct conversation across the coves, some of which are half a mile in breadth.

The whole of this district is peopled by a race, who speak a dialect differing from that of the tribes in other parts of Oman. They are also remarkable for their extraordinary attachment to their native wilds, and beyond hiring themselves out for a few months in the date harvest, on the Batinah coast, and an occasional visit to the Island of Larak, where a small party of them reside to catch and cure fish, they rarely quit their country. They likewise keep aloof from all their neighbours, and I have often inquired for them in the town without success. Before the visit of the surveying vessels they had never seen an European, and they testified as much surprise at the sight of looking-glasses, watches, and other objects of curiosity, as could have been exhibited by the veriest savage of New Holland. 'They are mostly very poor, wearing no other covering than a narrow cloth round their waist, which barely serves the purposes of decency. Their habitations are often small circular huts, constructed of loose stones, about four feet high, and usually erected on the strip of sea-beach already mentioned. Other dwellings are found within the space sheltered by some impending rock, the sides and front of which are built up in those spots which require it, but the greater number reside in caves and hollows. On one occasion when the surveying vessel drifted close to the shore, and it was feared she would ground, the hills, which, but a few minutes before, were without a solitary individual, instantly became covered with armed men, who had crawled forth from their caves to share in the expected plunder.

Their principal food is dates and salt fish, rice being nearly unknown to them, but they obtain, occasionally, a small supply of barley and wheat.

It has been asserted that this people are of a fairer complexion, and speak a language distinct from the other inhabitants of the province; but both opinions are incorrect. Those I met with were of a darker hue than the common race of Arabs, and their language differs no more from that used in Oman, than does the dialect of

Yemen from that of the Hijaz. A colony of Persians formerly settled in Kumzar (*Kumza*), and also in Khasab Bay, where their descendants still remain, and those who have seen them may have originated the supposition.

The number of those who inhabit this rocky wilderness is very considerable,- not less, as far as I could estimate, than fifteen thousand souls. Both the eastern and western shores are lined with villages. The Sheikh of Khasab can muster five thousand men under his government: the Sheikh of Bukha (*Bokh*) has nearly two thousand, and the chiefs of the other towns in equal proportion. They rear a small quantity of poultry within their dwellings, including a few ducks, which I never recollect seeing in any other part of Arabia.

CHAPTER 16
SEABORNE CONFLICT

M aritime Robbers - Forbearance of the Indian Government - Instructions to our Cruisers - Audacity of the Pirates - Anecdote - Capture of the Sylph - Massacre - Attack upon the Minerva - Captain attempts to blow up his Vessel - Crew offered up as a Sacrifice to the Prophet - Singular Ceremonies - National traits of Character - Respect for Women - Resolute bravery - Contempt of Death - Expedition against the Pirates - Mohammed Ali - Pirate Vessels - Reparation of Losses - Author engaged in Surveying the Arabian Coast - Additions to Geographical Knowledge - Danger of withdrawing our Squadron - Destruction of a Piratical Boat - Transportation of her Commander - Population - Tribes - Authority of Chiefs - Simplicity of their Domestic Habits.

It remains to notice the pirates, a race hitherto but little known, but whose power and influence was long felt by, and is still intimately connected with the political condition of the tribes in this part of Arabia. They occupy a part of the coast within the Persian Gulf comprehended between the mountain range and the sea-shore, and extending in that direction from Khasab to the Island of Bahrain,-a distance of three hundred and fifty miles. On the map, this portion bears the designation of the Pirate Coast.

The history of these maritime robbers may be traced back to a very remote period. Ibn Haukal, in his version of the Quran, informs us that before the deliverance of the children of Israel from Egyptian bondage, the subjects of a pirate monarch in these parts seized on every valuable ship which passed. The possession of a few ports within and near the entrance of the Persian Gulf, where it is not more than thirty miles across, enabled them to perceive and sally out on all passing vessels. Nor were their depredations confined to this vicinity alone; the whole southern frontier of Arabia, and the northern portion of India, were not exempted from their ravages. To the Portuguese during their brief career in India, they proved quite as troublesome as they did in the latter part of the eighteenth century to ourselves.

With these robbers the Imams of Muscat have been repeatedly at war. In 1805, Sayyid Sultan, uncle of the present Prince, encountered them near Bandar Lingeh (*Lingar*), and, after a desperate engagement, was slain. Sayyid Said has aided us in all our attempts to effect their extirpation.

It is needless now to inquire into the motives which then induced our Indian government so long tamely to suffer the repeated depredations of these marauders. The cause may, perhaps, be attributed to the brawls in which we were then entangled with the various powers in India. But, be that as it may, it is very certain that the Indian navy, constituting a force especially established and maintained for the suppression of piracy, received instructions, in no instance, to become the aggressors, but merely to repel any attack which was made on them. The following anecdote will serve to illustrate the singular relation which then existed between us.

Two Qasimi (*Johasmi*) vessels, lying in Bushehr (*Bushir*) [27] Roads in the Persian Gulf, stated to the British resident at that place that they were in want of gunpowder, and he, in accordance with his instructions from the Bombay government, to keep on pacific terms with them, directed a cruiser then lying in the harbour to supply the quantity they required. Hardly had they received it, than, with an audacity which could only be paralleled by the weakness which had furnished them with the means, they commenced an attack upon the identical vessel, which had treasure on board, as she lay at anchor; but, under the charge of a gallant young officer (whose name I regret being unable to supply), she cut her cable, and, after a brave defence, succeeded in beating them off.

I will add two other instances, which exhibit their mode of proceeding when successful in capturing a vessel :-

In 1808, the *Sylph*, a small ship of only one hundred tons, proceeding with the Persian Secretary from Bombay to Bushehr, was attacked, off the island of Kish (*Kenn*), by two large *baghlas*, each having a crew of upwards of two hundred men. After a short but desperate conflict, the vessel was carried, and the Arabs then commenced a deliberate massacre of the survivors. The work of death, however, was fortunately arrested by the timely appearance of His Majesty's ship *Nereid*, whose captain, perceiving how affairs stood, immediately fired into, and sunk the *baghlas*, with every soul on board. The other case, out of many which are before me, exhibits in its detail a still more harrowing and revolting picture of savage barbarity.

The *Minerva*, a merchant ship, proceeding to Bushehr, fell in with a large fleet at nearly the same spot, and after a running fight of two days, was carried, according to their usual custom, by boarding. The commander, Captain Hopegood, with the full knowledge of the cruel fate which then awaited him, attempted to blow the vessel up, but unfortunately he failed, and the slaughter of the victims commenced. The ship was first purified with water, and perfumes, and this being accomplished, the different individuals were bound and brought forward singly to the gangway, where one of the pirates cut their throats, with the exclamation they use in slaying cattle, "*Allah Akbar*" (God is great). They were in fact considered as a propitiatory sacrifice to their prophet. As if to show that even these lawless wretches retained some of those striking peculiarities of national character, which have rendered the Arab an anomaly in the history of savage nations, some nobler traits were mixed with their unrelenting ferocity. The persons and the virtue of females were always respected, and the contrary behaviour would have brought on them the deepest disgrace and contempt with their own tribes. An unresisting Muslim (*Mohammedan*) victim, after being stripped and plundered, they very generally spared; but death, or the immediate profession of their creed, awaited the unbeliever. And it is further due to them to acknowledge, that it was only when their vengeance became excited by a defence which cost the lives of many of their companions, that they had recourse to the remorseless measures which I have described here.

The most undaunted bravery was certainly theirs: if taken, they submitted with resignation to the fate they inflicted on others; and when they fell into the hands of the Persians, or other nations by which they are surrounded, they were never spared. After the destruction of one of their forts, several of them were brought on board our ships as prisoners. While uncertain of their fate, and before their wounds were dressed, it was asked what treatment they anticipated - "The same immediate death as we should have inflicted on you, had your fortune been ours," was the stern and characteristic reply.

Few merchant vessels, without the convoy of a ship of war, would now venture to sail between India and the Persian Gulf, while the native boats became subjected to almost certain interception and plunder. The trade in which great numbers of the latter were employed became almost suspended, and the patience or forbearance of Government was at length exhausted.

In 1809, an expedition under Captain Wainwright, in His Majesty's ship *Chiffonne*, several vessels in the Indian navy, and a detachment of the Bombay army under Colonel Smith, was sent against them. Their principal stronghold, Ras Al Khaimah, was stormed and taken, and fifty of their largest vessels burnt or destroyed. Leit, on the island of Qeshm, and several other ports, were reduced; and though this had the effect of checking them for a time, they soon rebuilt these ports, and gradually returned to their old practices.

About this period the success of Mohammed Ali's army in Arabia, and eventually the fall of their capital Diriyah, compelled a great number of Wahhabis to fly to the sea-coast, where the several tribes had already embraced the faith of their founder. To such restless, turbulent, and daring spirits, the roving and adventurous life of a pirate held forth every charm. It was but transferring the scene of a Bedouin's individual hostility to the rest of mankind, from a desert of sand to a waste of waters; and such numbers consequently joined them that their force soon became truly formidable.

Embarking from their ports in the southern part of the Persian Gulf, in large and swift sailing vessels, of from two hundred to four hundred tons, of which it is estimated they had then more than a hundred, and sailing together in large fleets, they kept the whole coast of Arabia, the entrance to the Red Sea, and the northern shores of India, in a state of constant excitement and alarm. Many and desperate were the conflicts which occurred at different periods between them and the vessels of the Indian navy, who now pursued a very different line of conduct to what they had done before. Though often repulsed or defeated, and even in one instance stormed with success in their principal strongholds, yet they never appeared to lose either energy or spirit for any considerable period. New vessels were built or purchased, other forts erected, and after a brief interval they again renewed their outrages.

Events connected with our operations in India against the Marathas (*Mahrattas*) occupied the attention and resources of Government so completely, that troops could not, without difficulty, for some time, be spared to punish them; but no sooner were these concluded, than their complete extermination was resolved on. The details of the expedition in 1819, are already too well known to render it necessary for me to describe them. I shall merely observe, that when Ras Al Khaimah, Sharjah, and the other ports again fell into our hands, all their boats were burnt or sold, and their forts razed to the ground. Certain information was likewise obtained that their fleets had often escaped the vigilance of our cruisers, by taking refuge in the numerous coves with which this part of the coast of Arabia is indented, and into which the fear of unknown dangers prevented our vessels from following them. When this was communicated to the Indian Government, it was at once resolved that a minute examination should be made of them.

Being employed in this investigation for a considerable period, I had the most favourable opportunities of collecting the information here detailed. To the expedition science is indebted for those magnificent surveys of the Persian and Arabian Gulfs. Notwithstanding the difficulties and privations they encountered from the perilous nature of the navigation, the jealous and hostile character of the natives, and the still more formidable effects of climate, the heat of which at certain seasons is almost insupportable, the surveying vessels successfully persevered. The result was so satisfactory, not only in adding to our stock of geographical knowledge, but in furnishing the Government with a full account of the several tribes, their condition and resources, that it was subsequently resolved to examine in a similar manner the whole coast of the Persian Gulf. To confine ourselves, however, to this portion, it was wisely foreseen that, with pirates, as with other thieves, the most effective way to disperse them was to lay open their haunts. So long as these remained unknown to us, a feeling of imaginary or real security would induce them to follow their former practices; but the circumstance of English ships "writing down" their coast, to use their own descriptive expression, was alone enough to give them an idea that we should possess a perfect knowledge of it.

The result has hitherto justified the anticipation, for the survey was no sooner completed, and a strict system of surveillance established, then their appliances and resources became, as a measure of necessity, turned from piratical to commercial pursuits. Petty quarrels between the boats of rival tribes still occur occasionally; but nearly the whole of their vessels now trade in the Persian Gulf, peaceably from port to port, and from thence to India or the Red Sea. It may indeed be questioned whether, from the very early period when commerce first dawned, and navigation, in the hands of the Phoenicians, made its infant efforts in the Indian seas, if in this part of Arabia an equal protection has been afforded to the bark of the merchant when sailing along its shores.

There is, however, reason to believe such security will exist no longer than we maintain our present policy towards the Arab chiefs. If our naval squadron was withdrawn from the Gulf for a single season, they would very soon make head again. All their towns have been rebuilt, and are perhaps more extensive than before; and when the treaty of 1819, by which they stipulated to refrain from fighting with each other by sea, had in 1835 expired, they addressed the Indian Government to be permitted to renew their ancient mode of settling differences, many of which during that period had arisen between them. As this was at once known to be merely a pretext for renewing their outrages on their more peaceful neighbours, it was of course refused them. But a few months before, a piratical boat fitted out by the Bani Yas (*Beni As*) tribe, seized and plundered an Indian vessel proceeding to Bushehr, but was encountered some days afterwards by the Honourable Company's sloop of war, *Elphinstone*. Nowise. daunted, the pirates awaited her approach, prepared for boarding; and it was not until they received a broadside of round and grape from the sloop's 32-pounders through their flimsy sides, that they became aware of the power of the foe they had defied. As they were but a few yards from each other, the slaughter was very great. The commander of the Arab vessel was subsequently taken to India, tried there in the Supreme Court, and sentenced to fourteen years' transportation.

The first part of this affair was intelligible enough to the several tribes along the coast, for we had no repetition of such attempts; but the sentence, which was carried into effect, puzzled them sorely; and during my travels I was repeatedly warned not to venture near to or within the territories of this tribe, as they had threatened to retaliate, by boiling in oil, the first European they could lay hands on.

Here, as in other parts of Arabia I have found great difficulty in ascertaining the amount of the population. Little reliance can be placed on the testimony of the chiefs; who are ever desirous of enhancing the power of their own, and depreciating that of other tribes; while, from their maritime pursuits, and their connexion with the pearl fishery, the amount of actual residents is constantly fluctuating. The number of their huts affords no surer guide, for, being built of the branches of the date palm with little trouble, when old and damaged by the wind, they are often deserted and left standing. The mean of my several inquiries induces me to fix their number at twenty thousand, exclusive of women and children. The principal tribes are the Qasimi, Manasir (*Menasi*), Bani Yas, and Mahama: the former is the most powerful. They not only possess all the chief ports of the Arabian coast, but have also established themselves on the Persian shore, where they have several large towns and flourishing villages. Their name is derived from a Saint Qasimi, who resided on a low tongue of land, and the tents of his followers, which were pitched around, gave the name of Ras Al Khaimah, or "Cape of Tents," to the promontory on which a town bearing the same designation was subsequently erected. The Qasimis very soon after its promulgation embraced the tenets of the Wahhabis, with whom they were always in strict alliance, and to this cause we are to attribute the bitter hatred of the Princes of Oman. Their present chief is considered to be wily and politic. In their peculiar mode of warfare he possesses great abilities, but is otherwise deficient in that boldness and frankness which characterises the Arab. His capital, Ras Al Khaimah, was wholly dismantled in 1819, but is now rebuilt, and, perhaps, of greater magnitude, and more populous than before. If our ships, therefore, were not kept in constant communication with him, there is little doubt, both from his ability and disposition, that he would occasion us some trouble.

The tribe next in importance to the Qasimi is that of Bani Yas. Its late Sheikh, Tanun, was an enterprising character, who possessed considerable power, and maintained a regular force of four hundred men, very well armed and equipped. Small as this number may appear, it was sufficient to give him considerable influence over his rivals, although the number of troops he could otherwise bring into the field was estimated at four thousand only. When the Imam, in 1829, undertook an expedition against the Island of Bahrain, he endeavoured, by the payment of a considerable sum of money, to secure the cooperation of Tanun; but when the hour of attack arrived, his lukewarmness was so apparent, that it is to this day believed he also received a bribe from the other side.

The surveying vessels, in 1828, received much attention from this chief, who was very fond, during their intercourse with him, of engaging in the several games with which the officers and men passed away their leisure hours, and equally happy if they would share in those of his own people. On these occasions the most perfect good humour existed. One day, an officer had been matched to run on foot against Tanun, who was in person rather short, but very active, and with abundant vivacity, and love of amusement. For some time after they had started the officer held the lead, but finding, as he approached the goal, that the longer-winded little Sheikh was about to pass him, he threw himself headlong before his path. Over flew Tanun, amidst shouts of laughter from his tribe; but, now is disconcerted or annoyed, the Sheikh arose, and, after joining most heartily in their mirth, congratulated his opponent on the success of his stratagem. In wrestling, leaping, and other athletic exercises, his Arabs generally were equally matched with, and, not unfrequently, had a decided advantage over our Europeans.

The authority exercised by these chiefs differs but little from that of the Sheikh government on which I have hereinafter touched. From the fierce and turbulent character of those they govern, their power is necessarily of a somewhat despotic nature, yet, in adjusting broils, and in matters connected with the general interest of the tribe, the opinion of their old men has great weight. The direct interference of the Sheikh is, in fact, neither sought nor often called for; and the tribe is ruled without the aid of frequent punishments; for, when its relations are so simple and so well understood as in Arabia, offences against the good order of society rarely occur. In their diet and mode of living these chiefs preserve the same simplicity as the Bedouin Sheikhs; a fact the more extraordinary, since they are not in the same manner shut up in a desert, but in constant communication with Indians, Persians, &c., and having more wealth and power, would experience no difficulty in supplying themselves with foreign luxuries. It follows then, that this self-denial, whilst retaining the national manners, must be considered as purely voluntary.

While cruising on this coast in 1827, I was proceeding with dispatches to the Sheikh of Sharjah, Sultan bin Saqr, when a strong breeze unexpectedly set in, and raised so heavy a swell on the bar, that our boat, in attempting to cross it, was capsized. This occurred some distance from the land, but, all being good swimmers, we reached it without much difficulty, and with no other inconvenience than a thorough drenching. After landing, the gale increased, and for three days we could not attempt to put off to the vessel. I then had some opportunity to study the private character of the people, as well as that of their rulers. Sultan was unremitting in his attention to me, a meal being every day prepared at, and sent from, his house. On one occasion he invited me to dine and pass the evening with him. I was received in a small room, furnished with only a rude table, two or three chairs, given him by the commanders of our vessels, and some carpets, on which, after I had declined the honour of the chairs, we all seated ourselves. Our dinner was, as usual, of the most frugal description, and, after its removal, the Sheikh's brother roasted and pounded the coffee, which the Sheikh himself made and handed round. A story-teller was then called in, whose tale, judging from the peals of laughter he drew from his hearers, must have possessed much entertainment; but I was then too ignorant of the language to understand it.

CHAPTER 17
CULTURE OF PERSIAN GULF

P*ersonal appearance of the Natives of the Pirate Coast - Pearl Fishery - Divers - Boats employed - Pearl Oysters - Expedient for retaining the Breath - Cruising on Pearl Bank - Atmospheric Heat - Effects on Europeans - Arab Swimmers - Anecdote of an Arab Diver - Diving for Fish - Saad bin Mutlaq - Advance of the Wahhabis - Termination of my Journey - Peculiar features of Oman - Oases.*

'The inhabitants of the Pirate Coast consider themselves to be far superior to either the Bedouins or town Arabs. The latter, especially those from Oman, they hold in such contempt, that a Muscati and an arrant coward are by them held to be nearly synonymous. They are taller, fairer, and, in general, more muscular than either of the above classes, until they attain the age of thirty or forty years, when they acquire a similar patriarchal appearance. Until this period some of their forms are perfect models of strength, and their development of muscle greater than that of any other Asiatic people with whom I am acquainted. Although by no means fond of exertion, when it can be avoided, yet, in cases positively requiring it, the manner in which they combine individual efforts is truly astonishing, their largest barks, of three hundred tons, being drawn by sheer physical strength above high water mark with no other assistance than rollers. Whenever our boats required to be launched, or hauled over flats, they were always happy to assist, in order that they might laugh at the puny efforts of the Lascars, for to save the Europeans in hot weather that class were not unfrequently employed in such operations.

When not at feud with any of their neighbours their time is devoted to fishing, diving for pearls, or passed in complete idleness, for the north-westerly gales which prevail throughout the greater part of the year in this gulf prevent them, during its continuance, from putting to sea, and their supply is then obtained from the creeks and inlets which intersect its shores. The pearl fishery only lasts from June to September, for at other periods they complain that the cold is too severe. During the season every person who can procure a boat himself, or obtain a share in one, is thus employed, and their villages have no other occupants than children, females, and men who are too aged to follow this pursuit.

The pearl bank extends from Sharjah to Biddulph's Group. The bottom is of shelly sand and broken coral, and the depths vary from five to fifteen fathoms. 'The right of fishing on the bank is common, but altercations between rival tribes are not infrequent. Should the presence of a vessel of war prevent them from settling these disputes on the spot, they are generally decided on the islands where they land to open their oysters. In order to check such quarrels, which, if permitted, would lead to general confusion, two government vessels are usually cruising on the bank.

Their boats are of various sizes, and of varied construction, averaging from ten to fifty tons. During one season it is computed that the island of Bahrain furnishes, of all sizes, three thousand five hundred; the Persian coast, one hundred; and the space between Bahrain and the entrance of the Gulf, including the Pirate Coast, seven hundred. The value of the pearls obtained at these several ports is estimated at forty lacs of Dollars, or four hundred thousand pounds. Their boats carry a crew varying from eight to forty men, and the number of mariners thus employed at the height of the season is rather above thirty thousand. None receive any definite wages, but each has a share of the profits upon the whole. A small tax is also levied on each boat by the Sheikh of the port to which it belongs. During this period they live on dates and fish, of which the latter are numerous and good, and to such meagre diet our small presents of rice were a most welcome addition. Where polypi abound they envelop themselves in a white garment; but in general, with the exception of a cloth around their waist, they are perfectly naked. When about to proceed to business they divide themselves into two parties, one of which remains in the boat to haul up the others who are engaged in diving. The latter having provided themselves with a small basket, jump overboard, and place their feet on a stone, to which a line is attached. Upon a given signal this is let go, and they sink with it to the bottom. When the oysters are thickly clustered, eight or ten may be procured at each descent; the line is then jerked, and the person stationed in the boat hauls the diver up with as much rapidity as possible. The period during which they can remain under water has been much overrated; one minute is the average, and I never knew them, but on one occasion, to exceed a minute and a half [28].

Accidents do not very frequently occur from sharks, but the sawfish (*Pristis zijsron* - Wellsted used the *Antiguorum* of Linneus) is much dreaded. Instances were related to me where the divers had been completely cut in two by these monsters, which attain, in the Persian Gulf, a far larger size than in any other part of the world where I have met with them. As the character of this fish may not be familiar to the general reader, I will add a few words in the way of description. They are of an oblong rounded form, their head being somewhat flattened from the fore part, and tapering more abruptly towards the tail. They usually measure from thirteen to fifteen feet in length, being covered with a coriaceous skin, of a dark colour above, but white beneath. The terrific weapon from whence they derive their name is a flat projecting snout, six feet in length, four inches in breadth, armed on either side with spines resembling the teeth of a shark.

Diving is considered very detrimental to health, and without doubt it shortens the life of those who much practise it. In order to aid the retention of the breath, the diver places a piece of elastic horn over his nostrils, which binds them closely together. He does not enter the boat each time he rises to the surface, ropes being attached to the side, to which he clings, until he has obtained breath for another attempt. As soon as the fishermen have filled their boats they proceed to some of the islands with which the bank is studded, and there with masts, oars, and sails, construct tents. They estimate the unopened oysters at two Dollars a hundred [29].

Pearl Diver attacked by a SawFish

Familiar with water from their youth, the natives are very expert, and the time they will remain upon it, as well as the distance they can swim, would sound incredible to European ears. There are well-attested cases of individuals who, without rest, have swam more than seven miles.

In 1827 we were cruising in the Honourable Company's sloop *Ternate* on the Pearl Banks. Whilst becalmed, and drifting slowly along with the current, several of the officers and men were looking over her side at our Arab pilot, who had been amusing himself in diving for oysters. After several attempts, his search proved unsuccessful. 'I will now," said he, "since I cannot gather oysters, dive for and catch fish." All ridiculed the idea. He went down again, and great was our astonishment to see him, after a short time, rise to the surface with a small rock-fish in either hand.

His own explanation of the feat was that as he seated himself at the bottom, the fish came around and nibbled at his skin. Watching an opportunity, he seized and secured his prey by thrusting his thumb and fore-finger into their expanded gills.

Tuesday, March 28th. Intelligence of Saad bin Mutlaq's advance on Bidiyyah, the details of which I have given in my account of that district, reached me this morning, and completely annihilated all hopes of being able, through his means, of reaching Diriyah. At the same time I also learnt that the Imam had dispatched messengers who, not finding us at Buraymi, as was expected, had gone on to Ibri.

As it therefore became necessary that I should now forego all present intentions of advancing further into the country, I determined to pass the few remaining days of the fair season on the Makran (*Macran*) coast, where, although a maritime survey, conducted at a considerable expense, has fixed the geographical positions of the towns, every species of information connected with its inhabitants &c., is wanting.

The general observations which follow embrace the several subjects which I have not embodied in the foregoing narrative.

I have not found it an easier task to fix the limits of this province, than I before experienced in ascertaining those of Hadramaut and Yemen. Under the denomination of Oman, some geographers comprehend all that tract which is encompassed by the provinces of Hadramaut, Al Ahsa, and Nejd. To the natives of the country, however, such a division is now unknown; and in speaking of Oman they merely refer to the space between the districts of Jaalan and Batinah. Where inquiries or research would produce in either instance no very satisfactory results, in my delineation of the province I have adopted the plan which appeared most natural, and consider that only as Oman which, in its general features, differs most prominently from the country by which it is surrounded, and which acknowledges the sovereignty of the reigning prince of Oman, though in some instances by a tie so slight, as scarcely to deserve the name.

Oman thus considered, may be described as a narrow strip of land of irregular width, never exceeding one hundred and fifty miles in its broadest part. It is bounded on the east by the Indian Ocean, on the west by extensive deserts, and extends in a direct line from the island of Masirah, in latitude 20° 48', and longitude 58° 56', nearly four hundred miles, to Ras, or Cape Musandam, in latitude 26° 24', and longitude 56° 39', where it terminates in the form of an acute angle.

By the natives of the country this part of Arabia is subdivided into four districts :-

1st, Jaalan, comprehending Beni bu Ali, and all that tract of country to the south-east of Bidiyyah;

2ndly, Oman from Bidiyyah, northwest to Maqniyat;

3rdly, Dhahirah (*Dhorrah*), from Maqniyat to Buraymi; and

4thly, Batinah, extending in a narrow strip along shore, from Seeb to Khor Fakkan.

The general features and outlines of the province may be thus laid) down. A range of mountains, forming a part of the great chain which almost encircles Arabia, traverses, in a direction nearly parallel to the shore, the whole extent of the province from Muscat to Sur. The hills take their rise close to the beach; but to the north of that port they retire considerably from it.

At latitude 23°, a second range, the Jabal Akhdar, or Green Mountains, still more elevated, run in a direction nearly transverse to the former; low parallel ridges, forming the roots of either branch, extending to a considerable distance from them. From the Jabal Akhdar the chain continues to Ras Musandam, throwing off in its course another branch or arm, which extends to Ras Al Khaimah, on the shores of the Persian Gulf. The space included within this bifurcation and the sea is broken into piles of mountains, which are singularly disposed and of various elevations; the width of the chain does not in general exceed twelve or fifteen miles, and the average height of the central or most elevated hills is from three thousand to three thousand five hundred feet. Some of the highest points of the Jabal Akhdar rise, however, nearly six thousand feet above the level of the sea. With the exception of this range, they are unwooded and barren. Feldspar and mica slate enter most commonly into the formation of the lower ranges, and primitive limestone into the upper.

By referring to the map and narrative it will be seen, that from Bani bu Ali to Nizwa, I traversed a line of oases, and that the space between them and the mountains on the seashore presents nothing but arid plains, destitute of either towns or villages. To the northward of Seeb, the width of the Tihamah (*Tehama*) or maritime plain (the Batinah of the map) is from twenty to forty miles. It rises with a slight but gradual ascent from the sea to the base of the principal chain, and although not crossed by any of the rivers which appear on our maps, it has nevertheless some very considerable streams, which continue for the greater part of the year to pour their waters into the sea [30]. Beyond, or to the westward of the mountains in the northern districts, few towns or fertile spots occur, and in some instances the margin of the Desert is but a few miles removed from them. From the summit of the Jabal Akhdar I had an opportunity, during a clear day, to obtain an extensive view of the Desert to the south-west of Oman. Vast plains of loose drift-sand, across which even the hardy Bedouin scarcely dares to venture, spread out as far as the eye can reach. Not a hill nor even a change of colouring in the plains occur, to break the unvarying and desolate appearance of the scene.

CHAPTER 18
AGRICULTURE OF BATINAH COAST

S oil and Agriculture - its general character - Batinah - Grain, Vegetables - Cultivation on banks of Streams - Description of the Oases - Irrigation - Subterranean Rivulets - Harvest - Seed-time - Soil of the Jabal Akhdar - Terraced Gardens - Progress of Agriculture - Crops - Wells - Mode of raising Water - Egyptian method Implements of Husbandry - Remarkable mode of Irrigation - Scriptural allusion - Arab Reapers -Trees, Plants, &c.

Oman may, therefore, be described as a desert thickly studded with oases, and containing amidst its mountains numerous fertile valleys; yet many of these are at a considerable distance from each other, and it must be admitted that the quantity of cultivated land bears but a small proportion to that which is incorrigibly barren; for the intermediate space between the oases to the westward and the great sandy Desert is an arid plain, either sandy or clayey, according as the aluminous or silicious particles prevail. A few succulent herbs, which are nourished by the nightly dews. and afford but indifferent grazing to their scanty flocks, spring up here; but the large tracks occupied by the beds of the streams have generally a layer of rounded masses of limestone, brought from the mountains, deposited on their surface, and are wholly destitute of every species of vegetation, save some dwarfish bushes on which the camel alone feeds. The soil in the Tihamah, in some spots, is hard and of a bad quality, but in others, whenever water can be conveyed, it is in a high degree susceptible to cultivation. In the narrow belt bordering on the sea-shore, called Batinah, large quantities of grain and vegetables are reared, and a continuous line of date-trees, often four or five miles in breadth, extends from Seeb to, Khor Fakkan a distance of nearly two hundred miles. Reference is repeatedly made in the Arabian authors to the palms of Oman. Much cultivation exists along the banks of the streams, and also in the vicinity of the towns. But the most remarkable feature in this country are the oases, which extend from Bani bu Ali, in a continuous line, to the west-north-west. They are usually of an oblong form, lying at right angles to the streams by which they are supplied. Their size varies from a circumference of seven or eight miles to one, or even less. The singular and laborious mode by which the natives convey water to them, I have already noticed in my account of the oases of Bidiyyah.

For the purpose of obtaining a better soil, and facilitating irrigation, the Arabs have removed the earth to the depth of six or seven feet, and they flood the whole or any part at pleasure. Some of these streams are public property, others belong to individuals or to companies. At a place called Om Taief, near to Muscat, the Imam constructed a *falaj* at a cost of forty thousand Dollars; but the water proved so brackish that they were forced to abandon it. An estate in North Oman, where these subterranean rivulets are very scarce, derives its value from its situation with regard to them. Some of the minor rills are exhausted, or their water is greatly diminished in the dry season, and the ground is then irrigated from the main streams. At Nakhl, near to Barka, four hundred Dollars were paid for a supply of one hour every fifteen days, and, as they have no watches, they have recourse to the stars, with the precise time of the rising and setting of some few of which they are well acquainted.

Water, it is well known, in a tropical climate gives an almost unlimited fertility to the soil. In the oases it is always saturated with moisture, and the leaves and other vegetable matter, decaying almost as soon as they are deposited, but little manure is required. Much of the cultivation is carried on beneath the trees, but open spaces are also left for grain or sugar-cane, which require the sun's rays to ripen them. Wheat is sown in the latter part of October, and reaped at the commencement or middle of March. Where they have the means of constant irrigation, the ground produces one crop of wheat and two of *dhurra*. Barley is sown a month after wheat. No rice is grown in Oman; and so far from any export of wheat existing, the natives have not a sufficiency for their own consumption, and import large quantities from Persia and Makran. In the oases wheat yields an increase from fifteen to twenty fold: barley the same: *dhurra* (*Sorghum bicolor - Holeus Sorghum*) from thirty to forty fold. The singular appearance which these groves present during the various stages of their vegetable produce, I have noticed elsewhere.

From the elevated position of the Jabal Akhdar, many of the valleys formed by the upper ranges differ from the plains below, both in their soil and mode of cultivation. The ground there is usually terraced, as in Palestine and China, and produces a great variety of trees and fruits not reared in other parts.

Agriculture has made but small progress in Oman. It has been already noticed that the prolific soil of the oases requires but small assistance; for where men fear nothing from the vicissitudes of the season, little management in the process of husbandry is required. But on the arable land in the open plains, where the earth, though of indifferent quality, is yet susceptible of considerable improvement, the natives bestow neither labour nor expense to remedy the defect. I must, however, except the country in the vicinity of Manah and Nizwa, which, in place of barren and neglected wastes but partially tilled, by which other towns are disfigured, exhibit extensive ranges of sown fields, rich in every kind of vegetable production.

Bullock pulling a water hide-bucket at water well

The crops in the plains depend, in some measure, on the rains, although many parts are irrigated from wells, some of which are of considerable depth. It is singular, considering the pains which have been bestowed on the rivulets by which the oases are supplied, that the inhabitants should not seek by mechanical means to abridge the labour which this process entails. Here, as in India, two pieces of timber, generally the trunk of a date-palm, are planted with sufficient inclination to plumb the centre of the well. Across a roller, affixed in the upper part of these, a bucket-rope traverses, the bucket being usually a bullock's hide, gathered up into the shape of a bag, with a hose at the lower part: to the extremity of this a small cord is attached, leading over a roller about two feet above the brink of the well. Bullocks are used for drawing the water; and in order to add the impetus of the animal to its strength, he is driven down a slope excavated for the purpose, at an angle of fifteen degrees. Both ropes are affixed to the yoke, and by the time the water is swayed sufficiently high, that made fast to the hose which has hitherto been kept in a vertical position, becomes tightened, drawing the mouth of the hose downwards, and the water is then discharged into a narrow reservoir.

When the wells are sufficiently shallow they practise the same method as is adopted by the Egyptians on the banks of the Nile. A pole being suspended in the middle between two supporters, the bucket is attached to one extremity, and a stone or some heavy article to the other: its weight assists the peasant, who sways on the rope attached to it. From the reservoir the water is conducted, by artificial rills, over the face of the surrounding country.

Their implements of husbandry are rude and ill constructed. The plough is of the same description as that of Yemen, which will be found figured by Niebuhr. After ploughing, they form the ground with a spade into small squares with ledges on either side, along which the water is conducted. Besides preventing its spreading, these embankments also serve to retain the moisture on the surface for a longer period. When one of the hollows is filled, the peasant stops the supply by turning up the earth with his foot, and thus opens a channel into another [31].

Within these enclosures they cast the seed by hand into narrow furrows, and afterwards cover it over, leaving the whole a plain surface. By this mode they affect a considerable saving of the seed, which can neither decay from exposure to the atmosphere, nor be carried off by the birds. Their corn is reaped with a small sickle of a semilunar shape, and notched like a saw. The man who reaps hands the sheaf to another, by whom it is formed, bound, and laid in a line parallel to that which his companion is clearing away. These are afterwards collected together, and a stone of considerable size is drawn over them by two oxen. In other parts a circular space, about twenty feet in diameter, is enclosed by a wall. To a stake in the centre a bullock is fastened by a yoke of peculiar construction, and he is driven round and round until the corn is trodden out in his progress. It is afterwards winnowed by means of palm branches, one of the party following and occasionally turning the sheaves with a rake. I was pleased on these occasions to observe that here, as in Palestine and other parts of the East, the ox was left unmuzzled.

Over the surface of the greater part of the intervening desert between the oases trees and bushes appear but thinly scattered. Some spaces are wholly destitute of them, but extensive tracts through which I passed, in the vicinity of Bani bu Ali, are thickly wooded with lofty acacias. The largest of these are called by the Arabs *Ghaf* (*Prosopis cineraria*), and *Simr*, A gum exudes from both; the true gum Arabic, however, is only obtained from the latter, although the produce of the former, of inferior quality, is not unfrequently substituted for it. These trees are used for making charcoal, and medicinal properties are attributed to the bark of the *Prosopis cineraria*, The wood is also made into agricultural implements, the stocks of matchlocks, and other articles requiring excessive hardness. No timber fit for building is found in Oman, the trunk of the date palm, commonly used in erecting their houses, scarcely deserving that appellation, since it is weak, and very soon decays.

Athel, or tamarisk bushes (*Tamarix aphylla - Tamarix Orientalis*) are numerous. Camels feed greedily on their tender branches and leaves, which the Bedouins collect by beating the trees with sticks, and receiving what falls upon a cloth spread beneath them. On the Jabal Akhdar there are, as I have noticed in the course of the Narrative, many indigenous trees not found in the plains. In some of the channels through which water has passed, lofty tamarind, *Sidr* (*Ziziphus spina-christi*), and *hithel* trees have taken root, notwithstanding the rocky nature of their bed; but, generally speaking, the summits and slopes of the mountains are unwooded and barren. Tamarind (*Tamarindus indica*) trees also grow most luxuriantly on some of the plains. They are large, wide spreading, beautiful trees, but the people of Oman, like the natives of India (*Hindostan*), entertain a belief that it is dangerous to sleep beneath them, especially at night.

In Oman I never met with either frankincense or dragon's-blood trees, although they are very numerous on the hills in the neighbouring province of Hadramaut. The Arabs report that they are not found to the westward of the Mahara district. On the borders of the streams aloes are very numerous. In the distribution of its leaves and its average height, the plant which is called by the Arabs *succul* is the same as the *Aloe perryi (aloe spiccata)*, found in Socotra, and on the coast of Arabia Felix; but it is of a sea-green, instead of a light brown colour; very succulent, and not so deeply serrated. I have seen a variety closely resembling this in India and Egypt, but am not aware that botanists have classed it. The natives collect a small quantity of the juice, but being of a more acrid taste than the better sort, it is not held in much esteem, and none is in consequence exported. *Senna alexandrina (Cassia lanceolata, senna maki)* (the sharp-pointed senna of Forskal) is found growing in great abundance in Oman, but the natives employ it very sparingly in their medicines. Many colocynth plants *Citrullus colocynthis* (*Cucumis colocynthis* of Linneus) are found in the vicinity of Bidiyyah, and also along the sea-coast. The melon, called by the Arabs *handal (hungil)*, is found in some places strewn over the ground in great profusion. Several bushes of the milk-hedges (*Euphorbia tirucalli*) are found amidst the mountains; and notwithstanding the peculiar acrid nature of its juice, which is sufficient to inflame and blister the skin, the goats eat the plants with impunity. Rue (Rice - sic) (*Ruta graveolens*), *Absinthium*, wild lavender, and many aromatic shrubs and plants are also seen: of these a large collection was made, but being of no utility to man and of little interest to the general reader, they are but slightly noticed here. The *champa* flower (*Magnolia champaca - Michaelis champaca*) and the Arabian *Jasminum* (*Jasminum sambac*) are cultivated for the sake of their perfume, which is in great request with the females. In north Oman two varieties of sorrel are found, of which the Bedouins, who consider them as a mild laxative, are very fond. Water-cresses grow on the borders of the streams; the Arabs use their seed for medicinal purposes. In the interior of the province all the oases, as well as the cultivated lands in the vicinity of its towns, are alike productive, and the following list applies to them collectively; but many of the fruits are not found in gardens near the sea-coast. I may be pardoned the dry detail of such a catalogue, since it will convey, better than any lengthened description, an idea of the natural productions of a country hitherto regarded as a desert. Nor must it be forgotten that all contained in this list, amounting to twenty different kinds, are often reared in a space not more than three or four hundred yards in diameter.

CHAPTER 19
AGRICULTURE AND LIVESTOCK

Fruits of Oman - Oranges - Limes - Lemons - Introduction of the Lemon-tree into Europe - Tamarinds - Mangoes - Beauty of the Mango tree - Grapes - Wine - Plantains - Pumpkins - Figs, inferior to those of Turkey - Dates - Seed of Male Palm - Grain - Vegetables, &c. - Wild Beasts - The Imam's Camel - Description - Food of the Camel - Value - Rate of Travelling - Burckhardt - Volney - Captain Burnes - Author's experience of Camel Travelling - Housings - Illustrations of Scriptural Quotations - Author in danger of being Shot - Imam's Horses - Value - Studs of Barka and Suwayq - Asses, their sureness of Foot - Buffaloes - Oxen - Poultry - Birds - Bedouin Sportsmen - Fish - Climate - Diseases - Arab Physicians - Meteorology - Geological Features.

Of oranges, limes [32], and lemons there are several varieties. Respecting the first, it may be sufficient to mention the sweet orange (*Citrus sinensis*); the Mandarin orange, so called in China and India; and a third sort, remarkable for the thinness and bright yellow colour of its skin, and its superior flavour. Of limes, there are the *Citrus aurantifolia* (*Citrus acida*), and three or four other species, also well known in India by the designation of sweet limes. Lemons are scarce and small; but the citron attains a very large size. The lemon-tree is said to be a native of Persia; but from its Arabian name, Limen, it would appear to have been brought to Europe by the Arabs. From the juice of limes, they make sherbet, a very cooling beverage, drank in large quantities during febrile disorders. Of tamarinds and mangoes there are also several kinds, differing considerably in size, flavour, and appearance; but the best are considered inferior to those obtained in India.

In the spring, when this tree puts forth its blossom, the whole of its foliage appears of a golden hue, which, with its wide spreading branches, and umbrageous foliage, entitles it to rank as the most noble among the vegetable productions of the oases. Fruits - [Wellsted wrote Quinces *Pyrus eydoma* and *Pyrus malus* - he may have meant the fruit known today as *Cydonia oblonga* and *Malus domestica*] are found on the Jabal Akhdar-the latter on the plains. A considerable quantity of this fruit is shipped off to India. Custard apples, *Annona reticulata*. Grapes are grown principally in the Jabal Akhdar, one of a white, and the other of a dark-purple colour; the former are used for wine, and from the latter they make raisins. Plantains also, of various sorts. Water melons, and pumpkins, all plentiful and good in their several kinds. Almonds, walnuts, figs, several varieties; the best, called *Tin* (*Ficus carica*, Linn.), are sweet and pleasant, but smaller, and inferior in richness and flavour to those of Turkey. The natives dry and string them on lines. *Sidr*, the fruit of the *Ziziphus spina-christi*. Dates. These form the principal, and often, particularly in travelling, the only food of the natives. Oman produces vast quantities. I have already noticed the extensive groves on the Batinah coast. The best kind here are considered scarcely inferior to those of Basrah and Bahrain, esteemed the best in Arabia. The natives are very fond of the seed of the male palm; it has a slight odoriferous smell, but its taste, I thought, could only be relished from habit. White and *jawari* grain *Sorghum bicolor*, (*Holcus sorghum*), wheat, and barley, are grown, but little rice. The vegetables are onions, lentils, radishes, carrots, *Brinjals* (the egg plant), parsley, several kinds of beans, peas, cucumbers, sweet potatoes, lettuces, and some greens, which, when boiled, taste not unlike our garden spinach. Potatoes have not been introduced; the *Semsem*, or *Sesamum orientale*, is grown in large quantities; from the seed an oil is expressed, which is much esteemed by the Arabs. They sometimes toast the seed, and make it into bread. To these we may add indigo, the cotton bush (*Gossypium herbareum*), the castor oil tree, and extensive fields of sugar-cane. Hemp is reared, but not manufactured; but its seeds form one of their natural inebrients.

The wild animals of Oman nearly resemble those common to other parts of Arabia. On the plains, jackals, foxes, hares, antelopes, and jerboas, the *Jaculus jaculus* (*mus jaculus*), are very numerous; hyaenas are only found near the mountains, where they shelter themselves in caves and hollows. Wild hogs, goats, and a description of small panther, are met with on the Jabal Akhdar.

Camels in all parts of Arabia are esteemed a gift of inestimable value, and those of Oman enjoy a deserved celebrity for strength and swiftness. Nejd is equally the nursery of the camel as of the horse; but the Omani in all ages is celebrated in the songs of the Arabs as the fleetest; their legs are more slender and straight, their eyes more prominent and sparkling, and their whole appearance denotes them of higher lineage than the ordinary breed of the animal. Anecdotes are told of two which the Imam formerly possessed, that appear almost incredible. I have heard it asserted by those on whose testimony I should place every reliance, that one of these favourite dromedaries carried a courier from Seeb to Sohar, an ordinary journey of six days, in thirty-six hours. Considering such frequent mention has been made of the camel from the earliest period, it is singular we possess no correct or even detailed information respecting its habits, character, or general appearance. I am not acquainted with a single illustrated zoological work which affords even a tolerable representation of one.

Wellsted's 'panther' the Arabian Leopard - Oman

The silence of travellers, in reference to an animal to which all have been so much indebted, may be accounted for on the supposition that each individual conceived the subject too important to have escaped his predecessors and naturalists in general, as in truth it appears to have done.

The following remarks, in addition to other scattered notices found in these travels, differ in many respects from received opinions; but very favourable opportunities of studying the subject enable me to submit them with confidence; and in other respects, that which is new may serve to supply a deficiency in the natural history of the most useful animal which the bounty of the Creator has bestowed on man.

All the camel's habits and instincts are adapted to its singular condition and the region which he inhabits. Let us contemplate the creature from the moment of its birth. Should this happen on a journey, the Bedouin [33] receives it in his arms, and for a few hours places it on the mother's back; but at the first halting-place, the little stranger is put down to receive the parent's caresses, and ever after continues, unassisted, to follow her footsteps.

Thus accustomed from its earliest age to long and toilsome journeys, little training is necessary, beyond proportioning the weight to its tender age, to inure them to the carrying of burthens; and they voluntarily kneel when about to be loaded for a journey, a position which their great height renders necessary. Kneeling is their natural state of rest; but when heavily laden on flinty or stony ground, it cannot be accomplished without pain. They then drop at once on both front knees, and in order to establish room for their hinder legs, are compelled in that condition, and whilst encumbered with the whole weight of the burthen, to plough them forward. The callosities on their joints, although nearly of a horny nature in the aged camels, seem insufficient to defend them, and it is impossible for the European to view the act without commiseration.

In consequence of this the Bedouins never make them kneel to mount themselves, but either cause the animal to droop his neck to receive their foot, and on their raising it the rider is enabled to gain his seat, or they climb up behind: it pleases them much when a stranger can accomplish either of these feats.

The camel of Arabia has only a single hump, which is round and fleshy, whilst the animal continues in good condition. No sooner, however, does he begin to feel the inroads of famine than a very remarkable change takes place. By a singular provision of nature, an absorption of this excrescence supplies the place of other nourishment; nor does the body exhibit any considerable diminution of bulk, until little more of the hump remains except it's frame-work of bones and muscles. Such is the universal report given by the Bedouins, whose ample means of observation entitle their opinions to respect.

Whilst young they are pretty-looking animals, but when aged and over-worked they generally lose their hair, and become very unsightly objects. In general they have a clean sleek coat, usually of a light brown colour, with a fringe of dark hair along the neck; but this covering in the Arabian or Desert camel is less profuse than in that of Upper Asia, which is better adapted to the climate of those regions. In Arabia I have occasionally seen one of these animals perfectly black; but the Bisharin (Bishyrean) camel, on the Nubian coast, is quite white. The eye of the camel resembles that of the gazelle; it is large, dark, soft, and prominent, and retains its peculiar brilliancy under the fiercest glare of the sun and sand. Its feet are large and spreading, and covered at the lower part with a rough, flexible skin, well adapted to a dry soil, but they soon fail them in wet or slippery places. Neither is the camel better pleased with a loose sandy soil than other animals; it is a hard but fine gravelly plain in which he delights; although, provided they are rough, he can ascend the steepest and most rugged paths with the same facility and secureness of footing as a mule.

Camels bear a high price in Oman. I have known one hundred and forty Dollars paid for one. Depth of chest and largeness of barrel constitute their chief excellencies. From thirty to fifty Dollars is however their average price.

The great length of the camel's neck enables the animal, without stopping, to nip the thorny shrubs which everywhere abound on the Desert, and, although the spines on some are sufficiently formidable to pierce a thick shoe, the cartilaginous formation of their mouth enables them to feed without difficulty. The Bedouin also, when walking, devotes a considerable portion of his time in collecting and feeding his camel with the succulent plants and herbs which cross his path. These, on a journey, with a few handfuls of dates or beans, form its ordinary food; but while encamped, he is fed on the green stalk of the *jowaree* and the leaves and tender branches of the *athel* [34], heaped on circular mats, and placed before the animal, who kneels while he is partaking of them. In Southern Arabia they are fed on salt, and even fresh fish.

During a journey it is customary to halt about four o'clock, remove the loads, and permit the camels to graze around. If the Arabs are desirous of preventing them from straying too far, they tie their fore-legs together, or bind the fetlock to the upper joint by a cord. 'The head is never secured, excepting whilst travelling, when the Arabs unite them in single file by fastening the head of one to the tail of his predecessor. Towards evening they are called in for their evening meal, and placed in a kneeling posture round the baggage. They do not browse after dark, and seldom attempt to rise, but continue to chew the cud throughout the greater part of the night. If left to themselves they usually plant their hind quarters to the wind. The male, as well as the female, voids its urine backwards, and, as the ground there becomes wet and uncomfortable, they continue slowly, without changing their recumbent position, to move themselves forward.

Authorities differ as to the period the camel can endure thirst. Buffon mentions five days as an extraordinary instance; Tavernier, a good authority, nine; but it appears that camels, like several other ruminating animals, when fed on succulent herbage, do not require water; and a friend, who has had ample opportunities of judging, assures me that he once travelled from Baghdad to Damascus, a journey of twenty-five days, without the camels once drinking - a sufficiency of moisture being afforded by the abundant vegetation there found at every stage.

Notwithstanding its patience and other admirable qualities, the camel is gifted with but little sagacity, nor does it appear to be capable of forming any strong attachment to its master, although they frequently do so to one of their own kind with which they have long been accustomed to travel. In protracted desert journeys the camel appears fully sensible that his safety consists in keeping close to the caravan; for, if detained behind, he never ceases making strenuous efforts to regain it. A recent traveller [35] represents the camel as a peaceful, quiet animal. He says that "they eat with a sort of regularity and order, a little at a time; and that, if either of them left his place, his companion appeared gently to reprove him, which made the other to feel his fault, and return to it again." On the contrary, I should say, they are the most quarrelsome brutes in existence.

After the hardest day's journey, no sooner is the baggage removed than the attention of the driver is constantly required to keep them from fighting; the "gentle approvals" being ferocious bites and lacerations of each other's ears.

Volney calculates the pace of the camels of Syria at three thousand six hundred yards per hour; and Captain Burnes, who has devoted considerable attention to the subject, found it in Turkistan to be nearly the same. In Oman I have however ascertained their average rate of caravan travelling to be considerably more, to determine which, I adopted the following method: By means of a good watch I on several occasions accurately noted the time which was occupied in passing between two places lying north and south of each other, the latitudes of which I had carefully fixed, and the result gives from two and a half to two and three quarters geographical miles-an-hour; and this, I observe, is the same as that reckoned by Burckhardt. But the usual pace of the Oman camels, when the Bedouins mount them for a desert journey, is a quick hard trot, from six to eight miles-an-hour. They will continue this for twenty to twenty-four consecutive hours; but increase their speed, on occasions which require it, to thirteen and fifteen miles-an-hour. The female is esteemed swifter than the male; nevertheless, the Bedouins, in consequence of its greater spirit, not unfrequently prefer the latter. The load of the camel differs very considerably. In Egypt, when supplied with abundance of food, they carry upwards of a thousand pounds; but the ordinary burden in a caravan journey is from two hundred and fifty to five hundred pounds. The motions and paces of the camel are ungainly; its walk, its trot at speed, its gallop, being equally violent and disagreeable.

They adorn the necks of these animals with a band of cloth or of leather, upon which are strung or sewn small shells called cowries, in the form of half-moons. To these the Sheikhs add ornaments of silver, so that, even in the present day, they would form a valuable prize to the spoiler. We possibly have here an illustration of several passages in Holy Writ, as Judges iii. 20. 26, when camel ornaments are mentioned in connexion with jewels and other articles of value. The shells are strung in a semicircular form; hence the phrase "ornaments like the moon."

The camel is subjected to but few diseases. In damp places its feet crack and ulcerate: the rot is especially fatal; hundreds, when the Syrian Hajj remains encamped at Aleppo and other large cities, being sometimes swept off by it. Petroleum is the most usual remedy. A. glandular swelling in the neck, which usually kills him in three or four days, and colics, are also said to prevail in the spring and autumn of the year. The actual cautery is put in requisition for all these.

When the camel on a journey refuses to rise, the Arabs universally abandon him to his fate. It is seldom they get on their legs again, though instances have occurred where they have done so, and completed a journey of several days. I have often passed them when thus abandoned, and remarked their mournful looks as with mute eloquence they gazed after the receding caravan. When the Arab is upbraided with inhumanity, because he does not at once put a period to the animal's sufferings, he answers that the law forbids taking away life, save for food; and even then, pardon is to be implored for the necessity which compels the act. When death approaches the poor solitary, vultures and other rapacious birds, which espy or scent their prey at an incredible distance, assemble in flocks, and, darting upon the body, commence their repast even before life is extinct. Thus, in well-beaten routes, the traveller continually sees remains of this faithful servant of man, exhibiting sometimes the perfect skeleton, covered with its shrunk and shrivelled hide, sometimes the bones only, altogether deprived of flesh, and bleached to dazzling whiteness by the scorching rays of a desert sun.

Those belonging to the Imam excepted, there are very few horses in Oman, and in some places the sight of them is unknown. On one occasion, when mounted on mine, and riding some distance ahead of the caravan, I was mistaken for a Wahhabi, and within an ace of being shot as such by another party advancing from one of the towns. To the fleetness of this noble animal, which, in compliment to its princely donor, I had named Sayyid, I was indebted, on another occasion, for the preservation of my life. On my return from Ibri to Suwayq, contrary to the wish of the Bedouins, who had received intelligence that the Wahhabis were lurking around, I left the village where we had halted alone, with my gun, in search of game. Scarcely had I rode three miles from the walls when, suddenly turning an angle of the rocks, I found myself within a few yards of a group of about a dozen horsemen, who lay on the ground, basking listlessly in the sun. To turn my horse's head and away, was the work scarcely of an instant; but hardly had I done so ere the whole party were also in their saddles, in full cry after me. Several balls whizzed past my head, which Sayyid acknowledged by bounding forward like an antelope. He was accustomed to these matters; and their desire to possess him unharmed, alone prevented my pursuers from bringing him down. As we approached the town, I looked behind me. A Sheikh, better mounted than his followers, was in advance, his dress and long hair streaming behind him, while he poised his long spear on high, apparently in doubt whether he was sufficiently within range to pierce me. My good stars decided that he was not; for, reining up his horse, he rejoined his party, whilst I gained the walls in safety. These were probably the same men who had murdered the two messengers despatched to me by the Imam of Muscat, and to which circumstance Said bin Khalfan (Sayyid ibn Kalfan) alludes in his letter, given in the Appendix.

The day before Sayyid came into my hands he had been presented to the Imam by a Nejd Sheikh. Reared in domesticity, and accustomed to share the tent of some family in that country, he possessed in an extraordinary degree all the gentleness and docility, as well as the fleetness, which distinguish the pure breed of Arabia. To avoid the intense heat, and spare their camels, the Bedouins frequently halted during my journey for an hour about mid-day. On these occasions Sayyid would remain perfectly still, while I reposed on the sand, screened by the shadow of his body. My noon repast of dates he always looked for, and shared. Whenever we halted, after unsaddling him, and taking off his bridle with my own hands, he was permitted to roam about the encampment without control. At sunset he came for his corn at the sound of my voice; and during the night, without being fastened, he generally took up his quarters a few yards from his master. During my coasting voyages along the shores of Oman, he always accompanied me, and even in a crazy open boat across the ocean from Muscat to India. My health having compelled me to return to England overland, I could not in consequence bring Sayyid with me. In parting with this attached and faithful creature, so long the companion of my perils and wanderings, I am not ashamed to acknowledge that I felt an emotion similar to what is experienced in being separated from a tried and valued friend.

Several of the Imam's horses are of the noblest breed in Nejd, some of his mares being valued at from 1500 to 2000 Dollars; and one horse, the most perfect and beautiful creature I ever saw, was considered to be worth an equal sum. He maintains a portion of his stud at Muscat; but the greater number is at Barka and Suwayq, where they pay great attention to the breed and rearing of these noble animals. Camels and asses are, however, more generally used for travelling in Oman; and although a Sheikh may occasionally think it derogatory to ride on the latter, all other classes are less fastidious. They are large, well made, and endure great fatigue. The Arabs take considerable care of them; and some of the better kind fetch from forty to fifty Dollars. Those which traverse the Jabal Akhdar, in point of size, sturdiness, and sureness of step, are almost equal to mules crossing the most difficult passes, over a smooth limestone rock, without a single false step. A great many asses are shipped from Oman to the eastern ports of Persia, and also to the Mauritius, where they are highly valued [36].

Buffaloes are unknown; oxen are not numerous, and they all have the hump which is supposed to be a distinguishing mark of the African species. Their value for agricultural and other labours is too considerable to allow of their being killed for food, excepting at the large towns. They are principally used for drawing water, for ploughing, and for treading out the grain. On the sea-coast, where there is a great scarcity of fodder, they are fed on dates, or fish, either fresh or salted.

Goats abound throughout Oman, but sheep are scarce, and usually of a black colour, and small size; but as they are mostly fed on aromatic herbs, of which there are great abundance, their flesh is sweet and well flavoured. The tail, though larger than that of the European breed, is less ponderous than those brought from the African shore. The Arabs do not castrate either sheep or goats, but destroy the generative principle in the male by means of a tight ligature.

With the exception of fowls, which are abundant and cheap, the Arabs of Oman have no domestic poultry. Game is scarce: the only water-fowl I saw there during my stay were some wild ducks, of the *Anas boschas* variety, and not in the slightest degree fishy. Doves, plovers, and pigeons are very numerous, but the Arabs never trouble themselves with killing them. Quails, the common brown, or Desert partridge, and a species of pheasant, are found in great abundance on the plains. The tenor of the Muslim law places a great restriction on shooting. Directly the bird falls, the sportsman runs up, and cuts his throat. If a sufficiency of blood does not flow from the wound, it is pronounced unfit for food. Eagles breed amidst the mountains, and three varieties of vulture are found on the plains. A great abundance and variety of sea-fowl frequent the sea-coast: of these the most common are the laughing sea-gull (*Ridibundus*), the noddy (*stolidus*), red-throated diver (*Gavia stellata - Septentrionalis*), the white spoon-bill (*leucorodia*), the Indian crane (*Antigone*). The whole line of coast abounds in fish, but as they are, with one or two exceptions, the same as those of India, I forbear to enumerate them.

Eagle (Aquila nipalensis) Oman

Muscat is often visited by a large grampus, which our sailors call the Muscat Tom, and the Arabs Ouey. It sometimes capsizes their boats, and plays, according to their report, other mischievous pranks, but I have never heard of its committing any serious injury.

Muscat Cove some years ago was so abundantly filled with the small fish called *sardinas* in the Mediterranean, that they might be obtained in any quantity, and a great number were preserved and exported; but about two years ago they wholly deserted their former quarters, and are now only found in the vicinity of Bandar Abbas (Gambrun) on the Persian shore. I have heard it related by the inhabitants, that about every fifth or sixth year the fish on the coast are visited by some epidemic, which destroys them in vast numbers, and many are then thrown up on the shore. In the running streams there are numerous small fry, but the natives do not eat them. The insects and reptiles are locusts, wasps, bees, tortoises, lizards, scorpions, and many others common to India.

A considerable diversity in the geographical features of the country produces in Oman a corresponding variation in the climate. Away from the sea-coast, to the westward of the mountains, the air is very dry in the cold, and excessively hot in the warm season; but in Batinah, the high mountains which retreat considerably from the coast arrest the progress of the vapours exhaled and wafted from the ocean, and it is comparatively cool and moist. The exuberant vegetation of the oases reduces the temperature, but the climate, at the same time, is especially obnoxious to strangers. Violent fevers, which have very generally a fatal termination, prevail all the cool season; indeed those who reside in the oases bear striking evidence of the fact that the air which is most favourable to vegetables, has a contrary effect on human life. They appeared during my stay among them to be constantly suffering from sickness, and have not the vigorous and healthy look of the Bedouins. Their houses, damp and gloomy looking edifices, which the sun's rays never warm, are built within their groves. Around them are swamps and pools of water, bordered by a rank and luxuriant vegetation, and the inhabitant steps from such a locality to the arid and burning Desert. The causes of such insalubrity are, therefore, fully as apparent as the effects. On the other hand, the district occupied by the Bani bu Ali tribe, the territories of the Bani Janaba, and the Batinah coast, are remarkable for their salubrity. People who have been attacked in the former with fevers, dysenteries, &c., aided by the pure air and plain diet, generally recover after a month's residence in the latter districts. The small village of Seeb, about twenty miles to the northward of Muscat, is especially celebrated for its restorative qualities.

Ophthalmia and other diseases of the eye seem very frequent, especially amidst those who reside in the oases. The sudden transition from the gloom of their groves to the glare of the Desert is sufficient to originate disease, and their uncleanly habits to continue it. They are perfect gluttons in medicine, and will swallow as much as is given them; but they laughed at, and wholly neglected my prescription of frequent ablutions. Some few cases of calculus came under my notice, but, I believe, they are not common, nor have they any knowledge of performing an operation to relieve it. I saw no instances of leprosy in Oman. Two cases of *dracunculus* [*Dracunculus medinensis*] were shown me: their mode of extraction is the same as that of India.

In the eleventh and twelfth centuries the Arabians are well known to have carried their research into the vegetable kingdom to a very great extent. They also possessed an extensive acquaintance with the science of medicine, and modern physicians gratefully acknowledge various articles of high repute for which their *materia medica* is indebted to the Arabs; but in neither of those branches do they at present possess even respectable attainments. In fevers they wholly abstain from animal food, drink copiously of sherbet, and partake freely of melons, cucumbers, and other cooling vegetables. At Nizwa, which contains nearly a thousand inhabitants, I found it impracticable to procure an individual who could let blood: Gunshot and sabre wounds, where everyone carries a matchlock and sword, are of frequent occurrence, but their treatment is equally simple, though, from their plain diet, and temperate habit of body, they are in many instances uncommonly successful.

Encircled as Muscat is by naked rocks, the sun's rays become there concentrated as into a focus, and the heat at certain seasons is almost intolerable. On the 10th of

April, at five in the evening, Fahrenheit's thermometer was 106, and then not a breath of wind was stirring. Very generally, however, during the day this extreme heat is moderated by cool and refreshing sea-breezes.

The general state of the atmosphere will be best exhibited by a reference to the abstract of the Meteorological Register which is subjoined. Rain falls from October to March, but rarely more than three or four days in each month, when the storms, though heavy, are partial. The lofty summits of the Jabal Akhdar arrest the clouds in their progress, and copious showers give rise to numerous streams, which flow down and cross the plains on either side the chain. Snow and ice in the winter months in those regions are not unknown, and in that of March hail-storms frequently pass over the plains below. The dews at night are singularly copious, leaving upon the trees and surface of the ground the same effects as would be produced by smart rain.

On the Desert the atmosphere is usually clear and cloudless, and in the day the sky is of the deepest blue. At night the stars shine forth with a brilliancy unknown in other climes. The cold at that season, as in all other sandy tracts, is proportionate to the heat of the day; but fevers appear to be unknown there; and the Bedouin who sleeps in the sand receives additional vigour and vivacity from the purity of the air he breathes in his slumbers.

Primitive limestone is the predominant rock in Oman, the principal chain of mountains being almost solely of this formation, and it enters largely into the composition of the inferior ranges.

In the northern provinces, and on the seashore in the vicinity of Muscat, hills rising one thousand five hundred and sometimes two thousand feet in height are composed wholly of mica slate, deposited in thin folds, and twisted into a variety of tortuous forms. In the vicinity of Ras Musandam there are basaltic rocks, in some places forming steep acclivities, and in others assuming the shape of mountain-caps. Arabia has been pronounced to be wholly destitute of the precious metals, but in this province we meet with silver associated as is usual with lead. Copper is also found: at a small hamlet on the road from Samad Al Shan to Nizwa there is a mine which the Arabs at present work, but the others are wholly neglected. Even in the vicinity of Muscat the hills are very metalliferous. No precious stones, as far as I can learn, have at any time been found.

CHAPTER 20
COMMERCIAL ASPECTS OF OMAN

Commercial Advantages of Oman - Simple Habits of the People - Deficiency of internal Commerce explained - Natives of the Sea-coast - Early Commercial Enterprise - Low State of Learning, Arts, and Manufactures - General Indifference to Knowledge - An Exception - Said bin Khalfan - Sugar Manufacture - Cotton Cloths - The Lungi - Silk-weavers - Bishts - Halwa - Sweetmeats - Honey - Vineyards - Artisans - Manufactory of Arms - Female Ornaments - Pureness of Gold - Religious Tenets - Population - Original Stock-Feuds - Honour and good Faith - General Character - Foundation of Quarrels - Morality - Ceremonious Behaviour - Salutations - Simplicity.

If we consider the advantageous position of Oman, as an emporium for the trade of India, Persia, and Arabia, it cannot fail to strike us with surprise that the province generally has never reached any considerable degree of commercial importance. We find, on the contrary, that, with the exception of Muscat, Sohar, and Qalhat, which collectively enjoyed but a scanty portion, even at the period when the main stream of that immense commerce flowed from India, past its ports, to Europe, enriching every country in its course, Oman alone was exempted from sharing in its benefits. But, in a country where, from the frugal habits of its people, the artificial wants are few, and its natural wants are, as in this instance, supplied by agricultural resources, there cannot exist much internal commerce. Its people are therefore in a measure independent of other nations, and too proud of their birth, country, and freedom, to mingle with their less fortunate neighbours : they have ever retained the same isolated and original condition. The only class who do engage in commercial pursuits are those residing near the sea, where we may infer that, while attending their fisheries along an extensive line of coast, they first acquired a disposition for enterprise and navigation. In the latter they must at an early period have attained considerable perfection, since we learn [37] that their ships, in the twelfth century, sailed from Sohar on distant voyages, even so far as China. At present nearly the whole of the commerce of Oman passes through the hands of the merchants at Muscat; and I have given in my account of that city all the necessary details. Its several branches at Sur, Barka, Sohar, and Shinas, are of minor importance, being principally confined to the exportation of dates, for which they receive in exchange grain, Indian cloth, and fire-wood.

The existing state of learning, the arts, and manufactures, does not in Oman rise superior to the low ebb at which they are found in other parts of Arabia: indeed, in all these respects, they are far inferior to their neighbours of Yemen. Though I purposely sought amidst the most intelligent persons, I found but one who had any knowledge of astronomy, or indeed of literature or of the sciences generally; nor do they possess a wish to cultivate them. We must not, however, on this account conclude that there is any want of capacity or intellect. One individual in particular, named Said bin Khalfan, who had been educated in Calcutta, was sufficiently versed in nautical astronomy to be able to take the sun with a sextant and artificial horizon, to calculate his observations, and to rate chronometers. He had been in command of several of the Imam's largest ships, and has on more than one occasion navigated the Liverpool (74gun) between Zanzibar and Muscat [38].

My instruments excited at first more attention than I desired; but this feeling soon died away when they were informed they were not made of gold. I could not, during my stay, obtain a book or manuscript on any other subject than commentaries on the Quran and divinity in general: on these points, together with reading and writing, their children are alone instructed.

At some of the principal towns sugar is manufactured in large quantities; but although the cane is of a very superior quality, the material, owing to some difficulty which they cannot get over in granulating it, has but an indifferent appearance; it forms, however, the principal export from Muscat, where, as well as at Nizwa, and several of the other principal towns, they manufacture large quantities of *halwa*, a mixture of sugar, honey, *ghee*, and almonds, boiled to a dense paste, of which large quantities are sent to India and Persia in shallow earthen basins about ten inches in diameter. They manufacture a sweetmeat similar to this in Syria, from the expressed juice of the grape; an inferior kind is also made from the *karrub* or locust tree, which, when boiled to the consistency of honey, is called dibs by the natives; and from the Arabian being the same as the Hebrew, that is most probably the article translated honey, with which the land of Canaan was said to abound. Wherever in Syria or Palestine there are vineyards, it is still met with; and when mixed with the juice of the olive, forms a principal article of food with the poorer classes. By adding the ground pulp of the *sesamum orientale* to this dibs, and baking both lightly in an oven, it is rendered into هليوى *halwa*. Cotton, canvass, and cotton cloths of a coarse texture, are manufactured by the men at their own houses. Of these, the *lungi* is the most common and valuable; they are mostly about ten feet long, and two feet six inches, or three feet broad, and striped horizontally with red and blue. They are used either to bind round the waist, or as turbans; their price varies from five to ten Dollars. 'The females spin and prepare the yarn. At Bani bu Hassan, I saw in an open shed about thirty silk weavers at work: the colours were good, but the workmanship was coarse, and the devices rude. In the northern provinces, the *bisht* is fabricated; but their quality is far inferior to those brought from Nejd.

I have elsewhere had occasion to observe that there are but few artisans in Oman. At the principal towns blacksmiths manufacture spear-heads, the crooked dagger, called a *jambiya*, and some rude knives: copper pots and dishes are also made by another class; but silversmiths are far more numerous than either. Considerable sums are lavished by the females in the purchase of various silver ornaments, and their children are literally burdened with them. I have counted as many as fifteen ear-rings on either side; and their heads, breasts, arms, and ankles are decorated with the same profusion. There are also many workers in gold, but the articles which they turn out of hand appear not well finished: the metal they use seems of the purest kind.

As regards their religious tenets, the people of Oman belong to the sect of the Kharijites (Khuwarijites) [39], a class of Muslims found also in other portions of the East, widely distant from the country I am now describing. The cities of Nafusa and Jarba, in Northern Africa, formerly subject to the Grand Signior, and that of Jabal Musib, a dependency of the Emperor of Morocco, still profess the peculiar doctrines of the Kharijites. These heretics the Sultan has made many efforts to chastise; but from the utter scarcity of water which prevails in the country intervening between him and them, his attempts have been in every instance unsuccessful.

Like the Moravians of Christendom, the Kharijites highly value themselves on being followers of the pure tenets of their prophet, unalloyed by any intermixture with the heresies which at different periods have sprung up in the Muslim world. We must, however, consider this to apply chiefly to the inhabitants of the Desert, and small inland towns; for as to the Arabs resident at the sea-ports, or in large trading cities, they, from causes similar to those which influence the professors of a purer faith, under similar circumstances, have become more lax in their religious discipline; and Shias, Sunnis, and Twelver Shia (Metawialis), sects which immigrated into Oman at a comparatively recent period, abound there. These, in the true spirit of Muslim proselytism, are incessantly labouring to gain over the pure Kharijites to their own way of thinking, though hitherto, I believe, with little success. At one period, also, a great number of the Kharijite Bedouins dwelling around the towns became followers of the Wahhabis; and since the defeat of those fanatics, have joined one or other of the heresies just alluded to.

As regards the ceremonial portion of the faith professed by this class, their practice seems distinguished by a much greater simplicity than belongs to most other Muslim sectaries. At the birth of a child, for instance, nothing more is at present thought necessary than the rite of circumcision at the usual age, common to all Moslem professors; for though some few voluntary ceremonies, including a sacrifice, were formerly admitted, these have been long laid aside. Their funerals are also conducted with little external display. They merely wash the body carefully, while one of those present recites certain prayers composed for the occasion. It is true that a few ignorant and extravagant persons sometimes spend great sums of money in providing sumptuous entertainments for the mourners; but among the higher classes of the natives these practices are unknown. In truth, they are directly opposed to the precepts of the Quran, where the Prophet commands food to be given to those only who have been immediately concerned in depositing the body within the grave.

The lawfulness or unlawfulness of the use of coffee, owing to the word signifying an intoxicating liquor, as well as a refreshing drink made from berries, has been a subject of controversy among Muslim professors, and is thus disposed of by the Kharijites in general. They affirm that a certain saint of distinguished piety, on one particular occasion, was desirous of passing the whole night in prayer and supplication to the Almighty, but sleep overpowered him. He therefore resorted to this drink, one of whose known effects is to produce extreme watchfulness; and finding that it completely banished his former drowsiness, he named it "coffee," that is, a stimulating liquor. The authority and example of this learned and pious Moslem, as well as the known fact, that many of the most eminent expounders of the law were equally favourable to its general use, had due weight with the Kharijites; and in consequence, the use of coffee became universal. They further assert, in defence of the practice, that not the slightest passage prohibitory of this favourite beverage can be traced in the Quran, or any other orthodox Muslim work [40].

One remarkable peculiarity in the opinions of the Kharijites consists in the jealousy with which they disclaim connexion with any of the numerous other sects into which the disciples of the Prophet have been split. "We approximate," says a native writer, indignant at the bare supposition that the people of Oman had ever been an offset of any one of these "we approximate not to any sect, nor does any sect approximate to us. How can we be in alliance with those innovators who oppose God's religion?"

In the true spirit of intolerance, he then proceeds to denounce all those whose faith differs from his own. "We conclude such to be devoted to ruin; enemies of God; infidels, whose portion hereafter shall be in *Jahannam* (*Gehenna*) for ever. They deny the eternity of future punishments; they diminish the enormity of sin; we enhance it. The portion of the wicked surely will be forever, for God is great! [41] Their doctrines content not our intelligent ones; away with it! away with it!"

The same writer mentions the existence of a tradition that the Muslims were to be divided into no less than seventy-three sects, of which, in course, only one could be orthodox; and hints the people of Oman is that one, grounding his opinion on the sense of the Arabic word ناحية which signifies "escaping," as well as "safe." In fact, the great points of contention between the Kharijites and their co-religionists may be said to spring from another famous and oft-disputed question, whether Mohammed actually saw the Deity or not?' The Sunnis strenuously maintain that he did, which their antagonists as strenuously deny, asserting that such an opinion is in fact infidelity; and "to say God can be seen, being to limit and circumscribe the illimitable and incomprehensible, is therefore absurd [42]." The Kharijites reject the interpretation of those verses of the Quran brought forward by the Sunnis to confirm their own peculiar views, and assert that these passages are to be received in a figurative, and not in a literal sense. Moses, for example, is said to have seen God; but this they will have to mean simply, that he witnessed the effects of His power and majesty, not that he viewed him face to face. Thus, again, as regards the Moslem belief respecting the scales of the day of judgment, in which all men are to be weighed; and the bridge Al Sirat, leading towards the 'gates of Paradise. The former, say the Kharijites, is a mere metaphorical expression, accordant with the usual style of oriental phraseology, which any one will readily comprehend; the latter means nothing more than the narrow path of truth.

The Sunnis again divide the wicked into two classes; the first consisting of infidels and pagans, the second of reprobates and apostates; but they refuse to style the *latter* infidels, however unworthy as Moslems they may happen to be. The Kharijites, on the contrary, more strict and more conscientious, consider all who have once renounced their faith to be unbelievers, distinguishing, however, the infidelity of grace from the infidelity of reprobacy; and look upon all pagans, in which denomination they include Christians, as coming under this latter class.

Furthermore, the Sunnis assert the infallibility and divine authority of the prophet's companions, saying it is a sin to disobey their concurring determination, and that they inherited the right of true judgment. This, also, the Kharijites deny, on the plea that if the son of Noah-the child of a prophet - did wrong, so might a prophet's follower.

They accuse both Sunnis and Shias of error, in making certain texts of the Quran apply only to the prophet's descendants, when, according to the interpretation of the Kharijites, they have reference to the faithful of every rank and station. Finally, they deny that the authority of the four first Imams is to he implicitly followed, as, in that case, both Ali and Abu Bakr were in error; the one for permitting a decision to be made by the Quran, the other for usurping an authority which was hereditary in the Prophet's family. Their own Imam they regard in two points of view-as a temporal governor, and an absolute indefeasibly appointed sovereign, whose authority is of God.

As to the derivation of the name of Kharijites, these writers assert that Muawiya I (Muwaiyah) having rebelliously opposed Ali, after some contest, finding himself about to be worsted, proposed a reference to the Quran. His adversary consented;

but some of Ali's followers protested against this mode of procedure, urging that rebels and sinners against God were not fit judges of the Imamship; that if they decided against him, his adherents must be regarded in the light of supporters of usurpation and tyranny, and that they could not accept an Imam of their choice. Ali refusing to listen to them, they departed from him; hence the derivation of the name of Kharijites-that is "seceders." Their first step was to appoint an Imam of their own, maintaining that Ali resigned his right to that office by allowing his pretensions to be decided upon by those who were not Imams, and thus rendered it lawful for the Kharijites to do the same. They likewise charge Ali with the slaughter of many of their sect, and that he died without repentance, since he exhibited none of the evidence which are considered necessary corroborations of such a state. Of two of these requisite proofs, viz., restitution and reparation, he certainly made no manifestation, nor did this sect ever suffer their faith to depend upon him, nor do they shape either their faith or their notions of right by the example of the great doctors, but from the harmonious concurrence of the "Book."

Respecting Harut and Marut, to whom considerable allusion is made in the religious treatises of the Moslems, they strenuously endeavour to combat the received opinion that they were angels sent by God to Babylon, where they committed adultery with Zahrat, or Venus. Even admitting them to have been angels, say they, we are not authorised in accusing them upon less evidence than the divine law enjoins; and, by the word of God, no believing person can be accused of that crime, except on the testimony of four eyewitnesses. Without such proof, those who originate the charge are to be received as liars, and are liable to the judgment appointed for such. The Kharijites do not regard Harut and Marut as celestial creatures, but as two eminent citizens of Babylon, commissioned by God to reveal to their fellow-men the difference between right and wrong; the indifferent and the permitted; with a knowledge of the nature and peculiarities of language. Indeed, the opinion that they were men, and not angels, receives some additional confirmation from the Arabic word applied to these beings, signifying 'kings or princes" only.

In closing my brief and imperfect sketch of this remarkable scion of Islam, of which, however, except in Sale's preliminary discourse, affixed to his translation of the Quran, I am not aware we have any previous information; I shall merely notice their peculiar interpretation of that famous passage where it is said that God and his angels pray unto Mohammed. "O ye who believe, pray unto, and salute him with salutations." Now Mohammed being a servant of God, how, consistently, can He be said to pray to him? Their writers, finding this a somewhat embarrassing question, meet it by a rather ingenious evasion. They assert that the words refer to a common expression of all Muslims, when speaking of their Prophet, viz., "The blessing and peace of God be upon him," and addressed by men to God, not to the Prophet. The phrase, "pray unto him," meaning in reality, pray with respect to him. In like manner is the same prayer addressed by angels to God in his behalf, just as they entreat him to grant pardon and forgiveness to all Moslems: that Mohammed was in a remarkable manner the deputy of God, being privileged to communicate with him by articulate sounds, by the hearing of the ear, and the utterance of the tongue; therefore, say they, in a minor sense, God prayed unto, i.e., requested him.

Although the Kharijites regard the Imamship, when once lawfully obtained, as a kind of pontificate almost infallible, their arguments upon the subject much resemble those which we might imagine a Transalpine Roman Catholic, who asserts the *sole* infallibility of the Pope, might urge, if that Pope became a heretic and schismatic, and wished to use his alleged infallibility for the enforcement of his opinions. He might justly argue that his opinions annulled his office, although the dilemma still remains regarding infallible opinions as fallible. We may further observe, that the discrepancies in Muslim sects are irreconcilable, being founded upon irreconcilable texts of the Quran, and tradition only, nor can it be determined which is the repealed, and which the repealing verse.

These remarks are grounded on native information. They were principally furnished by an Arab, a singular character, who thus concludes a very curious series of notes :- "From the Fakir, Servant of God, Nasir Ibn Abu Mihan, the Distressed One!" And verily, as regards his outward man, nothing could be more appropriate than the latter portion of this designation. When I last saw him he was clothed in rags, the personification of misery, and exhibited every symptom of squalid wretchedness. A beggar, however, by choice, his state of poverty was entirely voluntary, for the prince, his master, in consideration of his great endowments, has repeatedly offered him a permanent and comfortable asylum. This he obstinately refuses to accept, preferring a vagabond, unsettled condition before the favours of a court. He therefore depends for his daily sustenance upon alms, bestowed by pious Moslems, who regard works of charity as an essential portion of their religious observances. The manuscript itself is really a literary curiosity. Some small portion has been already quoted, verbatim, in these pages, and the reader will perceive it to be imbued with a spirit which too frequently pervades religious discussions in every country. He will discover excessive spiritual pride; the fiercest intolerance towards those professing opposite tenets; and a sort of monopoly of righteousness, cloaked beneath studied meekness and assumed humility. However, notwithstanding these defects, his treatise certainly displays great subtlety of argument, with extensive theological as well as historical reading. Like Hudibras,

He could a hair divide
Betwixt the south and south-west side.

And when considered in reference to the notoriously contradictory tenets of Islamism, it is an amusing specimen of that singular aptitude, possessed by some men, for making "the worse appear the better cause."

Nasir Ibn Abu Mihan resided in Muscat at the time I left Oman. Its population must be classed under two separate heads; those who reside permanently in the towns and oases, and the Bedouins, who inhabit the intermediate Desert. The latter are the indigenous inhabitants of the country, retaining all the personal characteristics of the true sons of Ishmael; the former are fairer, and somewhat more fleshy, although the difference is far less marked here than in other settled and civilized parts of Arabia. Both classes have mixed with their Kharijite conquerors, whose faith they embraced, and all distinction is now lost between them; but they have preserved another, which is forgotten, as far as I know, in other provinces. The Arabian historians derive the present population of Oman from two stocks; Qaḥṭan (Jactan) [43], the son of Abir (Eber) and Adnan [44], the descendant of Ismail (Ishmael) [45]. In Oman, the posterity of the former are styled Hinawi (Ummari), and that of the latter Ghafiri (Gaaffri); but these terms seem peculiar to the province, for by other writers the first are called Arab Al Arabi, or pure Arabs, and the latter Al Arab Al Mustariba (El Arab el Mustarab) [46], or mixed Arabs.

These two classes in Oman regard each other with mutual hatred. The town Arabs, independent of this distinction, are also divided into tribes, who engage as fiercely in quarrel with each other as their brethren of the Desert; and the detestable laws of blood revenge are, if possible, more strictly enforced. Their feuds most commonly originate either in these or with the Sheikhs, who have constantly some hereditary or personal quarrels with their neighbours. During their continuance, hostilities are conducted in the same manner, and on the same principle of good faith, as in the Desert. Such events do not disturb the general tranquillity, and a traveller passes through the districts of rival tribes without fear of interruption. The agricultural pursuits in which they engage are not considered disreputable, as in other parts of Arabia, nor do they produce the usual effects of abridging the invincible attachment to freedom - witness the late defeat of the Wahhabis, in a pitched battle by the inhabitants of Bidiyyah, who could only assemble a third of the force brought against them. Within this favourable estimate I cannot, however, include the inhabitants of the seacoast, especially the people of Muscat, whose poltroonery has been so often displayed, that with the other tribes a Muscati and an arrant coward are held to be nearly synonymous. The Arabs who inhabit the oases and the towns within them are a proud, high minded race, less corrupted or degenerated than those who, in other parts of Arabia, have passed from the pastoral to the agricultural state: their permanent residence and attachment to the soil has indeed stripped them of but few of those distinctive qualities which are possessed by their brethren of the Desert. They are hospitable, brave, and generous, but at the same time vindictive, irascible, and-in a high degree susceptible to insult.

The most bloody affrays have originated from causes the most trifling; and I will mention, by way of proof, an incident to which I became an eye-witness. A family from a neighbouring tribe being on a visit to another in Bidiyyah, the son, a boy about ten years of age, while engaged in a struggle with another lad belonging to the town, received accidentally a cuff, which was intended by the father of the latter, who had come to separate them, for his own son. The former went away crying to his family, who were highly exasperated, and immediately took their departure for their own tribe. On the following morning, a deputation arrived at

Bidiyyah to demand some explanation of the insult. They sat down at eight o'clock to debate upon it, and several times the messengers rose, unsatisfied, to depart, in which case hostilities must immediately have ensued. The elders of the party, however, induced them again to seat themselves; and it was not until sunset that the grave matter was finally settled. A feast the next day to about twenty of the offended tribe affected a perfect reconciliation.

A difference in the moral character of those residing in towns on the sea-coast, and such as occupy the inhabited parts of the interior, is also quite as striking in Oman as in most other parts of the world. An open profligacy of manners marks the lower classes within the former, and the habits of some of the higher orders are equally sensual and degraded; but I would not be understood to apply this generally, and the care taken to prevent such irregularities from becoming publicly known, is a sufficient proof that they are not wholly indifferent to the state of their moral character. As far as I could learn, in commercial transactions with each other very little good faith is observed: nor does a departure from its principle in their social relations affect them to any considerable extent. The discharge of the duties of hospitality is as strictly exercised by all classes in Oman as in other parts of Arabia, and the stranger is everywhere received with respect [47]. As I have treated the subject of their religion elsewhere, I here merely observe that the inhabitants of Oman are far more tolerant than the generality of Muslims.

The most distinguishing and predominant trait in the character of the Arabs is their plainness and simplicity. It is not only exhibited in every act of their social intercourse, but will also be found pervading every feature of their courts of law and of their government. This freedom from pomp and ostentation, so different from other Orientals, places their character to Europeans in a very favourable light, and is, I think, with others, a reason why we estimate them higher in the scale. The following are among their most ordinary modes of salutation:-

"*As salamu alaykum!*" (Peace be with you!) To this the person addressed replies-

"*Wa alaykum as-salam!*" (With you be peace!) - are words usually proffered upon entering a room, or in joining or passing a party on the road:

"*Sabah al-khair!*" (Good day!)

"*Masa al-khair!*" (Good evening!)

"*Fi aman Allah!*" (Under God's protection!)

"*Allah yahfazak!*" (May God protect you!) Either of these forms are used upon common or ordinary visits. Upon the entrance of the guest, the host and all who are present rise and return it, and continue standing until he has seated himself. In saluting a Sheikh or governor, they add his surname to either of the above forms; and if he is of superior rank, kiss his hand. Individuals meeting abroad clasp the hand of each other. The Imam rises to Europeans visiting him, and seats them on his right hand.

CHAPTER 21
FESTIVALS AND ORNAMENTS OF WOMEN

E*ntertainments - Evening Festivals - Author's ineffectual attempts to gain admission to - Ardent Spirits - Drunkenness - how punished by the Imam - Manufactory of Wine - Gaming - Divination - Love of Swinging - Musical Instruments - Martial Music - Feast of the "Eid (Aid)" - War Dance - Condition of the Inhabitants - Dress - Offensive Arms - Shields - Food - Person and Ornaments of the Women - Sprightliness - Anecdote - Freedom of Arab Females - Sheikh Government - Civilization.*

The inhabitants of the oases and towns are very fond of giving entertainment to each other, which are sometimes continued for three or four days. Contrary in their feelings to other Orientals, they are by no means insensible to the charms of natural scenery, and their guests are usually received in light buildings, (summer-houses we should style them) detached from their own dwellings, and often picturesquely situated beneath the shade of mangoes or tamarind trees. Within these they pass the day in feasting, and the night, if report does not belie them, very often in revelling and debauchery.

I have frequently joined these parties in the day-time, but the approach of sunset, when all retired to pray, served as a pretext to dismiss me, and I never could gain admittance afterwards. That they partake generally of the forbidden pleasures of wine can admit no doubt, for large quantities are brought from the hills; and whenever brandy or other spirits are smuggled on shore at Muscat, (where they are contraband articles) the greater part is immediately carried off into the interior. Upon my arrival at Muscat I found a ship direct from England lying there, and the selection of her cargo was somewhat singular for a Muslim port, for a very large proportion consisted of hams and brandy. I do not know how far they were successful in disposing of the former, but the latter, notwithstanding the strict prohibition of the Imam, found its way to the shore in large quantities; and I heard from him that nearly half the population of Muscat was intoxicated during the time the supply lasted. One of his relatives even ventured to make his appearance before the Imam in this state; but the next day found him on his way to Zanzibar, and I am told the offence was not repeated. The more rigid Muslims not only hold it unlawful to taste wine, or to press grapes for the making of it, but they also object to the buying, selling, or even maintaining themselves with the money arising from its sale. On the Jabal Akhdar large quantities of wine is made, of which the inhabitants at their meals partake most freely and openly; 'and at all the principal towns where sugar is manufactured, they distil from its refuse an indifferent rum, which in the country finds a ready sale. Gaming, although equally forbidden by the Quran, chess, and some few Persian games played with cards brought from India, are what they usually indulge in. Their other amusements are but few: they have their professed story-tellers, who also during their feasts amuse them with songs, which they perform in a falsetto tone to the utmost extent of their voices. Divination or augury is practised in a variety of ways. I have already mentioned the burning of bladebones, from which the practitioner pretends to obtain portentous information by means of certain mystical characters which appear after partial calcination. Certain days in the month are set apart as unlucky, and on these they will neither fight, land soldiers, or put to sea. They have also recourse, for the detection of theft, to the assistance of conjurors, who follow the same plans as those of India. Both sexes are remarkably fond of swinging, and sometimes pass hours in this exercise; they seat themselves on a stick attached to a single rope, which is usually fastened to the branch of a tree. It is singular that the Arabians, who, notwithstanding the prohibition in the Quran, have always been considered a musical nation, and in whose language many treatises on harmony have been written, should possess no musical instruments of their own, and that even keeping them in their houses should be considered disgraceful. They however neither 'object nor refuse to listen to slaves playing on such as they use, which are brought from Africa; the principal one being a rude guitar possessing six strings, which pass across a piece of parchment, spread over a wooden bowl, and produces notes by no means unpleasing. The drum, an invention of Arabia, is still used by the same class, an earthen jar being very frequently substituted for the belly of the instrument. It is often used as a call to collect the troops together; a long horn curved upwards is also applied to the same purpose.

At Suwayq, I witnessed the feast of the "Eid," instituted in commemoration of God staying the hand of Ibrahim (*Abraham*). It was less showy than I have observed it to be in other parts of Arabia; for the peculiar religion they profess enjoins individuals of every class to abstain from costly articles of dress. They have consequently no expensive Cashmere shawls, as at Shaer; nor do they paint their faces in the same manner, or load their persons with such a profusion of rings and silver ornaments. The men amused themselves with horse and camel races, and with the same description of war-dance as I have described in my account of the Bani bu Ali Arabs. They also practised another, which I have never seen elsewhere: two lines form at the distance of ten or fifteen yards, and approach each other to the sound of a drum, beaten by two slaves [48] stationed midway between them. They proceed at a slow and measured pace, until within about two yards from each other, and then either party, after simultaneously bowing their heads, retreated to the same distance as before; in this manner they continued to approach, bow, and retreat as long as I remained.

Celebration event Oman

The condition of the people is in general far better than that of most other Eastern nations; and if the good or ill government of a country may be estimated by the proportion of those who enjoy independence and comfort, or the reverse, that of Oman is entitled to hold a high rank.

Accepting at Muscat, and the other towns on the sea-coast, where they are mostly pilgrims, public beggars are very rarely met. The greater number of people appear decently clothed, have substantial dwelling-houses, are exempted from all imposts and taxes; and if the country boasts no capitalists nor extensive landed proprietors, it has also few in very low or indigent circumstances, Their wealth consists in a great measure in their date groves; every tree is registered, and marriage portions and legacies often consist of them alone.

The dress of the lower classes consists of a cloth bound round the waist, called *lungi*, a turban made of chequered linen, manufactured on the Barka coast, and a coarse cloak, or *bisht*. That of the higher orders is composed of a long shirt: over this they wear a thin cloth cloak, usually of a brown colour, and open at the front and sleeves; and above all a white or dark coloured *bisht*, of very fine texture, usually brought from Nejd: a Cashmere shawl wrapped round the head as a turban, and a girdle for the *jambiya (jambir)*, completes their costume. All classes use the same description of sandal. Their arms consist of a matchlock of the same description as those usually found throughout the East; the barrel of great length, and ornamented with inlaid gold and silver. Their sword is a straight, double-edged, thin blade, about three feet in length, having a long handle, without any guard. The *jambiya*, or dagger, is usually about ten inches in length, and the haft, with those who can afford it, richly ornamented with gold. 'Their shield measures about fourteen inches in diameter, and is usually attached by a leathern thong to the sword. The best kind, made from the skin of the hippopotamus, are brought from Abyssinia. Those who accompany the Sheikh on horseback, carry with them a lance about fifteen feet in length, ornamented near the end with a tuft of feathers.

In their diet the Sheikhs and superior classes partake of a great variety of dishes, which are cooked after the Persian mode. Kid, mutton, and camel's flesh-all these are somewhat dear, and the cost of a Sheikh's table, where hospitality is so freely dispensed, must be very considerable. In addition to these articles, rice, and large quantities of *ghee* or clarified butter, are principally consumed. The chief food of the poorer, and even the middle classes, consists of dates and fish; both so cheap and plentiful, that even their cattle are fed on them. The common people use very little animal food, but they have not the same aversion to beef as the inhabitants of Hijaz and Yemen. They are also very fond of wheaten bread made into thin cakes, and toasted on the embers of their fire, or baked in ovens, built up in the shape of a jar. These it requires but a small quantity of fuel to heat, and the cakes are placed against the sides: very little *dhurra* is eaten, as the natives say it produces flatulence and indigestion. Their corn is reduced to meal by the hand-mill which is so common in all parts of the East, and found even in Scotland, where it is called a quern. It probably may be considered the most primitive kind of mill in the world, consisting simply of a couple of circular stones, about two feet in diameter. The upper one is convex, and has a handle, the lower concave. The grist is supplied through an aperture in the former, which is whirled briskly round by the hand. Females are generally employed in this duty: the operation is slow, and more is not usually ground in a day than suffices for consumption during that period: the usual time for working it is in the morning, when they accompany the operation by a not unpleasing song.

Woman Muscat

Of fruit, which is produced in such abundance, they partake but sparingly; but seem extremely fond of sugar-cane, large quantities of which are daily sold at the market.

Of fish, the largest, such as the shark and dolphin, are, by some strange perversion of taste, the most valued.

In the country, females go with their faces uncovered; but at Muscat they wear a singular description of veil of an oblong form, about ten inches in length, and seven in breadth, embroidered with a gold border. In the middle, so as to cross in a vertical direction immediately over the nose, there is a piece of whalebone answering as a stiffener; and on either side of these two small apertures, through which they obtain a view of passing objects. Among the lower classes, their dress otherwise consists of a loose pair of drawers, with a running girdle, and a large gown or skirt of blue cotton; their arms and ankles are decorated with bracelets and ankle-rings of silver or amber; and in their ears they wear a variety of rings and other ornaments. The dress of the more respectable females is quite as simple, but the materials are silk of Indian manufacture; and over the gown, when abroad, they wear a large wrapper. They display their love of finery in the gold ornaments with which they decorate their heads. A singular custom also prevails of staining the entire person with henna. Shenna, a moss collected from the granite mountains in the Island of Socotra, is also used for a similar purpose. In addition to this, the lower classes aim at further enhancing their claims to personal beauty by exhibiting on their arms and faces various tattoo devices of a blue colour.

In their persons the females are tall and well made, with a roundness and fullness of figure, not, however, approaching corpulency. Their complexion is not darker than that of a Spanish brunette, and we may infer that this is their natural colour, since, excepting in the morning and evening, those who reside in the oases rarely leave their date groves, and in the towns they preserve their complexions with the same care. On the other hand, the Bedouin women, who are constantly exposed to the rays of the sun, are very swarthy; and the same is observed of the men, although the children are equally fair at their birth. The expression of their countenance is very pleasing; their eyes being large, vivacious, and sparkling; their nose somewhat aquiline; the mouth regular; and the teeth of a pearly whiteness. They are, without doubt, in point of personal attraction, superior to any other class which I have seen in Arabia. Of a gay and sprightly disposition, the smile of mirth constantly plays about their features; and any witty allusion in their conversation with each other, or ludicrous incident, however trifling, is sufficient to excite their laughter.

In the towns near the sea-coast, females of condition are secluded with as much care as in any other part of the eastern world; but the practice is optional with themselves, and they take the liberty of dispensing with it when they please. At the house of an Arab merchant whom I was in the habit of visiting, it was found impossible to restrain the curiosity of the females of his harem, who, desirous of seeing an European, were constantly flitting before the door of the apartment in which we were seated. My friend bore this with patience for some time, and strove by remonstrances to prevent it; but finding those ineffectual, he watched his opportunity when I next made my appearance, and turned the key of the harem upon the whole of them; but such an outrageous clamour was immediately raised by its inmates, that he was but too happy before I went away to release them. There is indeed little doubt that the Muslim ladies in Oman enjoy more liberty, and at the same time are more respected, than in any other eastern country. During civil commotions, they often take a part in public affairs, and in some instances have displayed the utmost heroism.

Amidst the most striking features in the condition of this interesting and singular race stands their Sheikh government, which, in its constitution and operative effects, is a political phenomenon in the history of nations. Although neither a republic, an aristocracy, nor a kingdom, it nevertheless possesses the elements of them all; and when we consider the ages for which it has endured, the slight degree of political restraint which it imposes on the people, the warriors it has reared and sent forth from time to time from its own unconquered wilds to devastate and ravage other regions, it furnishes a subject worthy our particular attention and study.

Arabia was among the first nations which felt the effects of civilization; and although it was here that the first large societies of men united themselves for mutual protection, yet, by an anomaly in the history of the world, their government has remained with but slight additions to its original simple and patriarchal form, from the earliest periods to which historical information reaches until the present moment. The remark applies especially to the southern part of this vast continent, for we learn by the traditions of the country, and the authority of eastern writers, that shortly after the deluge, a remnant of the few who were saved by divine mercy from that awful catastrophe, settled at Al Akas, in the province of Hadramaut. These were said to have been of the tribe of the son of Uz, the son of Shem, and from this stock Arabia is supposed to have been peopled.

CHAPTER 22
ARAB CULTURE AND GOVERNANCE

O*rigin of Bedouin Government - Authority of the Patriarchs - Bedouin Warfare - Invasion of Aelius Gallus - Defeat of Persians, - Turks, and Egyptians - Policy of Mohammed' Ali - Causes of the tranquillity of Oman - Power of life and death - Anecdote - Attachment to their Chiefs - Contrast between the Arabs of the Town and of the Desert - Notice of various Tribes - Independence of each other - Transfer of power - Price of blood - The Imam's Government - Court-Titles.*

It would be foreign to my present design were I to attempt to discuss in detail the origin and general history of the Bedouin government, the cause of its long continuance, or the circumstances which have induced the surplus population to migrate and carry but a portion of its elements to other parts. A brief abstract will nevertheless be necessary, in order to exhibit the political and physical relation of the two classes, which, as scattered pastoral tribes, or an agricultural and commercial people, inhabit the province of Oman, and which now, in their filiation, dialect, and advance in civilization, differ so materially from each other, that it has been necessary to treat of them severally. In the earlier stages of society mankind readily acknowledged obedience to the person to whom they owed their being. By a very natural chain of reasoning we can follow the extension of an authority which was vested in the father of a family over the different branches of it, or, in other words, a tribe. This would continue until the number of the tribe became too unwieldy to follow up their marches, or the scanty pasturage was insufficient for the increased number of their flocks [49]. It then became necessary that a portion should separate and seek for sustenance in more distant provinces. Age for a time would still continue to confine the authority to the patriarch, or his immediate descendants, who had conducted them in their wanderings; but, as the latter increased in number and ramifications, it must necessarily happen that the heads of the different tribes would select some person (though probably the nearer the parent stem the better) who, in their precarious mode of life, had made himself conspicuous by his valour or wisdom, and was adapted to be their leader during war, or to preside in their councils during peace. As they spread forth, they would still view with interest and affection the stock from whom they sprang, and, upon the appearance of a common enemy, would unite themselves by a voluntary and mutual contract to expel him. Should their strength at first be unequal to effect this openly, they fled to their deserts, at all times an impenetrable place of refuge, and from thence never ceased to harass and annoy the invader until they drove him from their country.

How successful their adoption of this natural mode of warfare has ever proved may be gathered from the result of the different invasions which have been directed against them. When Aelius Gallus penetrated from the shores of the Red Sea, the inhabitants, making but a slight resistance, retired before him; but no sooner had they drawn him by these means into the interior, where his troops began to be wasted by sickness, than they attacked him with so much fury that he was glad to escape with a miserable remnant into Egypt, and leave Arabia as unconquered as before. In the same manner they rid themselves at a subsequent period of the Persians, who at one time, under Khosrow I Anushirvan (*Nurshivan*), possessed the greater part of their frontier, including Oman; of the Abyssinians, who ravaged Hijaz and Yemen; and, finally, of the Turks, who for a period fixed themselves in Yemen.

It remains to be proved whether the wily policy of Mohammed Ali, who is supposed to contemplate the subjection of the whole peninsula, will surmount these difficulties. His former success against the Wahhabis affords no criterion by which we can judge; for those secretaries were considered by the more orthodox Arabians as a common enemy; and the union of several Arab tribes with his own troops alone enabled him to bring that war to a successful termination. The late destruction of his army-then well appointed and well commanded in the Asir country would rather induce us to anticipate no better conclusion to his efforts than, as I have just shown, attended those of former invaders.

The yoke which at several periods was imposed on these people proved so partial and endured for such a brief period, that no considerable change was effected in their general character and condition. Arabia, from this cause, as well as its peculiar position, has been exempted from the mighty tempests which have swept the neighbouring nations from the face of the earth, and left us nothing but their names. Even the mission of Mohammed, which shook and subverted the whole of the civilized world, failed to produce any permanent change. A history, therefore, of the whole or any part of Modern Arabia is valuable, since a picture of what they now are will exhibit, with but slight shades of difference, what they ever have been.

Although the Grand Sheikhs of the principal tribes have in some cases the power of life and death, and also that of declaring war and peace, yet their authority in every instance is considerably abridged by the aged and other influential men of the tribe. In civil and criminal affairs they act rather as arbiters than as judges, and cases of importance are sometimes debated by the whole tribe. With an authority so limited, I was in a particular degree impressed with the extraordinary care and affection which is generally testified by the tribes of Oman towards their persons. There is, in this respect, a marked difference between these Bedouins and the natives of the sea-coast of Oman and Hadramaut.

A few years ago two vessels richly laden were cast on shore to the east of Ras Al Had (*Roselhad*), within the limits of the Bani bu Ali Bedouins, who with the neighbouring tribe, the Bani Janaba, immediately plundered them. None of the crew were injured. There was a Jew on board who was sick.

When he was carried to the shore, a Bedouin took charge of him, and upon his promising to pay a certain number of Dollars, engaged to convey him to Muscat. Fearing, however, as he was very sick, that he might die on the road, and that he would then not only lose his reward, but perhaps also get into trouble, the Bedouin stipulated for a written engagement. As the Jew could not write, he dipped his fingers in ink, and left them impressed on the paper. Upon this the British Resident proceeded to Sur, and sent for the Sheikh of the former tribe, who resides some distance inland. Fearing the vengeance of the English, whose power he had already too severely felt, if he came, but dreading still more to refuse, he gave an unwilling assent, and proceeded, accompanied by the whole of his tribe, to the sea-beach. When there, they strove by tears and entreaties to dissuade him from his purpose of proceeding to the vessel, under a decided impression, as they explained to me, that he would be carried to Bombay, and imprisoned, as before. Nevertheless, he went, was received with much attention, and, after concluding a treaty, by which he bound himself, under condition of receiving a handsome salvage on future occasions, to collect and take charge of the property of any British vessels wrecked on the shores of his territories, he was again landed. The joy of his tribe, who remained in the greatest terror and anxiety during his absence, now knew no bounds; and, after being nearly suffocated by their anxiety to salute him, he was placed on the shoulders of two of their number, and carried away in triumph.

The Bedouins who traverse the frontiers of Oman, as well as those who occupy the intermediate space between the oases, have lost none of that attachment to a wandering life which characterises them in other parts of Arabia. It is true they acknowledge the authority of the Imam, since their chiefs secure presents by doing so, and nothing can be gained by pursuing an opposite course; but the obedience which is conceded to him does not exceed that rendered by the several minor Sheikhs to a great Sheikh, or "Sheikh of Sheikhs." He can, as with the agricultural class, command their services during war; but in peace they pursue, without any interference from him, their own nomadic and pastoral habits. Aware of the power which they would obtain over them, could the Bedouins be fixed in towns and villages, or their attention be turned to agricultural pursuits, every encouragement has been offered by the Imams to induce them to change their habits, nor have they been wholly unsuccessful.

Impure air, irregular diet, and other causes, increase the consumption of life within cities, while the Labourers who cultivate the oases are again less healthy than the hardy inhabitants of the Desert. In order to supply these deficiencies, a regular progressive migration must be kept up, or when it fails, as it has done of late years, large tracts of cultivated lands become abandoned. Several instances were, however, related to me of those who had passed from a pastoral to an agricultural state, but who could never forget their Bedouin habits, and frequently after a residence of many years in the oases, would again flee to the Desert. Facilities are afforded by those desirous of employing themselves in the cultivation of the land in Oman, which do not exist in other parts of Arabia, since they are neither kept in poverty nor ruined by the exorbitancy of the taxes.

In the course of this narrative of my travels I have given an account of the Beni bu Hasan, Bani bu Ali, and the Bani Janaba Bedouins; it only remains to notice a few others. The Beni Ghafiri muster eight hundred men: these, with the Yemeni and Al Arabi, are the most ancient and illustrious of the tribes of Oman. The latter boast of a descent from the Quraysh (*Korish*) at Makkah (Mekka). The Ghafiri were originally from Nejd, where the parent stem still remains. In the seventeenth century one of their number filled the throne of Oman, and their present chief, Musallam Ibn Massu, still refuses to acknowledge the sovereignty of Sayyid Said. I have already noticed that he resides in a castle near to Manah, from whence he occasionally sallies and annoys the surrounding country. The Beni bu Hasan amount to one thousand men. They live in various towns, but attend only to their camels, and, with the Janaba, the Meyan, and the Beni Kitab, are the carriers of Oman. Their wives and slaves occasionally till the ground, but the men would consider it a disgrace to do so.

The Bedouins who occupy the great Western Desert have neither houses nor tents, but live under the shade of trees.

It is by no means held binding here that the son should follow the occupation of his father. The former may sometimes reside in the town, and the latter on the Desert; but however long they may be permanently fixed, they never forget the tribe from which they sprang; and during the sojourn of Bedouins in Muscat or other towns, they are usually lodged with, and fed by such relatives.

Such are the principal tribes in Oman. I made myself acquainted with the names, number, &c., of upwards of a hundred others, but as they only vary in these respects, it would prove neither interesting or amusing to give the mere catalogue.

Each of these tribes being governed, in a measure, by its own ruler, acts on ordinary occasions as a civil community independent of its neighbours; but the smaller are commonly under the influence of the larger tribes. Yet this alliance hangs by so slight a thread that the veriest trifle is sufficient to sever it. If dissatisfied with their Sheikh, or they think they can better themselves, they quit his protection and obtain that of another, very possibly a rival. Thus, their numbers and strength are constantly changing, and the mal-administration of a single individual may reduce his rule over a powerful tribe to that over its mere skeleton. This is one of the principal features in the Sheikh government, and it is one to which they are indebted for a considerable portion of the liberty they enjoy. From their jarring interests and natural love of strife, they are generally at feud with someone, and if a tribe then finds itself unequal to maintain its position, it connects itself with another, or even with several others. These irregularities, so long as they are confined to themselves, are, in a measure, controlled by that part of their system which renders each particular tribe amenable not only to the Imam, but also to the several other tribes; and in cases where they suffer by any misconduct, and remonstrance is found unavailing, they do not scruple to avenge their wrongs by the sword. But these wars are neither very bloody, nor of very long duration. The price of blood, repugnant as it is to our feelings, seems not without its benefits, for, as compensation after these encounters is made for the slain, men's lives are too valuable to be wantonly destroyed; and the death of a few individuals rarely fails to bring the offending party to reason.

Thus they proceed in affairs amidst them selves; but if the matter, from the invasion of the interior tribes, or from other quarters, affects the safety or general interest of the province, the whole body, nomadic and agricultural, professing a common faith, which is regarded with great aversion by all other classes of Muslims, and recollecting their common ancestry, unite themselves firmly to deliberate upon and to oppose it. By such an union this isolated race have maintained their independence from the early period at which they first settled in this province, until the present time.

The details which I have given of the Bani bu Ali Bedouins indicate a deep-felt attachment for their tribe, and how freely they sacrifice life in defence of its fame. Indeed, if we contrast the character of the Bedouin, in general, with that of his neighbours, how immeasurably he stands before them! - his patriotism and natural independence rendering him as far superior to the Persian-a polished slave, - whose best energies are chilled by despotism,-as his superior physical strength, hardihood, and courage, place him before the placid, mild, enervated Hindu.

An Arab of the Desert knows and displays this in his behaviour and conversation. He believes himself to be the purest and best of the human race, and it is for the indulgence of these feelings that he infinitely prefers his own wilds to the comparative luxury of an abode in cities. Although disputes constantly occur between Arabs, accompanied by violent behaviour and gesticulations, yet, even in the extremity of anger, they never utter those disgusting epithets so familiar to the natives of India or Persia. An Arab's phraseology is simple and manly: for were he to give vent to expressions directly impeaching his opponent's honour and hospitality or those of his tribe, nothing short of the offender's blood would atone for the insult.

With the exception of Sohar, which has been under the dominion of another chief for some years, the whole of Oman formally acknowledged the sway of the reigning Imams; but in 1829, Shinas, and the ports from thence to the northward, threw off the yoke. The former has since returned to his authority, and its fort has admitted a party of Balouchi soldiers, but the other portion still, in a measure, remains independent of him.

None of the different forms of government in Arabia have excited more attention and discussion in Europe than that of the Imam, which, from its association of spiritual with temporal power, may be compared to that of the Pope. Niebuhr, in his visit to the coast in 1762, has furnished a full description of the constitution of the government of Sanaa (*Sana*), but that of the prince of Muscat differs in many most essential points: thus, the former rules through the intervention of a divan, which serves greatly to control his power and abridge his authority; while the latter, although he is content to leave the cognizance of civil affairs to the decision of the *qadi*, yet, in all such cases as require his interference he possesses the free exercise of his own will [50].

The rule at present exercised over those provinces of Oman which are subjected to the sway of the Imam of Muscat, is probably more mild, equable, and regular, than any other in Arabia, or perhaps any native dynasty of the East.

Yet, with all his able qualities, the Imam's government has on more than one occasion been placed in the greatest jeopardy. Ever restless, and incessantly on the look-out for some pretext to sanction their giving vent to a natural love of strife, his relations have usually taken advantage of his absence to Zanzibar to carry their views into effect. The defection of Sohar and the northern provinces has already been noticed: and in 1829 a party, headed by his nephew, obtained possession of Muscat, but the British government sent immediate intimation to the Imam of what was passing, and were prepared with ships and men to aid him in the recovery of it. This manifestation was in itself sufficient, when it became known, to arrest the progress of the rebellion, and the leaders, upon the arrival of the Imam, surrendered and threw themselves on his mercy. I believe the imprisonment of his nephew for about a week was the heaviest punishment which he inflicted on any one concerned. These irregularities appear inseparable from Muslim and eastern governments. The son no sooner comes of age than he plots against the father; and as the practice of polygamy has a tendency to confuse the order of succession, which here, as in other parts, is nominally hereditary, rival claimants seek by intrigue to establish and strengthen their cause at an early period, and before the death of the reigning prince. No sooner does this take place, than a general scene of strife and contention arises; the various Bedouin tribes hire themselves to different parties, and the contest lasts until the success of one individual more skilful or powerful than his competitors, obtains the prize. Compensation is then made to the friends of the slain, and things are restored to their original condition. On the death of the present Imam, the government will probably be contested by Sayyid Mohammed his nephew, and Sayyid Hilal, his son, the former of whom he is said to favour.

The reigning Imam has also to contend with another difficulty. Oman was formerly portioned out amidst a variety of Sheikhs, influenced by separate and jarring interests, and frequently setting the authority of the prince at defiance. Sayyid Said has in a measure remedied this, by granting these governments as they become vacant to his own officers, as a reward for military service. But in a country like Arabia, the life of an individual is too short, and the difficulties he has to encounter are too great, to enable him to establish a fixed and lasting principle of government. Yet this great prince, with his imperfect means, has done more than could be expected of him; and had he been backed by efficient troops, instead of the most indifferent to be found in Arabia, his career would, in all probability, have been boundless; but their want of bravery has occasionally subjected him to severe defeats.

His enlightened policy has greatly increased the commercial wealth and importance of Muscat, and he has more than doubled the extent of territory which was possessed by his ancestors on the coast of Africa. Beyond the general election of the several Chiefs, the theological discourse which is delivered by the Imam, and his vow to abstain from entering on board ships, no other oaths are required, nor are there any ceremonies of installation. His court is small, and almost entirely devoid of pomp; "*Sayyid na*" (*Said na*), "My Lord," is the title by which he is addressed, and those who approach him salute the back of his hand.

CHAPTER 23
THE IMAM OF OMAN

Administration of Justice - Family Feuds - Anecdote - Religious Toleration - Districts of Oman - Responsibility of the Sheikhs - Right of Appeal - Police - Revenge of Injuries - Government Resources - Revenue - The Imam's Household - His Munificent Character - Standing Army - Feudalism in Oman - Population - Towns - Map of Oman.

In the administration of justice at Muscat, the *qadis* take cognizance of all minor offences; but the Imam decides those of a graver cast. Although his power in every case is absolute, yet his aversion to the spilling of human blood might form a lesson to more civilized potentates: for murder, and murder alone, is the punishment of death inflicted. In the more distant towns, Sayyid Said has found it impracticable to abolish the sanguinary custom (which exists there in common with other parts of Arabia) of the friends of the deceased retaliating on either the slayer or his relations; but these quarrels are strictly forbidden in Muscat. As, however, they sometimes do occur, notwithstanding the Imam's vigilance, the relations of the person, as in Persia, are allowed their choice of demanding the life of the murderer, or accepting a compensation. At Sur, I saw an old man between seventy and eighty years of age, who constantly carried with him his matchlock loaded and primed; and upon inquiring the cause, was informed that he had a quarrel of this nature on his hands. It is one of the most remarkable traits in the character of the Arabs, that in the following up of these family feuds, they frequently permit years to pass before they have an opportunity of wreaking their vengeance on the individuals concerned. It is strange where religious toleration forms one of the most prominent features of the government, that a Muslim is permitted to compound for the death of a Banian, by the payment of a sum of money for the service of the mosque.

Oman is divided into districts, known by various designations, which also apply to their inhabitants. These, as I have just mentioned, are governed by Sheikhs, each of whom is responsible to the Imam for the good government of his respective district. All these chiefs acknowledge the supremacy of the Imam; and for rebellion, or withholding supplies of men when called on to furnish them, imprisonment and confiscation of property are inflicted. Sayyid Said seems, however, much more desirous to conciliate their esteem by presents, and to secure their cooperation for military purposes and the good order of his dominions, than to prejudice them against his person or his measures.

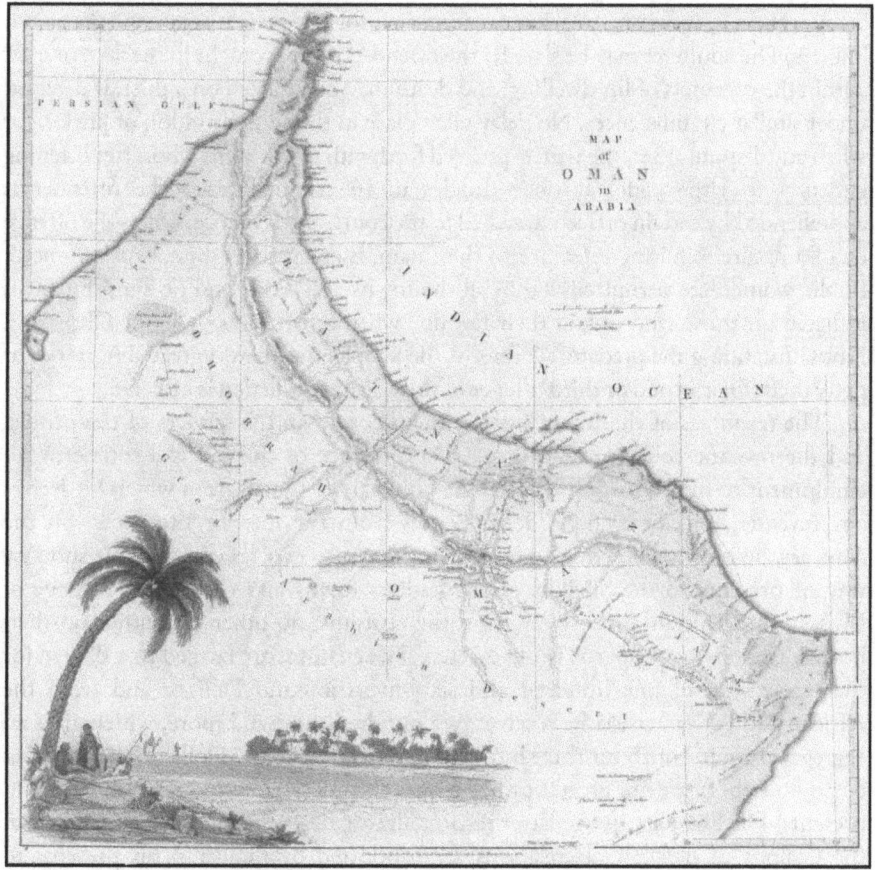

While the attention of the Imam is thus directed to the interest of his dominions generally, the details are left to these chieftains, and the power they possess in their several districts is still in consequence very considerable. It extends over the persons and property of the people, but not to their lives. A right of appeal to the Imam exists in every case, his decision being final and binding. A Sheikh would therefore find it very difficult to abuse his power, and personal security, as well as the rights of private property, are generally respected by them. They have no regular police for the maintenance of order; but the military retainers of these chiefs are usually employed for carrying the necessary measures into execution; and as the Imam supports but a small permanent force, the district Sheikh employs the same individuals for the execution of any order which he receives from him. The inferior Sheikhs exercise a like authority over their dependents, and the father over his family. Beyond the institutes of the Quran they have no regular code of laws; but when these are strictly administered, they appear admirably adapted to meet the cases which most commonly occur in such a country. It is, however, by no means unusual for the people to avenge their own injuries. The adulterer may be slain by the offended party if caught in the fact, or even within the precincts of his dwelling; and death may be inflicted on a thief, if detected under similar circumstances. No delay takes place in the administration of justice, for when any dispute arises, the parties proceed forthwith to the *qadi*, who, after listening patiently to either side, at once decides it. In criminal cases, the offender is apprehended by certain officers attached to the court, and sentence, unless the offence be of a nature requiring reference to the Imam, is executed as soon as pronounced. Public women are permitted within all the towns and oases, and no punishment is inflicted on those who obtain their favours, whether Muslims, Jews, or Christians. Notwithstanding the predatory habits of the people, they have a great abhorrence of petty theft; for a second or third offence of this nature mutilation is inflicted.

The resources of the Imam's government consist in the services of the people, and the revenue collected at Muscat. The produce of the soil is a source of no emolument to him. Muscat is indeed the only part of Oman from which he derives any revenue, for not a single dollar comes from the interior provinces; on the contrary, he is compelled during his stay in Arabia to expend considerable sums by way of presents to the Sheikhs of the various towns and oases. The revenue at Muscat and Mutrah arises solely from the customs, no other tax, either on their houses, persons, or property, being exacted. The customs are farmed to a Banian for the yearly sum of one hundred and sixty-five thousand Dollars; and from the African and Persian coasts he receives two hundred thousand more, which gives an aggregate revenue of about three hundred and sixty thousand Dollars. The expenses of his household are not great, but he lavishes considerable sums on his ships and in presents, His liberality in the latter respect almost rivals the tales which are told of the Caliphs of old. All his relations are supported by him, and his presents to strangers who visit him are magnificent in the extreme; and it rarely happens that the poorest Arab is allowed to depart without receiving some token by which he may remember the visit. Bedouins arriving in Muscat are fed at his expense, and when they depart are provided with as much food as they can carry away with them.

I was once present when one of the men entrusted with the charge of his horses entered the chamber, and reminded his Highness that when he had been looking at them on the previous evening he received no present. The Imam listened patiently to his tale, and then directed the treasurer to present him with ten Dollars. Such generosity is esteemed by the Arabs as the greatest virtue which a prince can possess, while the opposite extreme is held in equal detestation. Speaking of Sayyid Said, whose liberality has obtained for him the designation of the second Omar, they observe that he never refuses what is asked from him; and that for the customary offering to a superior so general throughout the East, the Imam usually returns its value one hundred fold; and for any works executed by his order, he pays a higher rate than other individuals.

The only permanent force which the Imam keeps at Muscat is a small body of four hundred men, accoutred in the same manner as the sepoys of India. Some of these are also his domestic slaves, but upon occasions which might require it, he could from Southern Oman collect in three days an army of ten thousand men and afterwards increase the number to thrice the amount, by the accession of several Bedouin Sheikhs and their followers, who would readily join for the sake of the share in the plunder, and the occasional presents which they obtain from him.

In conclusion, I cannot but notice that, in some of its prominent features, a considerable resemblance may be traced between the present government of Oman and that of the old feudal states in Europe. We have there, in the person of the Imam, the representative of the regal power: the chiefs, on whom he has bestowed governments, as a reward for fighting under his banner when called upon, resemble the feudal barons; while the people, released from all taxes, hold possession of the soil by the same tenure as the ancient vassal, viz., that of military service. A castle or tower is attached to each of these governments; and, whenever the authority of the Imam has not been well supported, the chiefs who held possession of them, like the barons, have called around them their retainers, and bid him open defiance.

Owing to the wandering habits of the Bedouins, it is very difficult to fix with precision the amount of the population of this province; but, during my stay there, I took considerable pains to obtain an account as accurate as possible. Southern Oman: is but thinly peopled, for the whole number, including women and children, does not exceed fifty thousand; but the northern districts are far more populous, and probably contain, including Muscat and Mutrah, two hundred and fifty thousand souls, which I am convinced is rather within than above the mark.

Valley in Oman - Wellsted

The Batinah coast, throughout its whole length, is thickly studded with towns and villages; and amidst the valleys, wherever the ground affords a sufficient space for tillage, are found hamlets of ten or twenty houses each.

With the exception of Rustaq, which is extensive and well built, there are no towns of any extent in the interior. Many of those which from native information have figured in our maps as large cities, and are even classed by Niebuhr as principalities, do not now rise into more importance than villages or hamlets. The ruins of houses, and the remains of former embankments, denote however both a superior population and more extensive cultivation; but, wherever irrigation ceases, the course of a few seasons converts the land, however fertile it may have previously been, into a desert.

All the towns, &c. are now situated either within or contiguous to an oasis; and these, with their inhabitants, have been so fully described in the course of this work, that it would neither amuse nor interest the reader were I to recur to them; but, in order to bring any peculiarity or additional information as much as possible into one focus, I have added on the face of the map a brief description of each.

The direction of my several journeys is also pointed out in the map. In order to show the degree of confidence to which this may be entitled, it is necessary I should state that all the principal towns, villages, and oases, are fixed from actual observation; and, with the exception of Rustaq, which is placed in the position it occupies from compass bearings, and Buraymi, the frontier station of the

Wahhabis, there is no place of importance in Oman, the geographical site of which has not been correctly determined. And here I may be permitted to observe that, although from untoward circumstances I was prevented from reaching Diriyah; yet, in adding a description of a province equal in extent to Syria to the scanty knowledge of Arabia which we previously possessed, I trust it will be apparent that the several months I remained there were neither inactively nor unprofitably employed.

CHAPTER 24
POLITICAL RELATIONS OF THE IMAM

H*abitations - Architecture - Interior of the Houses - The Harem - Slave - trade - The Imam's consent to its Abandonment - Reflections - Description and Amount of Slaves - How distinguished - Value - Kind Treatment - Punishment - Household Slaves - Education of Slaves - Historical Account of Oman - Our Political Relations with its Prince - Russian Invasion of India - By what Route - Importance of an intimate Alliance with the Imam - His Navy - Port of Muscat - Ungenerous Behaviour of the British Government - Conclusion.*

With the exception of Muscat and Rustaq, where they are constructed of stone, the houses throughout Oman are built either with sun-dried bricks or loose stones cemented with mud. They are, in consequence, far from desirable edifices, and a smart shower of some continuance scarcely fails to level many of them. As some protection from these accidents they use a cement composed of mud, straw, and pebbles, which is smoothed and consolidated by the hand alone. The larger sort of houses are of a square form, and built round an open court. Around each floor there runs a gallery, into which the several apartments open. These are usually spacious and lofty, with ceilings of wood, often painted in rude devices. The walls, which are whitewashed, are formed of cane; and around them on pegs hang their horse and camel trappings. They make their floors of earth smoothed and hardened by rollers, and usually cover them with a mat; but no furniture of any description is seen in their rooms, their meals being taken on a carpet spread for the purpose. These houses have but one entrance; they are surrounded by a wall, and seem designed to serve as places of defence. The dwellings of the poorer classes are of the same materials, and consist of only two square rooms, one above the other-the upper one answering for their harem, and the under for the reception of visitors.

Muscat is a great mart for slaves: nearly all those required for the supply of the shores of the Persian Gulf, Baghdad, and Basrah, are purchased here. The Imams formerly engaged in this traffic, and realized thereby an annual revenue of sixty thousand Dollars, or about thirteen thousand pounds; but Sayyid Said, in order to gratify our Government, who were then earnest in their endeavours to suppress the trade, with unprecedented liberality gratuitously abandoned the whole. For this he has received no equivalent. Is this generous? is it just? To Spain, a Christian Government; we gave two hundred thousand pounds for a similar abandonment, and remitted some millions of their debt; yet, to a Muslim prince, professing a faith which openly sanctions, if it does not actually enjoin, slavery, we have given-our acknowledgments !-at least, I hope we have, though I have never heard of any. *Proh pudor!* Let not England, who has hitherto stood forward in a cause which may be said to have elevated beyond all others the age in which we live, and to have stamped it with a die inscriptive of the purest practical essence of Christianity, be outrivalled in generosity by the ruler of a remote part of Arabia!

I am informed that at Muscat about four thousand slaves, of both sexes and all ages, are disposed of annually. They may be divided into three classes: the Towaylee, from the Zanzibar coast, who are known by having their teeth filed, sometimes to a point, and sometimes in notches like those of a saw. They have also some perpendicular incisions on either cheek, made with a penknife when the children are five or six years of age. The scars which remain denote the tribe to which they belong [51]. The price of a Towaylee is from forty to sixty Dollars. The Nabi, who come from the interior of Africa, are said to be vindictive and treacherous. The Bedouins, here as in the Hijaz, are the only purchasers. The Gallas, brought from Abyssinia, are highly valued; they fetch from one hundred to one hundred and fifty Dollars; the price of the females being about the same as that of the males, and strength, health, and good temper in the latter, are considered as a set-off against the comeliness of the former. They bring eunuchs occasionally from Darfur, which fetch from two to three hundred Dollars, and are mostly purchased by the Persians. It is some alleviation to learn, at the same time that we are made aware of the great extent of the slave-trade in these countries, that they are treated with considerable kindness. In Arabia, indeed, there is but little difference between servitude and slavery; for that can scarcely be deemed compulsatory where, if displeased with his master, the slave can go to the *qadi* and demand a public sale. This, however, very rarely occurs: the master's authority extends to selling, exchanging, and punishing them; but he cannot, even for crimes which the law deems worthy of death, inflict that punishment without a public trial. If a master furnishes a slave with a wife, and she bears sons and daughters, the wife and children are sold with the father. Upon the death of the master the slaves are usually set free. The Muslim law forbids the making slaves of Muslims; but a slave brought up in that faith, who has been once manumitted, can again voluntarily engage himself to another master. Arabs of condition have two or more slaves to assist them in their household establishment, besides others who are placed in situations of trust. In either instance they receive a degree of consideration and kindness which is not always extended to servants in Europe. When purchased young, they are brought up in the profession of the Muslim faith, are taught to read and write, and, when they arrive at a sufficient age, are often placed in command of ships or boats, and intrusted with most valuable cargoes.

During my stay in Oman, I made repeated efforts to obtain information which would enable me to draw up an historical account of the province; but the difficulties in a country where no one commits passing events to paper, are insurmountable. I give the result of my inquiries as far as they went, observing, in passing, that the silence of the Arabians themselves, the natural consequence of their unlettered condition, may, perhaps, be supplied from the annals of their neighbours the Persians [52]. In a summary of the religious tenets peculiar to this people already given, the reader has seen the motives which induced a considerable number of the Prophet's followers to desert their chief, settle in Oman, and choose an Imam or Caliph of their own. This event occurred during the wars in which Ali ibn Talib, the son-in-law of Mohammed, was engaged, in order to possess himself of the disputed Caliphate; and these seceders then received the appellation of "Kharijites," a term of reproach their sect still retains.

Excepting during the brief sway of the Portuguese, the sovereignty of Oman remained in the family of the Yarubi Al Azd for two hundred and fifty years. I think it will be considered sufficient if I begin with Saif [53].

This Prince, in 1658, drove the Portuguese from Muscat: he took Zanzibar, and several ports on the African, a few on the Persian, and one or two others on the Makran coast, with Bahrain, Qeshm, and many other islands in the Persian Gulf. His descendants lost Bahrain, which threw off the yoke towards the close of the last century, but have retained the others. Saif was succeeded by Sultan, Muhammad bin Nasir Al Ghafiri, and Saif bin Sultan II (*Seif, son of Sultan*).

The reign of Saif was stormy and unhappy. He deviated from those mild principles of government which had distinguished the reigns of his predecessors, and not only oppressed his subjects himself, but permitted his soldiers to plunder and annoy them. At the same time he forsook their frugal habits, addicting himself to wine, and other licentious pursuits, and even attempted the chastity of his subjects' daughters. His cousins, the elders of his tribe, reasoned with him in vain, until, finding the whole country was thrown into confusion, and that his subjects were gradually becoming more disaffected, they at length wrote to Ahmed ibn Said, the chief of Sohar, who bore the reputation of being the most politic of the princes of Oman. They stated that it was their intention to depose Saif, and elect Sultan bin Murshid, one of the same family, in his room, and required his sanction and cooperation. Ahmed replied that he should in nowise oppose their resolves, adding that, since the present Prince had shewn himself unworthy of their confidence, he would render allegiance to any person whom they might deem most fitting to succeed him. Before the plot was ripe for execution, Saif became in some manner acquainted with it. In the first transports of his rage he slew all those within his reach, and imprisoned others; but a remnant escaped, and proclaimed Sultan bin Murshid to be Imam. The greater part of Oman immediately submitted to this chief, and district after district continuing to fall to him, Saif at length found himself shut up in Muscat, his only remaining possession. His soldiers, still attached to him, from the greater license given them in the decline of his affairs to rob and plunder the inhabitants, garrisoned' the two citadels which command the town, and Sultan bin Murshid was unable to approach it. He, however, took possession of the neighbouring town of Mutrah, which has also a capacious port, and by reducing the duties, drew so many vessels there, that Saif, to prevent the utter ruin of Muscat, found himself compelled to solicit assistance from the Persians, and for this purpose he proceeded in one of his largest ships to Bandar Abbas. Nadir Shah, then King of Persia, who, with a force of ten thousand men, some months before, had made an unsuccessful attack on that town, immediately acceded to his request, and placed a force under Taqi Khan Shirazi (*Tiki Khan*), nominally at his disposal; but that general, at the same time, was instructed to lose no opportunity of possessing himself of the whole province. This being accomplished, Saif returned to Muscat, while the Persians landed at Ras Al Khaimah. After many conflicts the greater part of Oman surrendered to them, and at length they approached Muscat, but finding their troops were not admitted into the citadels, they invited Saif to a feast, and having plied him with wine until he was insensible, they attached his signature to a written order, requiring the governors to admit them into their forts. The order was obeyed without demur, and the Persians thus obtained possession without striking a blow. When the unhappy Prince awoke from his intoxication, he found himself betrayed, and, overwhelmed with the misfortunes which he had brought on himself and his country, in a few months afterwards died of grief. Sultan bin Murshid took refuge in Sohar, which had not yet surrendered, but against which the Persians now marched. The Imam was killed in a sortie, but Ahmed ibn Said defended himself nobly; and after a protracted siege of eight months, the Persians were constrained to permit him to retain his government, upon condition of acknowledging allegiance to their king. The death of Nadir Shah, which followed a few years after these events, drew great numbers of the invaders to their own country, and Ahmed found little difficulty in ridding himself of the remainder.

This effected, he convened a meeting of the chiefs and elders of the tribes, and reminding them that the government of the country belonged to the Arab family, invited them to name an Imam from that stock, and professed his willingness to obey whomsoever they might nominate. Mohammed bin Sultan then arose, and said that none could advance superior claims to those of the individual who had rescued his country from the yoke of foreigners, and taking Ahmed by the hand he proclaimed him Imam; which election was joyfully acceded to by the others, and ratified by the general voice of the people. But Ahmed was not destined to hold his office without a struggle. Bilarab Al Kamyar, a relation of Murshid, and Prince of Jabrin, when the intelligence was conveyed to him, immediately marched against the new Imam. After much skirmishing, Bilarab was slain by a son of Ahmed. By marrying himself to a daughter of Saif, Ahmed allied 'himself to the former dynasty, and gave his offspring additional claims to the sovereignty of the country.

An account of the fortunes and fate of the progeny of this prince may not at first sight appear very inviting; but I have inserted it, since it appears to me to furnish a more faithful picture of the interminable dissensions which the Muslim system entails on Eastern governments, than could be conveyed to the mind by the most elaborate disquisition.

Ahmed dying, left five sons-viz., Saif, Qais (*Kis*), Sultan, Talib, and Mohammed. Qais was chief of Sohar during his father's lifetime, and also at the time of his death. Saif, the heir apparent, was elected Imam on the decease of his father, and had a son called Ahmed, a wise prince, who conducted the affairs of his father's government. Ahmed, however, died, and the government then fell into such confusion, that the chiefs made Sultan Imam; but he was slain by the Qasimi (*Johasm*) pirates, and Kis sought to be chosen in his room. Sultan, however, had left two sons, the eldest, Said, who is now Imam, and Salem. Badr, the son of Saif, had left his own country and joined the Wahhabis; but when he heard of the death of Sultan, he quitted Heraiyat, and became the guest of his two cousins, who treated him with much attention, and it was agreed they should remain on terms of amity. They then attacked Qais, their uncle, and drove him back to his own government of Sohar; but as it subsequently appeared that Badr had great influence with the several Arab tribes, they were desirous of seeing him made Imam. He even concluded a treaty with the Wahhabis, by which he engaged to pay an annual sum of 50,000 Dollars, and to hold Oman as a tributary possession to their chief. It at length became apparent that his death would alone ensure Sayyid Said's throne and personal security; and he contrived to have him assassinated at a small village named Naaman (*Namhan*). not far from Barka, on the sea-coast. But although he thus rid himself of his formidable rival, Sayyid Said was not yet left to enjoy Oman without a struggle. Badr had previously concluded a treaty with Saud [bin Abdulaziz bin Mohammed Al Saud] , by which he stipulated to hold the province as tributary to that prince. This treaty Sayyid Said now refused to ratify; and, in consequence, the Wahhabi Chieftain despatched a body of 4000 men, under a warlike and enterprising chief, Saad bin Mutlaq, to enforce it. A series of petty warfare continued, with varied success, for some years, and the fortunes of Sayyid Said were at one time so low, that he was compelled to solicit the aid of the Persians; but eventually the death of his formidable opponent, followed by that of Saud, and the general dispersion of the Wahhabis, left him in undisturbed possession of his dominions, I cannot conclude the foregoing slight historical sketch without referring to the state of our present political relations with this Prince. The fears which have been so long entertained with respect to the advance of the Russians on our Indian possessions have induced us to regard with peculiar interest the various routes by which it is probable they might approach them. The Russian frontier now extends to within 120 miles of the sources of the Euphrates; and our late investigation of that river has shown that the passage of an army along its banks to the shores of the Persian Gulf might be accomplished without any considerable difficulty. It has here, as with the Red Sea, without due reflection, been suggested that a sufficient number of vessels could not be obtained to convey any considerable body of troops to India. I have little doubt Sayyid Said could collect enough of transports to convey an army of 20,000 men. His navy consists of four heavy frigates, two of fifty guns; three corvettes, from twenty-two to eighteen guns; and several smaller vessels of war. To these he might add his own merchant ships; those under Arab colours constantly trading to this port; and beyond all, on account of their great number, the services of the native boats or *baghlas*, some of which are upwards of 200 tons. The port of Muscat might, in a short time, in the hands of a skilful engineer, be made almost impregnable. Its situation commands the entrance to the Persian Gulf, and its harbours would offer shelter to any number of ships.

Whenever Russia strikes a blow, it will be done suddenly. We will not ask where this is most likely to be aimed, our duty is rather to guard every point to which it might be directed. The ships of the Imam of Muscat are constantly traversing the Persian Gulf. But one or two small vessels of twelve or eighteen guns are often the only force we have there. What is there then to prevent his squadron from forming a junction at some preconcerted period with the Russians at Basrah? This might be effected long before our naval force in India could be got together, or even if well arranged, almost before intelligence of such event could be conveyed to head quarters. Nor should it be forgotten, at certain seasons, that a month is the least period in which vessels proceeding from India can reach Muscat. In possession of the Imam's navy, the ships [54] of which are as well constructed and as well appointed as those of Her Majesty, and manned with Russian seamen, they would possess a force that would for some period give them the naval superiority in the Indian seas, With a power that may be wielded, if not precisely in this manner, yet in some other equally to our disadvantage, let us now inquire what are our present relations with respect to this prince. A reciprocal treaty of mutual alliance, defensive and offensive, was entered into with him, in which it was stipulated in Eastern phraseology that "his enemies should be our enemies, and his friends our friends;" and up to this feeling we have, until very lately, acted. But when the probability of our aid being solicited by this prince came a short time ago before the Supreme Government of India, the passage of the treaty which I have given being considered by them only in the light of an Eastern compliment, it was directed that no assistance should be afforded him, and the Bombay government have not therefore the authority to send a single vessel to the aid of one of their oldest and most faithful of allies. The sacrifice of so considerable a portion of his revenue to meet our wishes with respect to the slave trade, and his offer even to cede to us his territories in Zanzibar, for the furtherance of the same object, might, with many other instances, be adduced in proof of his sincere devotion to us. The knowledge that he possessed the support of the British Government has hitherto preserved his dominions to him; and was it for certainty known that these would be withdrawn, Oman would speedily be overrun by the Wahhabis, who are in intimate connexion with the Qasimi pirates, and who, once in possession of Muscat, might prove most troublesome neighbours. I think it can therefore admit of no doubt that the wisest, most politic, and most just line of action, which we can pursue in reference to this prince, would be to make our naval force, as with the native princes of India, in a measure subsidiary to his own, by which, without incurring any additional expense, we should at all times have a powerful armament at our command, in a quarter where it may prove of such vital importance, which could always, when required, be furnished from India with European seamen, where at present we have but a trifling force, and where, if the Oman government should fall into other hands, we might for a time have a most dangerous foe.

The magnificent seventy-four which his Highness presented but a few months since to his late Majesty [King William IV] had for its object, as he explained to me, his allying himself more closely with us; and I have not the slightest doubt but that whenever the above proposal is made to him, he will embrace it with the utmost willingness.

I conclude my observations on Oman with the detail of a short journey which I undertook in search of some inscriptions within the neighbouring province of Hadramaut.

CHAPTER 25
ARRIVAL IN BALHAF YEMEN

Ras Al Nashima (Ras ul Aseida) - Start for Nakab Al Hajar - Shells - Diyabit Bedouins - Shifting Sands - Excessive Heat - Ill behaviour of Guides - Caravanserai - Difference in Strength and Speed of Camels - Rak Trees - Curiosity of Natives - Kindness of an old Arab woman - Author recognised as an Englishman.

During our survey of the south coast of Arabia, while near the tower called Balhaf (*Ba-l-haff*), on the sandy cape of Ras Al Nashima, in latitude 13° 57' north, longitude 46 ¾° east nearly, the Bedouins brought me intelligence that extensive ruins, which they described as having been erected by infidels, and of great antiquity, were to be found at some distance from the coast. I was in consequence most anxious to visit them, but the several days we remained passed away, bringing nothing but empty promises on the part of Hamed, the officer in charge of the tower, to procure us camels and guides; and at length, in the prosecution of her survey, the ship sailed to the westward.

On the morning of her departure, April 29th, 1835, hopes were held out to me that if I remained, camels would be procured in the course of the day, to convey us to some inscriptions, but a few hours' distance from the beach; and in this expectation I remained behind with Mr. Cruttenden, a midshipman of the *Palinurus*, and one of the ship's boats.

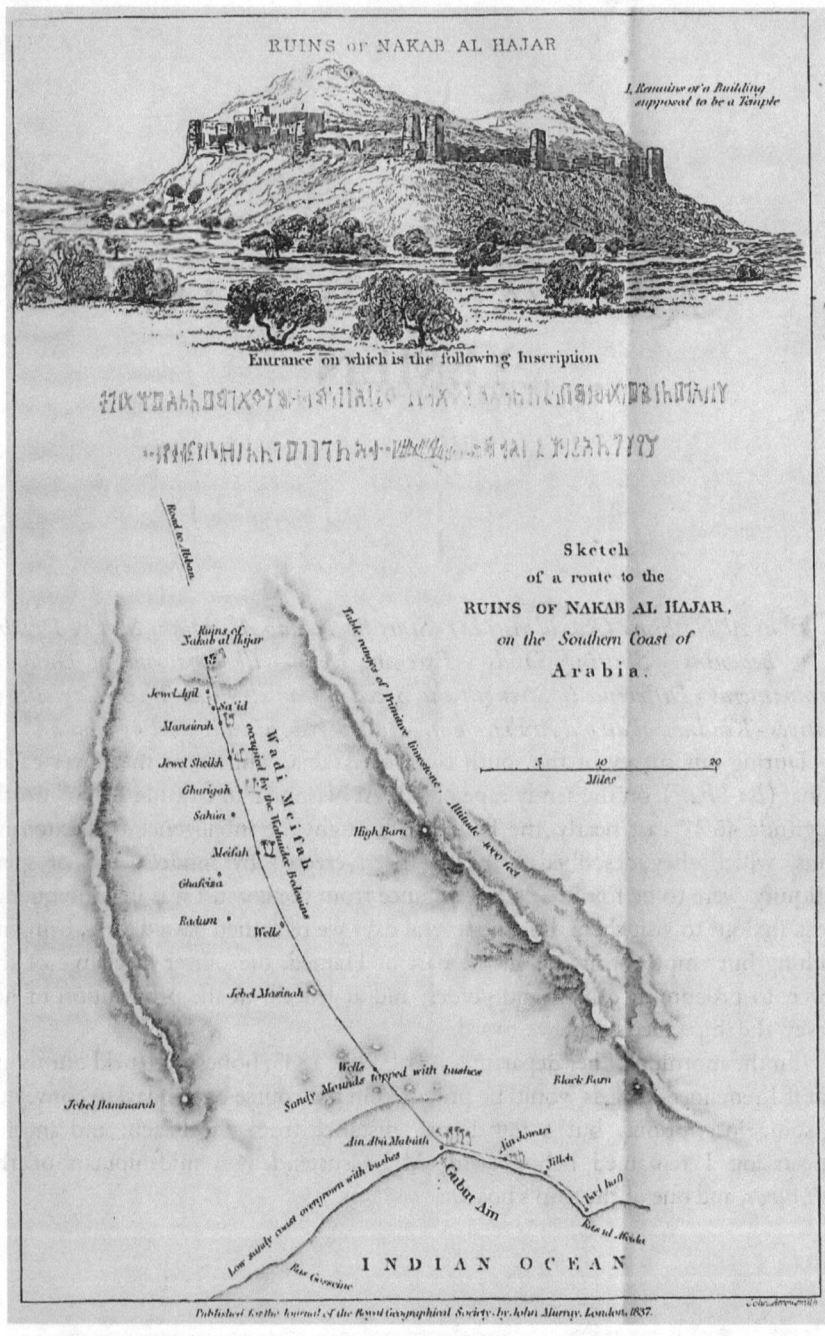

Nakab Al Hajar

Towards noon the camels were brought, and I was then somewhat surprised, after much wrangling among themselves, to hear the Bedouins decline proceeding to the inscriptions, but expressed their readiness to accompany me to the ruins I had before been so desirous of visiting. For this I was then unprepared, I had with me no presents for the Sheikhs of the different villages through which I had to pass, and only a small sum of money; but what (as regarded our personal safety) was of more moment, Hamed, who had before promised, now declined accompanying me, on the plea of sickness.

It was, however, an opportunity of seeing the country not to be lost, and I determined at once to place myself under their protection and proceed with them. Accordingly, I despatched my boat to the vessel, with an intimation that I hoped at the expiration of three days, to be at the village of Ain, on the seacoast, where it could again be sent for me. Having filled our waterskins, at three P.M. accompanied by an ill-looking fellow (styling himself the brother of Hamed) and another Bedouin, we mounted our camels and set forward. The road, after leaving Balhaf, extends along the shore to the westward. On the beach we saw a great variety of shells; among them the *Atrina vexillum* (*Pinna fragilis*), the *Solen*, the *Voluta musica*, and several varieties of Olives were the most common. Fragments of red tubular coral, and the branch kind of the white, were also very numerous. Under a dark barn-shaped hill, which we passed to the right, our guides pointed out the remains of an old tower, but as we were told there were no inscriptions, and as if its appearance from the ship indicated its being of Arab construction, we did not stay to examine it.

At 4:50 we passed a small fishing village, called Jilleh, consisting of about twenty huts, rudely constructed with the branches of the date palm. Along the beach, above highwater mark, the fishermen had hauled up their boats, where they are always permitted to remain, unless required for use. In their construction they differ in no respect from those which I have described in other parts of the coast.

At 7:20, leaving the seashore, we wound our way between a broad belt of low sandhills, and halted for two hours, about three miles from the village of Ain Jowari, to which one of our guides was despatched, in order to secure a supply of dates, the only food they cared to provide themselves with. Directly he returned we again mounted, and at eleven hours, the loud and deep barking of some dogs announced to us that we were passing the village of Ain Abu Mabuth; but we saw nothing of the inhabitants, and at one hour a.m. halted for the night.

We were now in the territories of the Diyabi Bedouins, who, from their fierce and predatory habits, are held in much dread by the surrounding tribes. Small parties, while crossing this tract, are not unfrequently cut off, and we were therefore cautioned by our guides to keep a good lookout for their approach. But after spreading our boat-cloaks in the sand, we were little annoyed by any apprehensions of this nature, and slept very soundly until the following morning.

The Diyabi Bedouins possess a great extent of country, and are very numerous and powerful. In their political constitution they differ from any other tribe in this vast peninsula with which I have become acquainted, either personally or by report. Instead of choosing a Sheikh or Sultan as their representative power, they are split into seven divisions, each governed by a chief, called Abu, who exercises what may be termed a patriarchal authority over them. These chiefs assemble for the discussion of all affairs connected with the general interest of the tribe, their decisions being regulated by a majority of voices. In certain cases this office of Abu is hereditary, but more generally it is filled by individuals whose superior sagacity, experience, and courage entitle them to that distinction. Some peculiar usages also exist among the Diyabi Bedouins, with respect to depredations committed on the property of each other. The Abu is answerable for all thefts occurring within his own district, and he makes restitution to the injured party, provided the offender be unable to do so. If, on the contrary, the thief has property, the Abu claims for himself a third, in addition to the value of the stolen property, as a further punishment, and compensation for the frequent losses he would otherwise be subjected to. The Diyabis have few spears, and no swords; their arms are a *jambiya*, a matchlock, and a shield: they are otherwise distinguished amidst the neighbouring tribes by the scantiness of their waist-cloths, and for the reputed levity and inconstancy of their females.

Thursday, April 30th. The Bedouins called us at an early hour, and after partaking of some coffee which they had prepared, we shook the sand (in which during the night we had been nearly buried) from our clothes, and at five a.m. at a slow pace again proceeded on our journey.

At seven hours we ascended a ledge about four hundred feet in elevation, from the summit of which we obtained an extensive but dreary view of the surrounding country. Our route lay along a broad valley, either side being formed by the roots or skirts of a lofty range of mountains. As these extend to the northward they gradually approach each other and the valley there assumes the aspect of a narrow defile. But on the other hand, the space between our present station and the sea widened, and was crossed by a barrier about thirty miles broad, forming a waste of low sandy hillocks. So loosely is the soil here piled, that the Bedouins assure me that they change their outline, and even shift their position with the prevailing storms. How Such enormous masses of moving sand, some of which are based on extensive tracts of indurated clay, could in their present situation thus become heaped together, affords an object of curious inquiry. They rise in sharp ridges, and are all of a horse-shoe form, the convex side to seaward. Our camels found the utmost difficulty in crossing, and the Bedouins were so distressed that we were obliged to stop repeatedly for them. The quantity of water they drank was enormous. I observed on one occasion a party of four or five finish a skin holding as many gallons.

At eight hours we found the sun so oppressive, that the Bedouins halted in a shallow valley under the shade of some stunted tamarisk trees. Their scanty foliage would, however, have afforded but slight shelter from the burning heat of the sun's rays, if our guides had not with their daggers dug up or cut off the roots and lower branches, and placed them at the top of the tree. Having Done so, they quietly took possession of the most shady spots, and left us to shift the best way we could. Within these burning hollows the sun's rays are concentrated and thrown off as from a mirror; the herbs around were scorched to a cindery blackness; not a cloud obscured the firmament, and the breeze which moaned past us was of a glowing heat, like that escaping from the mouth of a furnace. Our guides dug hollows in the sand, and thrust their blistered feet within them. Although we were not long in availing ourselves of the practical lesson they had taught us, I began to be far from pleased with their churlish behaviour. Every approach I made towards a good understanding was met by the most ungracious and repulsive return.

They now held frequent conversations with each other apart, of which it was evident we were made the subject,-and they not only refused water, except in quantities which they considered sufficient, but watched our movements so closely, that for a time, I found it impossible to take either notes or sketches.

Without anticipating dangers, still it was impossible not to feel that our situation must have been a critical one, had these men played us false. I knew that the natives of this district are considered especially hostile to those of a different creed; and that they had some years ago cut off the whole of a boat's crew of the only vessel that had previously touched on their coast, by seducing them with promises from the beach; I could not, therefore, but accuse myself of rashness, in thus venturing with no better pledge for our safety than their promised fidelity. There was, however, but little time for such reflections, and without evincing any change or mistrust in my manner, I determined to watch their conduct narrowly, and to lose sight of nothing which might be turned to our advantage.

At 10:30 our journey continued over the same sandy mounts as before; and at 1:30 we passed a sandstone hill called Jabal Masinah. The upper part of this eminence forms a narrow ridge, so nearly resembling ruins, that it was not until my return we were convinced to the contrary. We now left the sandy mounds, and crossed over table ridges elevated about two hundred feet from the plains below, and intersected by numerous valleys, the beds of former torrents, which had escaped from the mountains on either hand. The surface of the hills was strewn with various sized fragments of quartz and jasper, several of which exhibited a very pleasing variety of colours.

The only rocks we found in the valleys were a few rounded masses of primitive cream coloured limestone, of which formation are the mountains on either hand, and which is indeed the predominant rock along the whole southern coast of Arabia.

A few stunted acacias now first made their appearance, which continued to increase in size as we advanced. At four p.m. we descended into Wadi Meifah, and halted near a well of good light water. The change which a few draughts produced in the before drooping appearance of our camels was most extraordinary. Before we arrived, they were stumbling and staggering at every step; they breathed quick and audibly, and displayed other symptoms of exhaustion; but on arriving near the water, they approached it at a round pace, and appeared to imbibe renovated vigour with every draught. Then, after browsing for an hour on the tender shoots of the surrounding trees, they left as fresh as when we first started from the sea-coast. Notwithstanding the excessive heat of the day, and the heavy nature of the road, it may appear strange that these animals should have been so much distressed in crossing a tract of only forty miles. Camels however differ in Arabia, in point of strength and speed, more than is generally supposed. The animals we rode during this journey bore about the same resemblance to those on which I journeyed from Aden to Lahij (*Lahesdji*), as a first-rate hunter would to a post-horse in England. Whilst we loitered near these wells, an Arab brought several fine bullocks to water. They had the hump observable in those of India, to which, in size and colour, as well as in the stunted growth of their horns, they bear a great resemblance.

Rak/miswak trees [*Salvadora persica*] were very numerous, but taller, larger, and of a different species to those found on the sea-coast [55]. The camels ate greedily of those we found here, though they never feed on the latter unless pressed by hunger. This tree, common to Arabia, Abyssinia, and Nubia, is found in many places along the shores of the Red Sea, and the southern coast of Socotra abounds with it. Its foliage is of a lively green, which sends forth a most fragrant odour at certain seasons. The Arabs make tooth-brushes of the smaller branches, which they dispose of at Makkah and other parts of the East.

We observed also many tamarisks and acacias intermingling their branches with the other trees growing on this spot; the whole, at this season, putting forth young buds and shoots; so that after our journey over a dreary waste of burning sand, their verdure was an inexpressible relief to the eye.

At five p.m., again mounting our camels, we continued in a west-north-westerly direction along the valley. It is about one mile and a half in width, and the bank on either side, with the ground over which we were passing, afforded abundant evidence of its having been the bed of a powerful stream but a short time previous. The country also begins to assume a far different aspect. Numerous hamlets, interspersed amidst extensive date groves, verdant fields of *jowari*, and herds of sleek cattle, show themselves in every direction, and we now fell in with parties of inhabitants for the first time since leaving the sea-shore. Astonishment was depicted on their countenances, but as we did not halt, they had no opportunity of gratifying their curiosity by gazing at us for any length of time. But to compensate for their disappointment, one of our party remained behind, to communicate what he knew of us. In answer to the usual queries, who we were? were we Muslims? what was the nature of our business, &c.? his reply was, that we were *Kafirs* going to visit Nakab Al Hajar, in order to seek for treasure. Others he gratified with the intelligence that we arrived here to examine and report on their country, of which we were desirous of obtaining possession. In vain I endeavoured to impose silence, he laughed outright at my expostuation; while our guides, either disliking to be seen in our company, or having some business of their own, left us the instant we arrived near the village. They returned shortly after sunset, and we were preparing to halt near a small hamlet, when the inhabitants sent a message, requesting they would remove us from the vicinity of their habitations. Remonstrances or resistance, except on the part of our guides, who remained quiet spectators of all which was passing without an attempt at interference, would have been equally vain, and we were consequently obliged to submit.

Being now dark, it became evident that our guides had but an imperfect idea of the road, for we had not proceeded more than three or four miles, when we found ourselves climbing over the high embankments which enclose the *jowari* fields. The camels fell so frequently while crossing these boundaries, that at length the Bedouins, affecting to lose all patience, took their departure, and left us with them, an old man, and a little boy, to shift for ourselves. I should have cared the less for this, if before stealing off they had acquainted the latter with their destination, but they had not condescended to do so, and we were preparing to take up our quarters in the fields. Unexpectedly, however, we fell in with an old woman, who, as soon as she was informed of our situation, without the slightest hesitation promised to conduct us to her house. We gladly followed her, but having wandered far from the path, we did not arrive there until midnight.

We found our guides comfortably seated within a house, smoking their pipes and drinking coffee. Though excessively provoked, I was aware that remonstrance would be useless; and concealing my chagrin, I proceeded to secure a lodging for the night. But a large party had got there before us, and having taken possession of every apartment, were busily engaged with their pipes and coffee.

It appears we had arrived at a sort of caravanserai, one or more of which are usually found in the towns of Yemen, as in other parts of the East. We therefore requested the old lady, whose kindness did not abate when she heard we were Christians, to remove the camels from the court-yard, and there, after a hearty supper of dates and milk, we slept very soundly until about three o'clock, when we were awakened by finding our guides rummaging our baggage for coffee. At any other period I should probably have been amused at witnessing the unceremonious manner in which they proposed helping themselves, as well as the nonchalance they exhibited in piling, without ceremony, saddles, baskets, or whatever came in their way, upon us. But men are not in the best humour to enjoy a practical joke, when snatching a hasty repose, after a fatiguing day's work; and I therefore, with as little ceremony as they used to us, peremptorily refused to allow them to remove what they were seeking for. As we anticipated, they took this in high dudgeon; but their behaviour, unless they had proceeded to actual violence, could not have been much worse than it had been hitherto, and I therefore cared little for such an ebullition.

Friday, 1st May. Although it was quite dark last night when we arrived here, and we could not but be aware, from the state of the ground we had passed over, that there must be abundance of vegetation, yet we were hardly prepared for the scene that opened upon our view at daylight this morning.

The dark verdure of fields of *dhurra* [56], *dokhn* [57], tobacco, &c., extended as far as my eyes could reach. Mingled with these, we had the soft acacia, and the stately, but more sombre foliage of the date palm; while the creaking of numerous wheels with which the grounds were irrigated, and in the distance, several rude ploughs drawn by oxen; the ruddy and lively appearance of the people, who now flocked towards us from all quarters, and the delightful and refreshing coolness of the morning air, combined to form a scene, which he who gazes on the barren aspect of the coast, could never anticipate.

At six a.m. we again mounted our camels, and passing in succession the villages of Sahin, Gharigah, and Jewel Sheikh, arrived at another small village, where we had been led to anticipate we should meet the Sultan; but finding, to our very great joy, upon inquiry, that he had set off the day before for Abban, we pushed onwards.

Several people stopped us on the road, and saluted us, after the Arab style, with much civility. They appeared perfectly satisfied with the answer our guides now thought proper to give to them, namely, that we were proceeding to their Sultan on business. One man only recognised us in the course of our journey as Englishmen. He was a native of Hadramaut, who had heard of the English at Shaher, and was impressed with a belief that we were proceeding to purchase Hasan Ghorab from Abd Al Wahid.

At nine hours we passed Mansurah, and Said, and arrived at Jewel Agil, one of the largest hamlets of the group. Leaving several other villages to the left, we now passed over a hill about two hundred feet in height, composed of a reddish-coloured sandstone. From the summit of this, the ruins we sought were pointed out to us. As their vicinity was said to be infested with robbers, we were obliged to halt at a village, in order to obtain one of its inhabitants to accompany us to them. Our guides, as usual, having gone to seek shelter from the heat of the sun, had left us to make our breakfast on dates and water, in any sheltered spot we could find. The sun was nearly vertical, and the walls of the houses afforded us no protection. Seeing this, several of the inhabitants came forward, and offered with much kindness to take us to their dwellings. We gladly consented, and followed one of them. Coffee was immediately served; and it was with some difficulty, after a promise to return if possible in the evening, that we prevented our host from ordering a meal to be immediately cooked for us.

This circumstance, combined with several others which occurred on our return, convinced me, if we had been provided with a better escort, that after passing the territory of the Diyabis, we should have experienced neither incivility nor unkindness from the people.

CHAPTER 26

RUINS OF NAKAB AL HAJAR FORTRESS

Ruins of Nakab Al Hajar - Position-Ancient town - Inscriptions - Entrance - Materials used in its Construction - Vast Solidity - Interior - Excellent Masonry - Well - Antiquarian Remains - Anecdote - General Observations - Burckhardt - Origin of Nakab Al Hajar - Fertility of surrounding District - Kind Reception from Natives - Best mode of penetrating into the Interior - Return to the Ship - "Black Mail" - Anecdote of Diyabi Bedouins.

About an hour from the last village we arrived at the ruins of Nakab Al Hajar [58], and a rapid glance soon convinced me, that their examination would more than compensate for any fatigue or danger we had encountered on our road to them.

The hill upon which they are situated, stands out in the centre of the valley, and divides a stream which passes, during floods, on either side of it. It is nearly eight hundred yards in length, and about three hundred and fifty yards at its extreme breadth.

The direction of its greatest length is from east to west. Crossing diagonally, there is a shallow valley, dividing it into two nearly equal portions, which swell into an oval form. About a third of the height from its base, a massive wall, averaging in those places where it remains entire, from thirty to forty feet in height, is carried completely round the eminence, and flanked by square towers, erected at equal distances. There are but two entrances situated north and south from each other, at the termination of the valley before mentioned, A hollow square tower, each side measuring fourteen feet, stands on both sides of these. Their bases extend to the plain below, and are carried out considerably beyond the rest of the building. Between the towers, at an elevation of twenty feet from the plain, there is an oblong platform which projects about eighteen feet without, and as much within the walls. A flight of steps was apparently once attached to either extremity of the building, although now all traces of them have disappeared. This level space is roofed with flat stones of massive dimensions, resting on transverse walls. It is somewhat singular that we could not trace any indication of gates. The southern entrance has fallen much to decay, but the northern remains in almost a perfect state. The sketch on the map will illustrate its appearance and dimensions better than any verbal description.

Within the entrance, at an elevation of ten feet from the platform, we found the inscriptions. They are executed with extreme care, in two horizontal lines on the smooth face of the stones of the building, the letters being eight inches long. Attempts have been made, though without success, to obliterate them. From the conspicuous situation which they occupy, there can be but little doubt, but that when deciphered, they will be found to contain the name of the founder of the building, as well as the date, and purport of its erection. The whole of the wall, the towers, and some of the edifices within, are built of the same material, viz., a compact greyish-coloured marble, streaked with thin dark veins and speckles, and hewn to the required shape with the utmost nicety. The dimensions of the slabs at the base of the walls and towers were from five to six and seven feet in length, from two feet ten inches to three feet in height, and from three to four in breadth. These decrease in size with the same regularity to the summit, where their breadth is not more than half that of those below, where the thickness of the wall, though I did not measure it, cannot be less than ten feet, and, as far as I could judge, about four at the summit. Notwithstanding the irregularity of its foundation, the stones are invariably placed in the same horizontal lines, carefully cemented with mortar, which has acquired a hardness almost equal to that of the stone. Such parts of the wall as remain standing, are admirably knitted together; others which, by the crumbling away of their bases, incline towards their fall, still adhere in their tottering state without fracture; and those patches which have fallen, are scattered around in huge undissevered masses. There are no openings in these walls, no turrets at the upper part, -the whole wears the same stable, uniform, and solid appearance. In order to prevent the mountain torrent, which leaves on the face of the surrounding country evident traces of the rapidity of its course from washing away the base of the hill several buttresses of a circular form have been hewn from that part, and cased with a harder stone. The casing has partially disappeared, but the buttresses still remain.

Let us now visit the interior, where the most conspicuous object is an oblong square building, the walls of which face the cardinal points. Its largest size, fronting the north and south, measures twenty-seven yards. The shorter, facing the eastward, seventeen yards. The walls are fronted with a kind of free-stone, each slab being cut of the same size, and the whole so beautifully put together, that I endeavoured in vain to insert the blade of a small penknife between them. The outer unpolished surface is covered with small chisel marks, which the Bedouins have mistaken for writing. From the extreme care displayed in the construction of this building, I have no doubt that it is a temple, and my disappointment at finding the interior filled up with the ruins of the fallen roof was very great. Had it remained: entire, we might have obtained some clue to guide us in our researches respecting the form of religion professed by the earlier Arabs. Above and beyond this building there are several other edifices, with nothing peculiar in their form or appearance. Nearly midway between the two gates, there is a circular well ten feet in diameter, and sixty in depth. The sides are lined with unhewn stones, and either to protect it from the sun's rays, or to serve some process of drawing the water, a wall of a cylindrical form, fifteen feet in height, has been carried round it.

On the southern mound we were not able to make any discoveries, as the whole presents an undistinguishable mass of ruins. Within the southern entrance, on the same level with the platform, a gallery four feet in breadth, protected on the inner side by a strong parapet, and on the outer by the principal wall, extends for a distance of about fifty yards. I am unable to ascertain what purpose this could have served. In no portion of the ruins have we succeeded in tracing any remains of arches or columns, nor could we discover on their surface any of those fragments of pottery, coloured glass, or metals, which are always found in old Egyptian towns, and which I also saw on those we discovered upon the north-west coast of Arabia. Except the attempts to deface the inscriptions I have before noticed, there is no other appearance of the building having suffered from any ravages besides those of time; and owing to the dryness of the climate, as well as the hardness of the material, every stone, even to the marking of the chisel, remains as perfect as the day it was hewn. We were naturally anxious to ascertain if the Arabs had preserved any tradition concerning their buildings, but they refer them, in common with the others we have fallen in with, to their Pagan ancestors. "Do you believe," said one of the Bedouins to me, upon my telling him that his ancestors were then capable of greater works than themselves, "that these stones were raised by the unassisted hands of the *Kafirs*? No! no! They had devils, legions of devils, (God preserve us from them!) to aid them." A superstition generally credited by others.

The guides followed us during our stroll over the ruins, in expectation of sharing in the golden hoards, which they would not but remain convinced we had come to discover. When, as they supposed, they found us unsuccessful in the search, they consoled themselves with the reflection that we had not been able to draw them from the spirits, who, according to their belief, kept continual watch.

The ruins of Nakab Al Hajar, considered by themselves, present nothing more than a mass of ruins surrounded by a wall. But the magnitude of the stones used in its construction, and the perfect knowledge of the builder's art, exhibited in the style and mode of placing them together, with its towers, and great extent, would give it importance in any other part of the world. Here in Arabia, where, as far as is known, architectural remains are of rare occurrence, its appearance excites the liveliest interest. That it owes its origin to a very remote antiquity (how remote it is to be hoped the inscription will determine) is evident by its appearance alone, which bears a strong resemblance to similar edifices which have been found amidst Egyptian ruins. We have (as in them) the same inclination in the walls, the same form of entrance, and the same flat roof of stones. Its situation, and the mode in which the interior is laid out, seem to indicate that it served both as a magazine and a fort. I think, therefore, we may with safety adopt the conclusion that Nakab Al Hajar, and the other castle which we have discovered, were erected during a period when the trade from India flowed through Arabia towards Egypt, and from thence to Europe. Thus Arabia Felix, comprehending Yemen, Saba, and Hadramaut, under the splendid dominion of the Sabaean or Himyarite (*Homerite*) [59] dynasty, seems to have merited the appellation of which she boasted.

The history of these provinces is involved in much obscurity, but Agatharchides, before the Christian era, bears testimony, in glowing colours, to the wealth and luxury of the Sabaeans, and his account is heightened rather than moderated by succeeding writers. This people, before Marin (*Marbe*) [60] became the capital of their kingdom, possessed dominion along the whole of the southern frontier of Arabia, We are expressly informed that they planted colonies in situations eligible for trade, and fortified their establishments.

The commerce was not confined to any particular channel; on the contrary, we learn from an early period, of the existence of several flourishing cities, at or near the sea-shore, which must have shared in it. We know nothing of the interior of this remarkable country, but there is every reason to believe, as is most certainly the case with Nakab Al Hajar, that these castles will not only point out the tracks which the caravans formerly pursued, but also indicate the natural passes into central Arabia.

The inscription which it has been my good fortune to discover will create considerable interest among the learned.

Burckhardt, while regretting the absence of any information connected with the origin of the civil institutions of the Bedouins, remarks, "that perhaps the discovery of ancient monuments and inscriptions in Nejd and Yemen might lead to a disclosure of new historical facts connected with this subject." At the period of the promulgation of the Quran, two alphabets were used in Arabia, the Kufic, in which that work was written, expressive of the Quraysh dialect, and the Himyaritic, adopted by the people of Yemen [60]. The latter is now lost to us, and I know not on what grounds certain philologists have conjectured that it bore "a strong affinity to the Ethiopic;" but " when the Quran appeared in the Kufic character the inhabitants of Yemen were unable to read it [61]." It has frequently been a subject of regret that we were in possession of no inscriptions from the country by which these points might be determined. Niehbur's attention was particularly directed to it, although he was unable during his stay to obtain any: one was shown him at Mokha, which was copied some distance from the coast, but sickness had so reduced him, that he observes he was then more occupied with thoughts respecting his latter end, than any desire to copy unknown inscriptions; but conjectures, from recollection only, it might have been the Persepolitan, or arrow-headed character; but no resemblance can be traced between this and an inscription since found by Seetzin [63], on his road to Sanaa, nor those which I have given.

Owing to the locality in which the latter were found, and for other reasons, I venture to suggest that both they, together with those we discovered at Hassan Ghorab, are the lost Himyaritic writing. Should this prove correct, the resemblance to the Ethiopic is not conjectural, since a complete identity in many of the characters may be traced [64]. I am not sufficiently versed in oriental literature to pursue this subject further; and the above remarks are offered with some diffidence. Facsimiles of both, however, have been transmitted to the celebrated Gesennius, at Halle, and as they at present occupy his attention, we may venture to hope that the result will be a successful elucidation.

Nakab Al Hajar is situated north-west, and is distant forty-eight miles from the village of Ain, which is marked on the chart in latitude 14° 2' north, and longitude 46° 30' east nearly. It stands in the centre of a most extensive valley, called by the natives Wadi Meifah, which, whether we regard its fertility, population, or extent, is the most interesting geographical feature we have yet discovered on the southern coast of Arabia. Taking its length from where it opens out on the seacoast, to the town of Abban, it is four days' journey, or seventy-five miles. Beyond this point I could not exactly ascertain the extent of its prolongation; various native authorities gave it from five to seven additional days throughout the whole of this space. It is thickly studded with villages, hamlets, and cultivated grounds. In a journey of fifteen miles, we counted more than thirty of the former, besides a great number of single houses.

The date-groves become more numerous as we approach towards the sea-shore, while in the same direction the number of cultivated patches decrease. Few of the villages contain more than from one to two hundred houses, which are of the same form, and constructed of the same material (sun-baked bricks) as those on the sea-coast. I saw no huts, nor were there any stone houses, although several of the villages had more than one mosque, and three or four Sheikhs' tombs.

More attention appears to be paid within this district to agricultural pursuits, than in any other part of Arabia which I have hitherto seen. The fields are ploughed in furrows, which for neatness and regularity would not shame an English peasant. They carefully free the soil from the few stones strewn over it, and water the whole plentifully morning and evening, from numerous wells. The water is drawn up by camels, (this is a most unusual circumstance, for they are rarely used as draught animals in any part of the East) and distributed over the face of the country along high embankments. A considerable supply is also retained within these wherever the stream fills its bed. Trees and sometimes even houses are then washed away, but any damage it does is amply compensated by the mud deposited, which, although of a lighter colour and of a harder nature, is yet almost equally productive with that left by the Nile in Egypt. But beyond what I have noticed no other fruits or grain are grown.

Having now made all the necessary observations, on the ruins and the surrounding country, our Bedouins, as evening was approaching, became clamorous for us to depart.

About four p.m. we finished loading the camels, and travelled until near sunset, when we halted near one of the villages.

Our reception there was very different from that which we experienced at the first village on our journey from the well. Though about fifty men crowded around us, their curiosity, though much heightened by all they saw, was restrained within the bounds of good taste. The questions they asked respecting our journey were proposed with a degree of delicacy which surprised and pleased me. Milk, water, and firewood were brought to us almost unsolicited, for which we had nothing to return but our thanks. I much regretted on this occasion being unprovided with some trifling presents, which we might have left as a memorial of the Englishman's sojourn among them. What a different impression we might have formed of this people had we drawn our opinion from our guides or our first reception!

Saturday, May 2nd. Starting shortly after midnight, we travelled until four, but losing our way, halted until daylight. At this time a heavy dew was falling, and Fahrenheit's thermometer stood at 58°; it was consequently so chilly, that we were happy to wrap ourselves up in our boat-cloaks.

At eight hours we again halted at the well to replenish our skins, previous to recrossing the sandy hillocks, and then continued on our journey. From nine a.m. this day, until 1:30, we endured a degree of heat I never felt equalled. Not a breath of wind was stirring, and the glare produced by the white sand felt almost intolerable. At two hours our guides were so much exhausted, that we were obliged to halt for an hour. At 5:30 we arrived at the date-groves, near to Ain Abu Mabuth, where there is a small village, and some fountains of pure water, about fifteen feet square and three deep.

At seven hours we reached the beach, which we followed until we came opposite to the vessel. It was however too late for us to be solicitous about making a signal to those on board for a boat; and I was moreover desirous, from what we overheard between the Bedouins, who were with us, to defer our departure until the morning. Any disturbance we might have with them had better happen then than during the night. We therefore took up our quarters amidst the sand-hills, where we could light a fire without fear of its being observed by those on board.

It will readily be believed that if we felt fatigued it was not without reason. We had been seventy hours from our station at Balhaf, during forty hours of which we had been mounted on our camels. The whole distance, one hundred and twenty miles, might have been accomplished, on a quick camel, in half that time, and it was our slow pace during the excessive heat of the weather at this season, which formed the most toilsome and tedious part of the journey.

May 3rd. Being discovered at an early hour this morning from the ship, a boat was immediately despatched for us. Strengthened now with her crew, we settled with the Bedouins without any additional demand, and in the course of a few minutes were on board the vessel, where we received the congratulations of all on our return. Considerable apprehension had been entertained for our safety, when it was discovered that Hamed had not accompanied us.

It was not indeed until afterwards that we ascertained the extreme risk we had encountered on this journey; for the Diyabi Bedouins, finding we had passed through their territory, lay in wait for us, under the impression we should return by the same route. But the ship fortunately took up a second station, about twenty miles to the westward of the former one, and on receiving intelligence of that we returned by another and more direct road to her. Some idea may be formed of the reception destined for us from the following incident:- A few days afterwards, one of our boats was lying at anchor close to the shore; a party of this tribe appeared, and coolly kneeling, took deliberate aim, and fired into her. The midshipman in charge very quickly returned it, but no blood was shed.

The success which has attended this brief journey to the interior will, it is hoped, prove an inducement to others to follow up our researches. Had I been differently situated, I should have proceeded on to Abban, on the road to which there are at a village called Eisan ruins of nearly equal magnitude with Nakab Al Hajar. But independent of these ancient monuments, in themselves far more than enough to repay the adventure, the condition, character, and pursuits of the inhabitants, the productions, resources, and nature of the country, severally furnish subjects of peculiar interest, and would, there can be no doubt, amply repay the curiosity of the first European who should visit them.

In order to proceed, I imagine nothing more would be necessary than for any individual to procure a letter from the British Government to the Sheikh of Abban. A guard could be sent to escort him there from the sea-coast, and he could from thence be forwarded to the next Sheikh by a similar application.

By the assumption of a Muslim or even a medical character, and a sacrifice of every species of European comfort, he might, I have very little doubt, penetrate to the very heart of this remarkable country.

APPENDIX - LETTERS FROM SAID BIN KHALFAN

Extracts from Letters received from Said bin Khalfan (Sayyid Ibn Kalfan) [64], Secretary to the Imam of Muscat.

My Dear Sir, Muscat, 26th Dec., 1835.

I am glad to hear of the attention and civility you have met with in the dominions of His Highness; please God you may continue to do so, and succeed in your journey! Your letter to His Highness I have presented this day; and rest assured he is well pleased at hearing you are well satisfied with his subjects.

There is a Chief at Muscat of the tribe of Majira, who agrees for five hundred Dollars to conduct you from Buraymi to Diriyah, furnishing you all the way with camels, and a guard of seventy or eighty men. I am now waiting for your answer. There is no other way of crossing the Desert than in this manner with a caravan, You had better, as you suggest, take a Cashmere shawl for Fasil [65]. I will purchase and send you one.

I am, Sir
Your obedient Servant,
Said bin Khalfan .

My Dear Sir, Muscat, February 9th.

With much pleasure I acknowledge the receipt of your most esteemed letter, which reached me on the 4th; happy I am to find you are at Seeb, and recovering your health. Sir, the greatest benefit is to gain strength, and this I hear you are gaining; for this, in my daily prayers to Almighty God, I thank him. I explained to His Highness your fever at Nizwa: he said "it could not be avoided; that what Almighty God orders must take place." I enclose you a letter from him to the

Governor of Seeb, which you can read, as it is unsealed. He was quite pleased and happy to hear of your safe arrival at that place.
Yours faithfully,
Said bin Khalfan.

Muscat, 17th February, 1836.
I have received your letter this day at 8h.3'a.m. I have mentioned the route you intend to pursue, to His Highness; his reply is as follows: "That the road from Suwayq to Ibri is not safe for you; nor to Dharra." Do not run the risk; His Highness deems it not safe. The reason is, the Wahhabi tribe arrived from Diriyah; beyond Sohar, several places have been attacked and burnt; all the people are at present in confusion, particularly in those places connected with Ibri. They plunder and kill each other, and say it is the Wahhibis.

If you are therefore coming to Muscat, you had better get on board some *baghla* passing, as the weather is very hot to come by land.

Muscat, Sunday, February 22nd, 1836.
I received your letter last night, and perfectly understand the contents. Your determination to proceed to Ibri, I have told His Highness, and he has therefore given an order this day, that one of his officers is to conduct you to Ibri: viz., by this route he will first call at the town of Suwayq, to the country called Ghuzayn (*Gaizein*), of the tribe of Hawasanah; the said tribe will conduct you to the country of the Beni Kalban, who will take you to Ibri, the Yacknali tribe; there you must get them to conduct you to Buraymi.

The Sheikh at Buraymi, Saad bin Mutlaq, will conduct you to Diriyah. His Highness, to prevent accidents, will write to Buraymi by your guide, and to the Imam at Diriyah, that any orders from you for money drawn on him will be accepted and paid.

The Imam has given directions for camels to be furnished to convey you as far as Suwayq, that is, the last dominions of His Highness.
Yours faithfully,
Said bin Khalfan.

My Dear Sir, Muscat, April 6th, 1836.
I have to acknowledge the receipt of your letter, dated Seeb, April 5th.
Captain Hennell returned to Muscat in the *Coote*, and by her I have received several letters for you, which I send with this, without delay.
I never heard of the messengers the Imam despatched for you to Ibri; and I believe they were both murdered by the Wahhabis.
Yours faithfully,
Said bin Khalfan.
Thank you

THANK YOU 🙏 **for buying**
"Travels in Arabia"
I do hope you found it interesting.
A review will help let others know if it's right for them compared to other books.
It will also let us know what we need to improve.
Tony Walsh

APPENDIX - NOTATIONS

[1] The following communication from Captain W. H. Smyth, R.N., V.P.R.S., to the Author, is here alluded to:-" It may strengthen your conviction of the substantial claims of Bruce to the applause of his country when I tell you that Mr Salt admitted to me that he (Salt) had drawn his conclusions too hastily and from preconceived impressions. The late Dr. Gillies, the historian of Greece, who criticized Bruce so severely in the Monthly Review, also assured me that he afterward altered his opinions entirely in favour of him. Indeed, those who have made journeys in the present day can readily estimate what must have been his courage, address, and perseverance, to have accomplished so much at that time;-and when I first visited Algiers and Benghazi, he was not entirely forgotten.

"It is curious that Dr Gillies married the sister of the enterprising Captain Beaver, who, in his ' African Memoranda,' renders due tribute to the merits of Bruce, and emphatically styles him 'the Prince of Travellers.'

[2] Vol. vi. p. 51.

[3] The following is a copy of one of these Official Documents:- Persian Department, No. 17, of 1835. These are to certify, that Lieutenant Wellsted is proceeding, with the sanction of the Right Honourable the Governor in Council of Bombay, through various parts of Arabia, and all those who are desirous of maintaining the friendship of the British Government are requested to show him every attention and civility. By order of the Right Honourable the Governor in Council, W.H. Wathen, Sec. to Government. Bombay Castle, 7th November 1835.

[4]* Sometimes spelt "Muscat" by English writers, but more properly "Maskat".

[5]* Situated in the Wadi Beni Hanifah: it is one of the defiles by which alone the Nejd el Arid can be entered. Tchan Numa, p. 523.

[6]Jarab was the son of Sultan, the son of Eber, and brother of Peleg, and from him, the ancient Arabians derive their ancestry. The Yarubi, therefore, who claim the nearest approach to the parent stem, trace their genealogy further back than the other tribes in Arabia, and may, undoubtedly, be pronounced the oldest family in the world. Saba, the grandson of Sultan, founded Saba, and the Sabeans are supposed to be identified with the Cushites, who dwelt upon the shores of the Persian Gulf, This was the position the Seceders occupied at the period of the dispute between Ali and Muawiya for the caliphate, and it throws a ray of light upon the mist that envelopes the history of this remote period, when we find some direct evidence bearing on a point which has heretofore been a matter of mere conjecture. The name of Arabia, with some show of reason, has also been derived from the Jarib here alluded to.

[7]* Geographa, lib. vii. cap. 6, p.153

[8]. #Edrissi writes it مسقط

[9]* A rude description of vessel of various burthens, from fifty to three hundred tons. The term is, most probably, from *bagala* or *bagla*, a kind of heron. (Ardea Torre.)

[10]* See Captain Thompson's Report, dated 18th November 1820, -Asiatic Journal, vol. xi. p. 593.

[11]

The Imam, with the remnant of his army, accompanied our troops during their march, and it would be an injustice to the noble and gallant character of this prince, were I to omit mentioning the resolute bravery with which he maintained his ground, even when wounded, and his determination to retreat no farther than Beni bu Hasan, if he had not been deserted by a large portion of his army.

[12]

In January, 1821

[13]* In March, 1821.-Asiatic Journal, xii. 364.

[14]* I had with me some cigars, but, knowing the aversion those of that sect have to the use of tobacco, I refrained from producing them;-but, by some means, they discovered they were in my possession, and insisted on my smoking, which, to relieve myself from their importunities, 1 was compelled to do.

[15]* The Bedouin still retains that passionate love of song for which his race has ever been distinguished. Whether tending his flock, beguiling the tediousness of a journey, or seated after his evening cheer at the fire, the Arab constantly breaks out into some ditty, the theme of which is either love or war, Seated cross-legged

under the scanty shade of the date-palm, I have often listened to one of them thus amusing himself for hours. The only accompaniment is a rude guitar with two strings. Although nothing can be further removed from our idea of melody, yet their sentiment and expression are admirably suited to the scenes they describe, and are also strikingly illustrative of the peculiar character of their minds. Combinations the most harsh and rugged form the most striking feature of their music, as often, when their movements are grave and slow, as when they are brisk and lively. In the former they often exhibit much grave and melancholy thought, in the latter they not unfrequently spring up simultaneously, and join, to the full extent of their voices, in a rude chorus. I found no surer way of exciting a kindly feeling towards myself, when among this rude people, than by listening with apparent interest to these performances.

[16]* Cissus Arborea of Forskal. The smaller branches of this tree are used in Arabia for tooth brushes. It was held in such high estimation among the ancient Arabs and Egyptians as to be celebrated by their poets,

[17]
* The supply of water is so plentiful in Oman, that we seldom had occasion to carry it with us; when we did, it was placed in skins called *girbars*, and all the hides of the sheep or goats killed during our journey were kept for this purpose: those of kids or lambs serve for milk, while the larger are used for either wine or water. They are tanned with the bark of the acacia, and the hairy part, which is left without, is generally, though not invariably, cleansed. The apertures through which the legs protruded are closed up, and the fluid within is discharged through the opening of the neck, which is gathered together, and fastened by means of a leathern thong, its extremity being cut in the form of a tongue or spout. They are slung alongside their camels, and a Bedouin when thirsty may frequently be observed drinking from them whilst in that position. They answer better than jars, because if the camel run against trees or his fellow beasts in the caravan, they are not liable to be broken, and from the evaporation constantly going on, the water is also kept perfectly cool, but whilst new, sufficient attention is not paid to cleansing them, and their contents thus acquire a loathsome taste and smell, A disagreeable appearance is also imparted to the water from grease, with which the Arabs lubricate the inner side to prevent it from oozing through. How immutable are Eastern customs! These are the bottles so frequently alluded to in the Scriptural narrative; and in the Antiquities of Herculaneum, vol. vii. p. 197, will be seen as the representation of a female pouring wine into a vessel from a skin precisely similar to what 1 has here described.

[18]* The genealogy of the Wahhabi chiefs is as follows :-Fasil, the present Imam, as he is now styled, Ibn Furkey, Ibn Abdallah, Ibn Mohammed, Ibn Saoud, Ibn Abdulaziz, and Ibn Saaud, who, in 1747, became a proselyte of the reformer Abdul

Wahhab. Abdulaziz here referred to is the individual who, in 1801, pillaged and burnt the town and magnificent mausoleum of Imam Hussain, and with ruthless barbarity butchered indiscriminately all the men, women, and children that fell into his hands.

[19]* Lieutenant Whitelock's route from Muscat is laid down on the map. It led along a narrow road, through a wilderness of broken mountains. He passed a few spots where there were date plantations, but the country was generally barren, and destitute of water.

[20]* I could not learn that any manna is here procured from this tree, as in the vicinity of Mount Sinai.

[21]* "No God but the God; and Mohammed is his Prophet.'

[22]* "Tn the name of God."

[23]#"Praise be to God."

[24]* Spelt Nizzuwah in the accompanying Map, which seems to be the more correct orthography. This town is called Tama in ldrisi's printed epitome.- Geog. Nub. page 54. In the Oxford MSS. it is spelt نزوة

[25]*These streams are styled Tas'l

[26]* This custom appears to be of great antiquity - See Herodotus.

[27]Properly Abu-sher

[28]* This was in the presence of the British Resident, Col. Stannus. One man of some hundreds present, for a reward of a few Dollars, remained one minute and fifty seconds. In Ceylon they rarely exceed fifty seconds.

[29]* Of the several duties assigned to the Indian navy, that of cruising on the Pearl Banks is by far the most harassing and unpleasant. It is admitted by those who are well qualified to judge, that the heat of the atmosphere in the Persian Gulf During the warm season is not surpassed by any other spot in the known world, The nights being short, neither earth nor sea has time to cool. Even when on the horizon, the sun is sufficiently warm to be disagreeable: the sailors say it rises red hot; and a few minutes afterwards the intensity of its beams elevates Fahrenheit's thermometer ten degrees. From this period until about eleven in the forenoon, when the sea-breeze sets in, the heat is almost intolerable. Under double awnings, their heads not unfrequently bound with wet cloths, the seamen are seen lying on the deck, or stretched along the gunwale, looking for the first welcome indication of the breeze, absolutely panting for breath. Without the smallest exertion, a copious perspiration streams from every pore. Water increases, instead of allaying thirst; the skin is in such a state from irritation, that no clothes can be endured, and the slightest movement, by causing it to crack, is accompanied with great pain.

[30] * There are, I am told, two exceptions, viz., the stream near to Ras or Cape Qurayyat (*Kuriat*), and that at Seeb, along the bed of which lies the road to Nizwa.

[31]* An allusion to this custom, of the gardener changing with his foot the channel of a stream of water, furnishes the King of Assyria, in his threatening message, with a very appropriate image. "With the sole of my foot," says he, "1 have dried up the rivers of besieged places." The practice of Arabia is also familiar to the modern Portuguese husbandman.

[32] * Large quantities of limes are dried in the sun, and exported to the Persian Gulf.

[33]* He is joyously welcomed with the exclamation, " Another child is born unto us."

[34]* *Tamarix aphylla* (Tamarix Orientalis)

[35]* Ali Bey. Badhea

[36]*There are no vehicles of any description either carried or drawn in Oman, nor, as far as I have seen, in any other part of Arabia.

[37]*Geo. Nubiensis

[38]* As a specimen of his proficiency in the English language, I present the reader, in the Appendix, with letters addressed by him to me. Besides exhibiting a considerable portion of natural talent, they are curious in many other points of view. The polished blade-bone of a camel serves them as a tablet to write on, and they use a kind of ink easily obliterated.

[39]*Called also "Biazi"

[40]* Notwithstanding this, I must observe that the Imam, and some other strict Moslems, from religious scruples, entirely abstain from this beverage.

[41]* From a MS. in the Author's possession.

[42]* MS. quoted above.

[43]*Jactan the son of Hebra.

[44]#The Arabs trace their descent as far as Adnan, but not to Ishmael.

[45]+Robinson's Calmet, Boston Ed. p. 570. Ante, a.p. 1817.

[46]~Mos-Arabes, or Mostae-Arabes.

[47]* In Oman travellers are often entertained in the mosque.

[48]* In the course of the Narrative it has been mentioned how powerfully the organs of these people are affected by their rude instruments ; it seems curious, therefore, that they should not improve on them.

[49]*Gen xiii. 7

[50]* The title of Imam, implying " Vicar of Mohammed," is ecclesiastical in Arabia, and synonymous with Emir el Nunumim, or Prince of the Faithful. It appears to have been assumed by the successors of the Prophet.

[51]* Some remarks on this practice may be found in Mr. R.Lander's Travels.

[52]* After all, I do not think that my want of success in these researches will be deemed of much consequence. It will be seen, by what I have laid before the reader, that the history of the province presents nothing but a series of petty wars and

intestine broils, and our attention is so divided by the number of personages who figure on the stage, that we soon cease to feel an interest in any.

[53]* The genealogy of the preceding Imams is Saif ibn Sultan, Ibn Malik, Ibn Adul Arab, el Yarubi ul Uzde, ul Quaitani.

[54]* Built in the dockyard at Bombay, and stored, &c., direct from England.

[55]* The former is the Salvadora Persica, well described by Forskall as the Cissus Arborea; the latter is the Avecennia nitida. -Delille, Voy. en Arabie de Léon lu Borde.

[56]*Sorghum vulgare

[57]# Sorghum saccharatum

[58]* Nakab Al Hajar signifies " the excavation from the rock."

[59]* The ancient people called Himyari by the modern Arabs were probably called Homeiri by their ancestors, as their territory corresponds with that of the Homerite of Ptolemy.- Geogr. vi. 6., p. 778.

[60]. #The Mariaba of the Grecks.-Sirabo, xvi

[61]* Conder's invaluable Modern Traveller. " Arabia." Page 41

[62]. #Ibid, p 42

[63]* Mines d'Orient. p. 282.

[64]It also bears some similitude to the rude undeciphered characters cn the Lat of Firoz Shah at Delhi-As. Res. vii. pl. 7-10.

[65]*This gentleman, an Arab, was educated in Calcutta, and I have given a literal transcript of his English letters,

[66]#The Imam of the Wahhabis.

PHOTOGRAPHS & IMAGES

Photographs - Arabesque
 except
 A Valley in Oman - Wellsted
 Bishyrean camel - Wellsted
 Nakab Al Hajar - Wellsted
 Banian Hindus in 19thc - James Forbes
 Map - Wellsted and Arrowsmith
 Sawfish Pristis pristis townsville - unknown
 Woman in Face mask - unknown photographer
 Ships in Muscat - 'Muscat Cove', British Library: Visual Arts, Photo 355/1/47, in Qatar Digital Library
 Papers, Photo 496/6/7, in Qatar Digital Library
 Captain Sir Charles Malcolm - George Englehart
 Sayyid Said bin Sultan - unknown artist
 Sheikh Muhammed bin Nasir - S.B. Miles

INDEX

A

- **Almonds:** 46, 55, 66, 69, 135, 146
- **Aloes:** 101, 132
- **Arrowsmith, John (Mapmaker):** v, xxiii
- **Asses (Donkeys):** 12, 23, 24, 54, 64, 65, 74, 77, 78, 89, 100, 112, 141
- **Athel (Tamarisk) trees:** 64, 132

B

- **Badr bin Seif:** 89, 178,
- **Baghlas (Ships):** 8, 11, 14, 22, 42, 50, ,91, 110, 117, 179, 198
- **Balhaf (Yemen):** 181, 183, 194
- **Bani bu Ali (Tribe & town):** xiii, xviii, xx, xxi, 3, 21, 27-31, 35, 36, 39, 40, 41, 42, 45, 79, 94, 97, 127, 129, 131, 143, 156, 163-165
  - British expedition against: 28-30
  - War dance: 35, 79, 156
- **Bani bu Hassan (Tribe & town):** 26, 29, 41, 42, 147
- **Bani Ghafiri (Tribe):** 56, 164
- **Bani Janaba (Tribe):** xiii, 29, 36, 39, 40, 42, 143, 163, 164
- **Bani Riyam (Tribe):** 71
- **Bani Yas (Tribe):** 120, 121
- **Banians (Indian Merchants):** 8, 9, 10, 11, 22, 169, 170
- **Barka (Burka):** 18, 89-92, 129, 141, 146, 157, 178
- **Batinah Coast:** v, 52, 113, 114, 126, 127, 128, 135, 142, 143, 172

INDEX

- **Bedouins:**
- Character and habits: xii, xiii, xiv, xx, xxiii, 3, 4, 9, 11, 16, 17, 18, 25, 26, 27, 29, 32-44, 49, 51-52, 54-55, 60-61, 64, 72, 77-80, 83, 85, 88, 91, 94-95, 98, 100, 103, 107, 118, 122-123, 132, 136-137, 139-140, 143-144, 147, 151, 159, 161, 163-166, 170-171, 175, 181, 183-184, 187, 191-192, 194, 195
- Guides (Conduct of): 184, 186
- **Bidiyyah:** 28, 45, 48, 52, 106, 113, 125, 126, 129, 132, 152
- **Birkat Al Mawz:** 55, 70, 74, 76, 77, 83
- **Bombay:** viii, ix, x, xi, xii, xvi, xix, 2, 11, 29, 30, 82, 94, 117, 118, 163, 179
- **Bombay Marine (Indian Navy):** vi, vii-viii, x
- **Bruce, James (explorer of the Nile 1730–1794):** xxiii, 54
- **Buraymi:** xviii, xix, xxi, 18, 48, 83, 86, 106, 107, 110, 112, 113, 125, 126, 172, 197
- **Burial: 104-105**

- C

- **Camels:** xii, xiv, xxiv, 3, 15, 16, 17, 22, 24, 25, 33, 35, 36, 38, 40, 44, 47, 48, 51, 52, 53, 55, 61, 77, 78, 79, 83-86, 88-89, 99, 100-102, 107, 112, 114, 128, 132, 135-141, 156-157, 164, 174, 181, 183-184, 186-188, 193-194, 197
- Diseases: 139
- Speed and endurance: 36, 138-139
- **Castles** – see forts
- **Climate/Weather:** 13, 19, 20, 36, 40, 46, 52, 64, 70, 86, 129, 142-143
- **Coffee:** vii, x, xv, 1, 7, 8, 10, 11, 12, 33, 38, 66, 70, 79, 122, 148, 184, 187, 188
- **Coinage (Dollars/Thalers):** vi, xii, xxi, 9, 59, 61, 64, 78, 87, 92, 93, 94, 97, 98, 103, 107, 111, 112, 113, 124, 125, 129, 137, 141, 147, 163, 170, 171, 175, 177, 178, 197
- **Customs (Duties/Revenue):** 10, 11, 61, 92, 95, 111-113, 170, 175, 179

- D

- **Dariz Ibra:** 48
- **Dariz Ibri:** 105
- **Dates/Date Palms:** xii, xv, 5, 10, 11, 18, 20, 22- 24, 26, 29, 38, 40, 42, 46, 47, 48, 55, 68, 73, 74, 76, 79, 83, 84, 86, 87, 91-93, 99, 100, 101, 103, 107, 108, 112, 113, 114, 121, 124, 128, 130, 131, 135, 138, 140, 141, 146, 157, 159, 183, 186-188, 193, 194
- **Desert (The):** xiii, xix, xxi, 26, 32, 34, 36, 39, 43, 44, 45, 46, 48, 51, 52, 55, 72, 77, 78, 79, 85, 114, 118, 122, 126, 127, 128,

INDEX 211

- 131, 133, 137, 138, 139, 140, 141, 143, 144, 147, 151, 152, 162, 164, 165, 172
- **Dhurra (Grain):** 129, 157, 188
- **Dibba:** 113
- **Diseases:** 143
- Fever (Malaria): xv, xvi, 8, 47, 52, 55, 82, 83, 86, 143, 144, 187
- Ophthalmia: 103, 143
- **Diyabi Bedouins:** xii, xv, 183, 184, 188, 195
- **Dress (Costume):** xix, xx, 3, 9, 14, 53, 59, 77, 96, 98, 118, 140, 155, 157-158

E

- **East India Company:** v, vi, viii, xviii, 82, 120, 125
- **Exports and Imports:** 10, 11, 22, 92, 93, 108, 129, 146

F

- **Falaj (Irrigation system):** 46, 77, 84, 129
- **Falaj Bani Rabiah:** 99, 100
- **Feasts and Festivals:** 155
- **Fish/Fishing:** 12, 17, 39, 83, 92, 114, 120, 123, 125,
- **Food and Diet:** xi, xv, 7, 11, 17, 23, 35, 38, 53, 67, 68, 72, 76, 79, 97, 99, 100, 122, 138, 155, 157, 174, 188
- **Forts & castles:** xi, xiv, xviii, 5, 7, 22, 25, 26, 28, 29, 30, 49, 53, 54, 56, 58, 60, 76, 77, 85, 86, 89, 94, 95, 97, 103, 104, 105, 110, 112, 113, 164, 166, 171, 192

G

- **Geology & geography:** 17, 64, 75, 144
- **Ghaf Trees:** 16, 42, 98, 131
- **Government, Oman (Structure):** xx, 3, 4, 5, 7, 8, 24, 79, 95, 110, 115, 122, 153, 156, 160, 161, 165-171, 176, 177, 178, 180
- **Gum Arabic:** 38, 43, 131

H

- **Hadramaut:** 1, 4, 126, 132, 160, 163, 180, 188, 192
- **Haines, Captain Stafford B.:** vi, xi, xvi-xvii, 82
- **Halwa (Sweet):** 59, 146
- **Hamed (Guide Oman):** 44, 52, ========sort spelling Hamid
- **Hamed (Guide Yemen):** 181, 183, 195

- **Hamud bin Azzan Al Said (Sheikh of Sohar):** xviii, 110, 111
- **Henna:** 15, 159
- **Hilal, Sayyid bin Mohammed Al Said:** xviii, 89, 94, 95, 96, 98, 99, 109, 110, 111, 167,
- **Horses:** xvi, 3, 36, 38, 52, 77, 98, 100, 135, 140, 141, 156, 174, 186
- **Hospitality:** xiii, 53, 67, 72, 78, 94, 153, 157, 165
- **Hugh Lindsay (Steamship):** ix, xvi

I

- **Ibadhi (Sect):** vi, 29, 111
- **Ibra:** 48, 49, 56, 58
- **Ibri:** xxi, xxii, 86, 99, 104, 105, 107, 109, 110, 113, 125, 140, 198
- **Imam of Muscat (His Highness Sayyid Said):** xii, xiv, xvii, xviii, xix, xx, xxi, xxiv, 3, 4, 5, 8, 13, 22, 24, 25, 27, 35, 50, 56, 58, 86, 87, 94, 95, 99, 101, 103, 106, 110, 111, 117, 164, 167, 168, 169, 171, 175, 178, 179, 180, 197
- **Indigo:** 99, 108, 135
- **Inscriptions (Ancient):** 105, 180, 181, 183, 190, 191, 192, 193
- **Irrigation:** 25, 129, 172

J

- **Jaalan (District):** 21, 24, 33, 45, 55, 103, 126
- **Jebel Akhdar (Green Mountains):** xxi, 3, 58, 62, 67, 68, 72, 77, 126, 127, 129, 132, 135, 141, 144, 155
- **Jews:** 7, 9, 81, 110, 163, 170

K

- **Kharijites:** vi, 147-151, 176
- **Khor Fakkan:** 93, 113, 126, 128

L

- **Locusts:** xv, 142
- **Lungi (Cloth):** 97, 146, 157

M

- **Malcolm, Sir Charles (Bombay Marine):** viii, ix, xii, xxiv
- **Malcolm, Sir John (Bombay Governor):** viii,
- **Manah:** 55, 56, 57, 59, 130, 164

INDEX

- **Maqniyat:** 103, 104, 126
- **Medicine & cures:** 18, 47, 78, 112, 132, 134, 143
- **Miskin:** 101, 103, 105
- **Moresby, Captain Robert:** ix, x, xi, xxiv
- **Muscat:** vi, viii, xiv, xvi, xvii, xviii, xix, xx, xxi, 1-5, 7-11, 16, 20-21, 29, 38, 40, 58, 59, 61, 70, 81-84, 86-87, 91, 94, 95, 97, 110-111, 117, 123, 126, 129, 140-146, 151, 152, 154-156, 159, 163, 164, 166-168, 170, 171, 174-177, 179, 180, 197
- **Musannah:** 92
- **Music and Instruments:** 14, 35, 155, 203
- **Mutlaq bin Mohammed Al Mutairi:** xviii
- **Mutrah:** 10, 14, 15, 170, 171, 177

N

- **Nakab Al Hajar (Ruins in Yemen):** 182, 186, 189, 191-193, 195, 206
- **Navy (Imam's):** xix, 19, 179
- **Nizwa:** xvii, xviii, xxi, 55, 58, 59-61, 64, 74, 77, 82-84, 127, 130, 143, 144, 146, 197

O

- **Oases:** 45, 46, 48, 52, 77, 84, 113, 127-132, 135, 143, 151, 152, 154, 159, 163, 164, 170, 172
- **Ormsby, Henry:** viii, xvi, xxiii

P

- **Palinurus (Ship):** v, vi, ix, x, xi, xii, xv, 82, 181
- **Pearls/Pearl Fishery:** 9, 10, 11, 120, 123-125, 205
- **Persian Gulf:** vii, viii, ix, 1, 5, 7, 9, 11, 22, 70, 110, 113, 116, 117, 118, 119, 120, 124, 126, 175, 177, 179, 202
- **Persia/Persians:** xvii, 4, 5, 7, 8, 10, 12, 14, 18, 46, 59, 87, 96, 107, 110, 113, 115, 119, 121, 122, 124, 129, 134, 141, 142, 145, 146, 155, 157, 162, 165, 168, 170, 175, 176, 177, 178,
- **Piracy/Pirate Coast:** 29, 112, 116-120, 123, 124, 178, 180
- **Portuguese:** xv, xvii, 4, 5, 110, 117, 176

Q

- **Qalhat:** 20, 21, 23, 145
- **Qasimi (Joasmi) of Sharjah & Ras Al Khaimah:** vii, 117, 121, 122, 178, 180

R

- **Ras Al Khaimah:** vii, xviii, 70, 112, 118, 119, 121, 126, 177
- **Ras Al Nashima (Yemen):** 181
- **Ras Musandam:** 112, 113, 126, 144
- **Red Sea:** vii, ix, x, xi, xv, xvi, xxiv, 10, 11, 17, 20, 39, 119, 120, 162, 179, 186
- **Religious Tenets:** 9, 28, 113, 121, 147, 151, 176
- **Ruins:** xiii, 5, 20, 21, 22, 30, 74, 148, 172, 181, 183, 185, 188, 189, 191, 194, 195

S

- **Saad bin Mutlaq (Wahhabi commander):** xviii, xx, xxi, 47, 98, 106, 112, 125, 178, 198
- **Said bin Khalfan (secretary to Sayyid Said):** 140, 146, 197, 198
- **Salutations:** 84, 150,
- **Samad Al Shan:** xx, 24, 52, 56, 144
- **Samail:** 84, 85
- **Sayq:** xxi, 66, 94
- **Sayyid Said bin Sultan see Imam of Muscat:**
- **Seeb:** xvi, xxi, 83, 85, 86, 87, 88, 107, 127, 128, 135, 143, 197
- **Shinas:** xviii, xxiv, 107, 110-113, 146, 166
- **Shirayjah:** 65-68, 70, 74-76,
- **Slaves/Slave Trade:** xi, xx, 8, 11, 33, 35, 55, 78, 79, 85, 92, 93, 96, 97, 99, 155, 156, 164, 165, 171, 175, 180
- **Socotra:** x, xi, xii, xiii, xv, xvi, xvii, 132, 159
- **Sohar:** xviii, xix, 86, 92, 95, 99, 101, 110, 111, 135, 145, 146, 166, 176, 177, 198
- **Steam Power:** viii, ix, x
- **Sugar/Sugar-cane:** 55, 59, 99, 108, 129, 135, 146, 155
- **Sur:** xiii, xx, xxi, 3, 20-25, 29, 39, 51, 81, 126, 146, 163, 168
- **Suwayq:** xxi, 77, 93, 94, 95, 97, 98, 99, 109, 140, 141, 155, 198

T

- **Tanuf:** 62, 64, 66, 74
- **Thesiger, Wilfred:** xiv
- **Tihamah (Tehama):** 127, 128
- **Transliteration (Names):** v
- **Trees:** 5, 38, 39, 69, 84, 93, 101, 134, 135, 146, 155, 157, 185, 186

W

- **Wahhabis:** xv, 6, 7, 48, 81, 107, 112, 113, 140, 178, 198
- **Water/Wells:** 7, 16-18, 21, 23, 25, 33, 37-40, 44-46, 52, 54, 55, 59, 64, 66, 70, 75, 76, 77, 83, 84, 85, 88, 113, 129, 130, 131, 132, 141, 143, 185, 186, 191, 193, 194, 203
  - **Weaving & spinning:** 15, 43, 59, 147
  - **Wellsted, James Raymond:**
  - Biography/Family: vi-xvii
  - Death: xvi
  - Illness/Fever: xv, 82-86
  - Service in Bombay Marine: vi-xii
  - **Whitelock, Lieut. F.:** xx, xxi, xxiv 53, 82, 106, 204
  - **Wine:** 33, 66, 68, 69, 72, 96, 135, 154, 155, 176, 177, 203
  - **Women (Arab):** xiv, xx, 9, 26, 30, 33, 38, 74, 91, 121, 159, 170, 171

- **Z**

  - **Zanzibar:** vi, xix, xx, xxi, 8, 146, 155, 166, 175, 176, 180

www.ingramcontent.com/pod-product-compliance
Lightning Source LLC
Chambersburg PA
CBHW011406070526
44577CB00003B/387